9/27

Human Development and the Spiritual Life
How Consciousness Grows toward Transformation

The Plenum Series in Adult Development and Aging

SERIES EDITOR:
Jack Demick, *Suffolk University, Boston, Massachusetts*

AGING AND HUMAN MOTIVATION
Ernest Furchtgott

THE CHANGING NATURE OF PAIN COMPLAINTS OVER THE LIFESPAN
Richel R. Thomas and Ranjan Roy

THE DEVELOPMENT OF LOGIC IN ADULTHOOD
Postformal Thought and Its Applications
Jan D. Sinnott

HANDBOOK OF AGING AND MENTAL HEALTH
An Integrative Approach
Edited by Jacob Lomranz

HANDBOOK OF CLINICAL GEROPSYCHOLOGY
Edited by Michel Hersen and Vincent B. Van Hasselt

HUMAN DEVELOPMENT AND THE SPIRITUAL LIFE
How Consciousness Grows toward Transformation
Ronald R. Irwin

HUMAN DEVELOPMENT IN ADULTHOOD
Lewis R. Aiken

PSYCHOLOGICAL TREATMENT OF OLDER ADULTS
An Introductory Text
Edited by Michel Hersen and Vincent B. Van Hasselt

PSYCHOLOGY OF THE CONSUMER AND ITS DEVELOPMENT
An Introduction
Robert C. Webb

A Continuation Order Plan is available for this series. A continuation order will bring delivery of each new volume immediately upon publication. Volumes are billed only upon actual shipment. For further information please contact the publisher.

Human Development and the Spiritual Life
How Consciousness Grows toward Transformation

Ronald R. Irwin
Brockville, Ontario, Canada

Kluwer Academic/Plenum Publishers
New York • Boston • Dordrecht • London • Moscow

ISBN: 0-306-46606-6

©2002 Kluwer Academic / Plenum Publishers, New York
233 Spring Street, New York, N.Y. 10013

10 9 8 7 6 5 4 3 2 1

A C.I.P. record for this book is available from the Library of Congress

All rights reserved

No part of this book may be reproduced, stored in a retrieval system, or transmitted in any form or by any means, electronic, mechanical, photocopying, microfilming, recording, or otherwise, without written permission from the Publisher.

Printed in the United States of America

Preface

In this book, I propose a theory of the development of consciousness that at first makes ego appear center stage as the agent of socialization and culture. Ego is defined as what makes self become object to itself so that self-control and self-regulation are enabled. This process builds on representational capacities that are an outcome of natural selection.

The gaze of others (a prerequisite to moral behavior) becomes internalized as the self observing the self, the self reflecting on itself, the self making an object of itself, so that the light of moral consciousness dawns. But as ego becomes more substantial, more solid, so does repression and alienation from the sources of our being.

But the story of ego is not all that occupies the landscape of consciousness and development. The importance of ego as an agent of self becomes eclipsed with aging, so that the predominance accorded self-control can be attenuated. Ego can be relaxed, and as the executive functions become more automatic, there is more room to breathe. The straitjacket of ego on consciousness is loosened. As ego loosens, so too does much of what is taken for granted by convention as necessary to moral and social behavior. As ego is transcended, we enter the *postconventional*, the *postrepresentational*, and the *postpersonal*. In the separate but related domains of intellectual, self, moral, and consciousness development, we find a self more porous and permeable, open and unbound, more naked and free, unshackled by self-scrutiny and self-observation.

Consciousness still observes itself, but without the ubiquitous need for self-control. Self-observation is now no longer driven by the directive of obedience, nor structured by the scripted routines inherited from childhood. Self-observation can become mindfulness and receptiveness, and serves as a bridge to self-transformation and liberation instead of self-strangulation.

In what follows, I review some of the literature on identity and narrative as preparatory to this process and then, separately, outline the fields of intellectual, self, moral, and consciousness development that I see as constituting converging lines of evidence indicating that consciousness development can indeed transcend conventional ego development.

ACKNOWLEDGMENTS

I would like to thank several reviewers for their suggestions: Gisela Labouvie-Vief for commenting on the section on her work; Cheryl Armon for reviewing the section on the Good Life model; Susanne Cook-Greuter for reviewing her work on Loevinger; Julia Guttmann for reviewing the section on Charles Alexander's work; Joel Funk for commenting on my Wilber section; Michael Basseches for reviewing the section on dialectical thinking; Jan Sinnott for reviewing the section on relativistic thinking; Mark Tappan for reviewing the section on narrative; and Angela Sumegi for comments on the section on meditation.

Contents

Part I: A Sketch for a Theory of Psychology

1. The Relevance of Psychology to Spiritual Development 3

    What Development Is About............................ 3
    Meditation and Development 8
    East and West....................................... 16
    Spirituality and Religion.............................. 19
    Science... 22

2. The Nature of Development 25

    Agency and Communion.............................. 25
    A Conception of Development and the Nature of Universality 29
    Ego: Bounded Self and Identity 31

3. Evolution 35

    Mind as Simulation.................................. 35
    Childhood as the Artificial Amniotic Environment 40
    Ego as Mediated Being 44

4. Impulse Control and Repression 49

    Repression and Happiness 49
    Repression and Childhood Coping..................... 53
    A Comparison with Object-Relations Theory 59
    Transcendence as Derepression 62

5. Cognition 65

Fixation of Belief... 65
The Primacy of the Social 67
Biological Architecture 70
Cognitions about Self 75
Cognition as Representation of Sensation, Perception,
and Action 76

6. Language 79

Language as a Cultural Prosthesis 79
Language as an Autonomous Domain of Simulation 81
Language as Cultural Determination 83

Part II: On the Threshold of the Spirit

7. Identity 93

Identity as Development and as Achievement 93
Identity as Fiction and as Constraint 99

8. Narrative 109

Introduction: The Transition to the Postconventional
via Language 109
Freedom as Rewriting 112
Temporality 113
Cognitive Structuring 115
Cultures, Stories, and Symbols 117
Lives as Texts 119
Nature of Reality 120
Breaches and Ruptures 121
Therapy as Narrative Repair 122
Transcending Narrative 125

9. Epistemic Knowing 137

Relativistic Knowing 137
Dialectical Knowing 145

10. Knowing the Self **149**

    Robert Kegan 149
    Changes in the Vertical Organization of Ego 153
    The Midlife Crisis in Development 158
    Juan Pascual-Leone 164

11. Social and Moral Knowing **169**

    Lawrence Kohlberg 169
    Cheryl Armon 172

12. Cosmic Knowing **175**

    Susanne Cook-Greuter 175
    Ken Wilber 178
    Charles Alexander 183
    James Fowler 186

Conclusion **191**

References **195**

Index **201**

PART I

A Sketch for a Theory of Psychology

CHAPTER 1

The Relevance of Psychology to Spiritual Development

WHAT DEVELOPMENT IS ABOUT

When investigators of human development have written about "higher" or more adult stages of development they often indicated that such development is spiritual. Clear examples of this can be found in the work of the earlier of the adult developmental theorists, including Kohlberg, Erikson, and Jung. Kohlberg's (Kohlberg & Ryncarz, 1990) speculations regarding a seventh stage of moral judgment had a clearly spiritual nature: individuals focus not only on how to be moral, but also on why they should be moral from a nondualistic perspective. Erikson's higher stages of psychosocial development—the Generativity and Integrity stages—included a concern for others rather than oneself, an orientation away from ego and its identity and its conformity, toward both egolessness and a greater breadth of vision. Jung's account of the process of individuation at midlife included transformations of the personality that expanded it to include not only previously repressed or unacknowledged aspects of the self, but also the release of archetypal images from the collective unconscious, the content of which Jung identified with the central images and motifs of the world's mythological and religious traditions (Campbell, 1971).

Whether we examine moral development, psychosocial development, or midlife individuation, the descriptions of phenomena at these higher stages often contain characteristics that can be interpreted as spiritual. It is as if developmental researchers are finding that human development "naturally" tends toward spiritual development, that spirituality is a part of both normal and optimal development. In fact, because it occurs in the later stages of life, not only is spiritual development normal, we can also draw the inference that it is "higher" or more "evolved." This point will be clarified in what follows.

If we agree that developmental psychology is a form of science, then we can conclude that science, in another form, has revealed an aspect of spirituality from a new perspective, as others have argued that the physical sciences are revealing truths known to wisdom literatures (Zukov & Finkelstein, 1994) or cognitive science is uncovering truths long known to Eastern traditions (Hayward, 1987) or that psychoanalysis arrived at insights compatible with Zen Buddhism (Fromm, 1960).

Conceptions of the highest stages of development inform what developmental researchers conceive earlier development to consist of. Such conceptions inform the way that observations are interpreted, the way frameworks are used to categorize descriptions, and the way methodologies and measurements are constructed, articulated, and refined. In the adult development field it is commonly accepted that Piaget left out the higher developmental stages, and that this, in turn, shaped and informed what he conceived earlier development to consist of (Commons, Richards, & Armon, 1984; Commons, Sinnott, Richards, & Armon, 1989; Commons et al., 1990).

Many have criticized the exclusively intellectual focus of Piagetian work, and this can, in part, by explained by the endpoint to development that Piaget postulated. His project of *genetic epistemology* was intended to analyze the development that occurred from the child's sensorimotor contact with the physical world to the fully developed logical competence of the mature scientist. *Formal operations,* defined as the highest stage of development in that scheme, are the structural competence necessary to employ systematic scientific reasoning. With this hypothesized endpoint to development, it was only natural for Piaget to construct measurements and methodologies that could articulate his goals as a researcher. But by focusing only on this framework, Piaget did not include other aspects of development within his predominately epistemological and intellectual orientation.

We may regard theories in terms of their *breadth* or their *depth*. On the one hand, regarding the dimension of breadth, Piaget neglected aspects of social, interpersonal and affective development. On the other hand, regarding the dimension of depth, later possibilities and transformations in human potential were left out.

> How narrowly or uni-dimensionally one conceives of cognitive processes and their capacity for integrated growth determines not only the breadth and upper boundary of development, but also one's formulations of all lower stages, which are invariably cast as sequential approximations of the final stage. (Alexander et al., 1990, p. 290)

If one defines higher development as spiritual development—as I shall try to show in the following—we will articulate new and higher stages of human potential to be added to our models of human psychology, and that will also mean that earlier stages of development will have to be reformulated as well. If the general path of development is not solely about the equilibration of logical-mathematical structures—as it was for Piaget—then what is it about? What is the dimension or underlying process or structure that develops? As researchers reframe the question of what they are looking for, they will begin to discover new data as the methodological criteria for what constitutes data changes.

When the theoretical sweep is widened in terms of breadth, many researchers have posited *social* or *ego* or *self* development as the underlying structure that accounts for the many changes in behavior, thinking, and feeling that occur over the life span. The self, as it is understood from this perspective, is an essentially *social* self. Processes essential to its development include internalization, imitation, perspective-taking, interpersonal relations, socialization, modeling, and so on. Often the social domain is conceptualized as prior to the individual, constituting it and constructing it.

But how can a model that posits *spiritual* development as the endpoint to which earlier development leads, as I am proposing, be explained by a theory that explains development primarily in terms of *social* development? Positing social development as the superordinate construct affects how we think of what spiritual development is. Is spiritual development then a more attenuated or refined kind of social development? A theory that holds that social development is the source out of which all development and psychology proceeds implies a form of social constructionism, and therefore, in all likelihood, implies moral and religious relativism. What would then become of the emphasis in spiritual traditions on human and religious universals? What would become of "truth" if everything is socially constructed?

Theories that emphasize social development sometimes neglect the individual component of the equation, and this is consistent with social constructionism. A truly interactionist theory of development has to accord a greater role to individual psychological reality than that accorded by social constructionism. This means that psychological processes cannot be reduced solely to social processes. An interactionist theory has to acknowledge and articulate the contributions of biology, a cognitive architecture, and an individual phenomenology that interacts with social processes. Socialization is therefore only a *part* of development.

If researchers opt for an interactionist theory, and if they also elect to include increasing the depth as well as the breadth of their theoretical reach, then they might turn to a theory that postulates *consciousness* as the underlying structure that develops over the life span. Socialization is a part of that development, but as the shift of focus changes to the higher reaches of the life span, investigators will have to make room in their theories and models for phenomena that are by no means reducible to socialization. I believe that consciousness is a construct that might enable us to incorporate cognitive development, social development, and spiritual or religious development under one theoretical umbrella.

* *

In the West, we tend to see development as eventuating in autonomy and will, the rational and self-directed agent. This can be seen, for instance, in the theories of Freud, Piaget, and Kohlberg. For Freud, maturity was achieved when the ego was securely adapted to reality, using secondary process thought, and the superego and the id were securely in their place as subordinate aspects of the personality. For Piaget, formal operations as the endpoint of development were the high point of self-regulated behavior. Individuals in possession of formal operations are able by means of purely internal logical operations to anticipate all physical perturbations to their psychological equilibrium. For Kohlberg, stage six postconventional reasoning was free of the pressures of both social conformity and social systems, making moral judgments from a kind of Olympian height of self-chosen moral principles.

I believe that this kind of orientation reflects the trends of both Enlightenment rationality and bourgeois society. As we explore a theory of development that holds that consciousness is the central structuring principle, I shall suggest that the implicit values and frameworks of researchers will have to become realigned as they explore a conception of development that does not posit autonomy, will, or rational self-regulation as the highest achievement of development.

* *

We may define *consciousness* as the dominant structuring of our awareness. By contrast, *attention* is what infants have. Attention creates their awareness; infants do not, however, possess consciousness, as I am defining it. When learning and society begin to mediate the structures that control attention and awareness, then we can speak of consciousness. But consciousness also transcends social mediation in the higher stages of development, so that while ego structures remain as part of the overall repertoire, they need not always regulate attention in specifically learned ways. Attention and awareness develop a degree of autonomy, a space to breathe, apart from ego, which is itself a learned structure. This is facilitated, for example, by practices involving meditation.

One aspect of *ego* is the self's cognitive representation of itself. The ego begins to develop in early childhood as a social accommodation to external powers; it enables self-control so that the child can insert him- or herself into a predictable and regulated social world. Children can control themselves and relate to others in the social world better if they can represent themselves as objects in relation to other objects in their world. Early ego controls are based on primitive mechanisms such as guilt and shame, which are methods of internalizing the social sanctions of discipline and punishment. As the ego becomes more general, more abstract, and less bound to the interpersonal context and to the superego, developmental researchers refer to it as *identity*. Identity is simply a more evolved form of ego, a form of ego uniquely characterizing adolescence and adulthood, when early identifications are resynthesized in the light of abstract concepts and logical reflections, when the force of the superego is attenuated, and the more conscious *ego ideal* comes to the fore to embody the values, goals, and beliefs of the individual. In the developmental literature, there are significant changes in this identity that have implications for, and suggest a readiness for, spiritual development, a development that transcends both ego and identity.

If higher consciousness has a developmental dimension to it, then consciousness at higher stages may mean development that goes beyond early forms of ego control, development that goes beyond self-monitoring and self-surveillance, and the continual self-talk required for us to be conscientious citizens. Consciousness acquires a spaciousness, an openness, and a receptivity to inner realities and depths, without the operation of the ego's defenses and conditionings. It is an openness to the entire sensorium free from the imposition of thought formations that always enforce an interpretation with reference to a center. It is a letting go, a surrendering, that leads to a nonattached acceptance of things as they are.

Consciousness has its origins in the prepersonal and the prelinguistic, in a state not characterized by the subject–object duality, in the nondifferentiated ground. Consciousness is subsequently structured through development by a series of mediations that alienate the self from itself in the form of ego. First, society mediates between the individual and nature, that is, between the organism and the external world. For the self then to relate to and interact with society, an ego is constructed. The ego is used as a cognitive representation by largely linguistic structures that are internalized from the prevailing culture as identity. With maturity, these representations of self are taken to be identical to the self. Until this point, development can be described as alienated. But with the beginnings of postpersonal development this alienation is transcended.

While childhood and adolescent development can be understood as primarily social development, optimal adult development can be understood more properly as *postsocial* development. Adult development investigators commonly speak of *postformal* operations (Commons et al., 1984), *postconventional* morality (Kohlberg & Ryncarz, 1990) or *postpersonal* stages (Wilber, 1996a), or *postlinguistic* (Cook-Greuter, 1990) or *postconformist* (Loevinger, 1976) stages of ego development. All of these descriptions indicate that the individual goes beyond phases of development that are readily characterized by means of conventional language. Because the content of such stages is described by the use of a type of prefix—indicating that they can be more easily described by what they *are not* than by what they *are*—we may assume that development at the upper reaches goes beyond language and what can be agreed on by means of social consensus.

While aspects of postsocial development have characteristics that are associated with wisdom, compassion, and selflessness, and are illustrated by many of the spiritual luminaries known throughout history, such as Gandhi, Christ, the Buddha, and the Dalai Lama, nevertheless, we should not overlook the less conventional and less socially acceptable aspects of postsocial development that I believe may be illustrated by the lives of such people as Friedrich Nietzsche, Michel Foucault, Jack Kerouac, or William Burroughs. While the latter group may not have matured as smoothly as the former, both their successes and their plights need to be understood, and a solid adult developmental theory provides one means of such understanding.

MEDITATION AND DEVELOPMENT

In the East, meditation is taught and practiced to facilitate spiritual development. Meditation cultivates qualities of mind that require that the mind change itself. Meditation begins a process that, in my view, uncovers, unravels, and untangles much of the ordinary process of socialization, conditioning, habitual thinking, and adaptation that have made us into socialized beings. This whole process of socialization has a history, and the history has to have reached a point of maturation, a point of saturation, as it were, before it can be ready for development beyond conventional socialization.

Throughout this book I shall discuss meditation in general, but I should note that my own studies and practice have chiefly been with the Buddhist *shamatha* and *vipashyana* meditation practices, practices that are taught in Tibetan Buddhism, as well as in *Theravadin,* or Southeast Asian, approaches, from which they originate. While I believe that my comments are generalizable to many, if not most, meditative practices—particularly *zazen* practice as it is taught in the *Soto* Zen Buddhist school of Japan—my own experience and reading are restricted mainly to Buddhist methods, and of those particularly *shamatha* and *vipashyana* techniques. Within Buddhism, there are other meditation techniques, and in other spiritual traditions there are other techniques as well. But I hope that my comments are general enough to apply to those other practices in important ways.

Shamatha and *vipashyana* meditation are generally taught in conjunction. *Shamatha* meditation is focused on developing a sense of focus, detail, precision, and clarity in the moment, and on training or "taming" the mind to stay in the moment. It is concerned with slowing ourselves down enough to begin to notice how much we speed ourselves up. Once we have tamed the mind into returning to the present every time it wants to jump away, we are ready for *vipashyana.* *Vipashyana* takes this gentle focus and expands it to include the whole environment, the space in which breathing and sitting are occurring. But, inevitably, we lose ourselves in thoughts, which are as legion as dust motes in the sunlit window, and which we are to regard as no more substantial. Always, we must remember to come back to the breath, back to *shamatha.*

The basic instructions involve how we arrange our body, breath, and mind.

Body. We find a comfortable way of sitting. Contemporary meditators use a *zafu* and a *zabuton.* A *zafu* is a round hard cushion, about one foot in diameter, about eight to ten inches thick. A *zabuton* is a flat square cushion approximately three feet by three feet and about one or two inches thick. It is preferable to sit on a *zafu,* which is placed on a *zabuton,* but sitting practice can be done even while seated on a chair. If we are going to practice on the cushion, we place the *zafu* at the back of the *zabuton* so that there is room for our crossed legs on the *zabuton.*

The purpose of the *zabuton* is to soften the surface on which we place our knees. We position the *zafu* at the back of our behind so that our knees touch the *zabuton* firmly. If our knees are not so limber, we can simply sit cross-legged. In order to center ourselves on the cushion, we gently sway back and forth until we come to a balance.

We hold our backs straight, not rigid, neither too tight nor too lax. To straighten the spine, it helps to imagine that the tops of our heads are being pulled up by a rope. We can place our hands in the traditional zen *mudra,* one hand inside and on the other, fingers lined up, thumbs lightly touching as if we are holding a thin piece of paper between them. Or we can use the "resting the mind" *mudra*, simply placing our hands in a relaxed fashion on top of our thighs so that our arms are extended comfortably.

Our shoulders are held straight to align with the ears and slightly back so that the chest is open and exposed. The chin is tucked down a little, but the back of the neck is straight. The jaw is kept loose, as if to exhale with an "AH" sound, with the mouth slightly open and the tongue placed gently on the back of the upper palette. Eyes are kept open. The gaze should be softly pointed to a position on the floor about four to six feet in front of your legs.

The aim is to physically bring the body to a stillness and a presentness that the mind, of course, will try to fight. It is important to be rooted firmly on the ground, but it is equally important for the head to rise to the sky. You are here, and cannot for the duration of the sitting, go anywhere else. While it is essential to be firmly present in the here and now, if discomfort and pain arise, it is alright to shift or move slightly to avoid obsessing about certain pains.

Breath. Meditation practice is not like the practice of *pranayama* in yoga. The breath should not be manipulated artificially. The breath should simply be allowed to relax and settle into its own natural rhythm. In addition to allowing the breath to relax and settle, attention should be placed lightly on the out-breath. But it is not necessary to strive for concentration. In fact, Trungpa (1995) states that only about 25% of attention should be placed on the breath in vipashyana and warns against aiming to develop forceful types of concentration. The breath is merely a conveniently located instrument that we use to return our wandering minds back to the present. The convenience is because the breath is always there.

Attention is made to follow the breath in and out, but the out-breath does get the greater emphasis. A good point of focus for following the breath is just beneath the nostrils, a tip where the inhalation and exhalation can be felt most clearly. As the breath goes out, we let our mind go out into the gap, which without effort is soon filled with the in-breath. Then we simply follow the air back in until it fills us and then we let it go, again and again, over and over and over. Without our manufacturing it in any way, the breath will become deeper and fuller, relaxing us and affording a deeper perception of the richness of the practice.

Using the breath as an object of meditation is not about knowing the breath or about becoming better breathers or even better meditators. The breath is really just a handy tool or instrument by which we begin the taming process of the mind.

Mind.

> We are instructed to let the thoughts come and go as if touching a bubble with a feather. (Chodron, 1997, pp. 54–55)

In sitting practice, we work to develop mindfulness, but it will appear to many, in trying to meditate, that the mind wants to do anything but be mindful of the present. We use any thought that bubbles up out of the mind as an excuse to elaborate trains of thoughts that take us off into the future or back into the past. But these thoughts should be treated as no more than secretions. The practice consists not in attempting to stop these thoughts, nor in overtly suppressing them, but in simply labeling them as "thinking," and returning to the breath.

We don't *stop* thinking; we let it go. Anything that comes up is fair game, but always the instruction is to label the thought as "thinking" and return to the breath. There will be good thoughts, bad thoughts, silly thoughts, sexy thoughts, scary thoughts, boring thoughts. All just thoughts. So just say to yourself "thinking" and go back to the breath. Don't judge, don't cling, don't grasp, don't hold.

Some thoughts are trivial and some thoughts are epic. "I must remember to put the roast in the oven." "I have to finish that report." "I wonder what so-and-so thinks of me." "Will this meditation session ever end?" "I wonder what we are having for lunch." All thoughts are part of the on-going chatter and commentary by which we situate ourselves in our little worlds, binding us to our egos and isolating us from each other and ourselves.

> When we cling to thoughts and memories, we are clinging to what cannot be grasped. When we touch these phantoms and let them go, we may discover a space, a break in the chatter, a glimpse of open sky. This is our birthright—the wisdom with which we were born, the vast unfolding display of primordial richness, primordial openness, primordial wisdom itself. All that is necessary then is to rest undistractedly in the immediate

present, in this very instant in time. And if we become drawn by any thoughts, by longings, by hopes and fears, again and again we can return to this present moment. We are here. We are carried off as if by the wind, and as if by the wind, we are brought back. When one thought has ended and another has not yet begun, we can rest in the space. All compassion and all wisdom come from that. (Chodron, 1997, pp. 106–107)

The body is the place where we rest our minds. Part of the body is the feelings and emotions that continually arise. Face each feeling and let it go to take its course. Above all do not try to construct a storyline around each feeling or try to place it in some appropriate place in an evolving drama. Sink into and then let go of each feeling as it flows and surges, sitting still and firm and open on the cushion. Being mindful of feelings and emotions as they are, without acting on them, brings a richer sense of the energetic quality of feeling. Being mindful also softens the ego's tendency to solidify feelings as concrete reference points in the play of phenomena.

One of the points of basic vipashyana practice is developing what is known as the knowledge of egolessness. That is to say that the awareness that develops through the vipashyana experience brings nonexistence of yourself. And because you develop an understanding of the nonexistence of yourself, therefore you are freer to relate with the phenomenal world—the climate, atmosphere, or environment we have been talking about. (Trungpa, 1995, p. 105)

The goal of meditation, and we really should not place goals in the way of mindfulness, is egolessness. But it is not really egolessness that is attained. The ego never disappears. It is rather that the solidity and the reality of its constructed fiction is seen through. The ego becomes transparent so that the whole panorama of its situation is opened up. Whereas before the ego was taken as certain and firm, now it is lightly relinquished. But the ego itself is not a given. It has evolved over the lifetime, beginning in infancy and developing by means of the structuring of consciousness.

* *

There are a number of things that are considered basic to Buddhism: accepted by the Theravada, the Mahayana, the Zen and the Vajrayana schools. These include: The Four Noble Truths, the Eightfold Path, the Triple Refuge, and the Three Marks. The Three Marks are said to characterize the phenomenal world. And the practice of meditation brings us face to face with this phenomenal world and to the realization of the nature of these three marks: *dukkha, anicca, anatta.*

Dukkha: sorrow, that life is suffering (also the first of the Noble

Truths). Life is inherently unsatisfactory. Pleasure is unattainable. Any action or thought predicated on ego-oriented desire is going to lead to more suffering. We always want what we do not have and we do not want what we do have. Suffering cannot be removed or rationalized away by social engineering; suffering is intrinsic to conditioned existence.

Anicca: impermanence, all things are impermanent; all things pass away. *Everything* that arises passes away. But we try to hold on to things, we aim for permanence, and this desire is always frustrated—hence our suffering. Because nothing really exists in itself. As one of Joseph Goldstein's meditation teachers said, it is all "empty phenomena rolling on."

Anatta: selflessness, of all the things that do not last, that do not exist in themselves, the most salient to our experience, is the self. Fundamentally, the self, as an enduring, fixed, unchanging essence, does *not* exist. But it is the clinging to this very nonexistent idea that is at the heart of suffering.

In meditating, we learn to feel the pervasiveness of these three marks. We learn in the letting go of thinking and the letting go of breath to let go of our private and personal burdens, our anxious identity concerns, our territories, and our credentials. But in this letting go, we are not diminished. We learn to live as warriors: open-hearted, brave, honest, skillful, saying yes to whatever experience brings, tender and vulnerable.

> Life feels spacious, like the sky and the sea. There's room to relax and breath and swim, to swim so far out that we no longer have the reference point of the shore. (Chodron, 1997, p. 120)

> Our usual experience is that, just when our perception is getting vivid, we get jumpy. The world is always displaying itself, always waving and winking, but we are so self-involved that we miss it. The experience of sticking with it, of not giving up, is one in which the whole world, everything that we see, becomes extremely vivid and more solid, and at the same time, less substantial and more transparent. We're not talking about seeing anything other than the person sitting in front of us. . . . The things we see all the time can pop us out of the painful cycle of samsara. (Chodron, 1997, p. 129)

The apparent solidity of the experienced world gives way to an all-pervasive feeling of energy and space. Practicing a mindful witnessing to what is passing in our minds without judgment, meditators learn to accept their minds as Buddha-nature, to accept themselves as they are and not as they or others think they should be. Such openness to oneself allows for an openness to the phenomenal world and to others. The machinations and contrivances of ego, with its credentialing and its posturing, are let go of—not suppressed—but let go of with a patient forgiveness for what is at bottom a confusion and not an evil.

* *

If meditation does indeed aim toward the development of consciousness, then the success of meditation depends on the developmental level of the meditator. In much of the following, I hope to elucidate precisely what I mean by "developmental level." Meditation is said to work by drawing on the possibilities contained within a person's consciousness, and these possibilities vary from person to person. In the East it is believed that what you experience and do in the present life is due to your past *karma*. I am going to argue that the level of development you have achieved in the present life is part and parcel of your karma as well. Karma determines when you are ready to hear certain messages and karma determines when you are ready to achieve certain insights.

One of the preliminaries to spiritual practice *(ngondro)* in the Vajrayana tradition of Tibetan Buddhism is the contemplation of the uniqueness of the human condition. It is believed that the human realm is one of many, in fact, one of six realms, and to be born as a human is considered of enormous benefit to the practice of dharma. It is said that you are as likely to be born a human as it is likely that a tortoise, swimming in all the oceans of the world, coming up for air once in a thousand years, will stick its head out precisely at the place where a ring floats on the surface. My approach is to further refine the description of the probability of self-transformation. Not only is it rare and unusual to be born a human, it is also rare to evolve high enough within the life span to be ready for spiritual understanding. Data derived from research to be considered below indicate precisely how rare an event a truly human maturity is.

Developmental research has relevance of a practical nature when it can be shown that the success of psychological interventions—and here I intend to treat meditation as on a par with other psychological interventions—depends on the level of development of the individual. This holds true whether we speak of the success of psychoanalytic treatment interventions or cognitive–behavioral interventions. Wilber (1986a, b, c) writes about treatment modalities and shows that most known modalities can be arrayed along a continuum, where the continuum is defined in terms of his model of the spectrum of consciousness development. Each of the methods or techniques is most useful when it is appropriate to addressing the issue being negotiated at that point on the continuum. Meditation can be understood then as one such treatment modality, appropriate only to those of a certain developmental level or within a certain range of developmental levels.

Of course, this depends on precisely how the success of the intervention is operationalized. Some might argue that if we define success as progress along the developmental continuum, then we are asserting a tautology. But I think that this is precisely what a developmental approach entails. I believe that the success of psychological interventions is, most broadly conceived, the facilitation of personal development. If a psychologist defines success in other ways, then the interventions are restricted to removing dysfunctional symptoms, or ameliorating pain, or providing coping strategies to enable adaptation to the status quo. While these are worthwhile and necessary, I do not think that these interventions address the most important concerns clients bring to therapy.

Some of the variability in the success of meditative practice can be explained by the fact that different people are at different levels of readiness to take up a spiritual practice. Meditation requires that consciousness be ready to transcend past levels of development, which I am defining here in the first half of life as chiefly development of ego. Some people may not be mature enough for meditative practice; for some people, meditation may not even be advisable. It is said "You have to be a somebody before you can be a nobody." In other words, you have to have an ego before you can transcend it.

If development is necessary to spiritual practice, then we may ask how we can identify when somebody is ready to take up a spiritual tradition or meditative practice. What are the characteristics that indicate a readiness for spiritual transformation? Are there stage levels that have to be achieved before an individual is "mature" enough to enter a spiritual path? Stationing a psychometrist at the front doors to meditation centers, ashrams, and temples, assigning prospective seekers of the truth a "spiritual potential" score, may seem absurd; nevertheless there is a rationale behind the notion. On the one hand, some people may not be ready for the type of spiritual practice required in meditation. On the other hand, spiritual practices, and not traditional psychological interventions, may be precisely what is needed for those at higher developmental levels.

Many individuals may be attracted to meditation for the wrong reasons, and these wrong reasons may have something to do with their development. Perhaps some individuals at conventional or conformist levels of ego development may be drawn to exotic teachings and practices because these practices may be seen as providing a solution to the problems of identity with which they are grappling. Or they may be searching for something to believe in—an ideology or a creed. Perhaps an individual who is functioning at an even lower instrumental or preconventional level may be trying to evade responsibility, shrugging his shoulders and saying "What difference does it make if we don't exist anyway?"

Many spiritual traditions may already possess methods of turning away those considered too immature or not developed enough to benefit from their teachings. They may have methods that do not explicitly turn such people away but that provide them only with some comfort or reinforcement for where they are in their lives, but without real transforming depth or insight. Developmental research could at some time provide these teachings with a more formal and rigorous method of selecting initiates.

The problem is different when applied to individuals at higher levels of development. For example, depression may require cognitive–behavioral modification of one sort or another at more conventional levels of development, but may require a more existential or spiritual approach for those entering the postpersonal and transpersonal levels of development, which I shall describe later. While there are signs that the field of psychology as a whole is shifting away from its disdain for religion (e.g., see *The APA Monitor*, August 1996), because of the field's secular bias it has probably often been the case that people who have had problems requiring a sensitivity to the existential and humanistic issues particular to the transpersonal developmental stages have not been treated appropriately. I suspect that many psychologists and others in the mental health field are simply neither prepared enough in training nor developed enough in their own consciousness to handle issues that emerge with a transcending of the personal stages of development.

EAST AND WEST

Western psychology is the objective study or science of the psyche, or mind. Its aim is to create a body of knowledge that can be understood by a professional and used for the benefit of all. In its applications, a practitioner will use this psychology on others to alleviate their suffering, provide insight, enhance self-actualization, or empower the disenfranchised. By contrast, Eastern philosophy is about introspectively studying one's own mind and dealing with one's own particular suffering, as well as that of others. Its aim is not so much the creation of an objective body of knowledge, but rather to address problems with lived experience and to transform that lived experience.

Western psychology tries to fulfill people's desires. It either tries to satisfy those desires directly or else tries to help the individual satisfy them for him- or herself. Happiness is thought to consist in the fulfillment of desires. Some desires may be secondary or perhaps even distorted desires, but they are nevertheless accepted at face value. Western psychology is oriented to helping people get more out of life. Eastern philosophy, by contrast, tries to cast a light into the regions from which desires arise, questioning those desires and the reality of the existence of the person having those desires. For Eastern philosophy, happiness cannot be achieved by fulfilling desires; desires are, in fact, obstacles to inner peace. Happiness is a state of being free of attachment to such desires.

Western psychology attempts to empower people by enhancing their self-esteem, encouraging optimistic thinking, improving self-efficacy, increasing ego strength, or teaching mastery of one's life and thoughts, enabling people to operate from a sounder, more secure, and more self-possessed foundation. Eastern philosophy teaches egolessness; happiness cannot be achieved so long as *someone* must have that happiness. Eastern philosophy teaches surrender, letting go, nongrasping.

Western psychology locates itself securely within a world that accepts and celebrates the reality of the individual. It assumes that the reality in which that individual lives and operates is true. Personhood is cultivated, celebrated, and reinforced. Eastern philosophy steps outside the world in which self-contained individuals operate and questions the reality of personhood, the reality of the individual, and the reality of the world in which the individual is situated.

When psychology focuses on development of the person, development is usually described as culminating in individual autonomy. Childhood is described in terms of what it lacks relative to the fully formed adult individual. Individual rationality, choice, autonomy, individuation, differentiation, self-actualization, agency—all are indicators of progress in development. The individual is the apex of what the social and natural order is about, the *telos* of the forces of both nature and culture. What does not lead to this autonomy and individuation is not defined as development; in fact, it is often labeled as regression or pathology.

While we in the West may believe that our conception of the autonomous self is the self that is the most free, in the following I shall try to show that it is precisely this autonomous self that is not free, that this self is really a socialized self, a conditioned self, a determined self—that is, the ego. And true freedom—spiritual freedom—is found beyond ego in the real self beyond the straitjacket manufactured by civilization.

One of the principal themes of this work is that the concept of development as we understand it in the West is biased, and we can picture this bias easily if we contrast it with Eastern conceptions. One aspect of this bias is the Western focus on studying autonomy, agency, self-directedness, individuality, and so forth. From Freud to Piaget, conceptions of development have proposed as their apex a conscious and self-possessed personhood. By contrast, this conception of personhood is radically questioned when one adopts the point of view of Eastern philosophy.

When Eastern philosophy speaks of paths to spiritual development, higher states of consciousness are equated with deindividuation, release from the ego, the relinquishing and surrendering of personal autonomy and agency. Positive virtues within Eastern philosophy are those emphasizing wisdom regarding the illusion of self and those emphasizing compassion for others, virtues not centered around the self or ego, but rather virtues that are directed toward other sentient creatures and the universe outside the individual.

However, in spite of the foregoing, I believe that the East can learn something of value from Western scientific studies of human development. These studies have identified constraints, limits, and ceilings as to what can be learned by individuals and what can be expected of individuals as they develop through the life span. Mind, consciousness, ego, self, and personality are not simply faculties that can be assumed to come fully formed at birth. They have an ontogenetic history. The understanding of this ontogenetic history can be applied in a number of ways. As applied to Eastern spiritual practice, I hope to show that not all persons are ready to adopt meditative or spiritual disciplines in an across-the-board, or over-the-counter, fashion. And this, in turn, can explain something of the variability of the success of spiritual practice for different people.

Despite the pejorative connotations of the word *ego* when used in colloquial discourse, ego for most psychologists is identified with positive traits and positive development. Ego represents those aspects of the mind that are oriented to reality, adjusted to the social order, and those in control of emotions. Persons without functioning egos are identified as pathological, or requiring therapy. Anxiety is defined as that which threatens ego. Ego strength is equated with ability to cope. We seek to reinforce ego assuming that ego is necessary to motivate actions. Ego is considered a prerequisite for happiness and joy. Ego is the platform from which you set forth into the good life. Ego is what puts you in touch with reality. And, to a certain extent, this is true.

In Eastern philosophy, ego is an illusion; something to be transcended. Ego is that aspect of consciousness that gets in the way of direct perception and insight. Furthermore, ego is the source of suffering. In Eastern philosophy, ego is what makes us cling to experience, impeding the experience of happiness and joy which is our birthright insofar as we are all aspects of Buddha or God. This original nature is described as obscured by ego. Ego is the prison your mind creates from moment to moment.

SPIRITUALITY AND RELIGION

Spiritual development is about being naked to the universe. It is about getting to know your true self. The knowing that is sought is not the knowing that is defined by the categories of society. Spirituality is about knowing outside of the categories—the roles and the rules—employed by society. It is about transcending the mediational processes that have constructed us as social-linguistic beings alien to our own natures.

It has become the fashion in intellectual circles to argue that we are socially determined; that society and language define us in essential ways. When we feel and think, we are doing so in ways that are prescribed for us by the social realities in which we are inextricably embedded. But I think that the social constructionists are wrong when they argue that we are *only* our social determination. We can be free and we can be natural, but perhaps only with higher development.

For most people, society is underneath their skin. It is inside them and they cannot feel it as other than themselves. But spiritual development is about transcending society *and* getting out of our skin. Getting out of our skin is what enthusiasm and ecstasy are all about. It is what meditation, trance, rapture, devotion and love are all about.

While it may appear as romantic to some, in the following I am going to make the case that spirituality in adulthood is largely about transcending socialization and all that is entailed in becoming socialized. But, by this I do not mean that we shed our socialization in the process of becoming more spiritual. Spirituality is not an *undoing* of socialization; it is a development *beyond* socialization. I am going to introduce a conception of development that holds that development has a progressive direction to it, that it is not the same thing as *change*, that it leads to *improvement,* that it builds on and incorporates all that has gone before, but also transcends or surpasses. The higher stages of development are about transcending socialization, a socialization that is nevertheless necessary for biological and social survival. We call this development, because the socialization is not shed but only backgrounded by cognitive means, to be described later. The socialization is incorporated in later stages of development in a hierarchical process of integration and differentiation that creates the possibility for transcendence.

This might not be the way that all Zen Buddhists or Vedantists or Sufis understand what it is that they teach, but I think that is because a notion of *society* is not really a part of their discourse in the way it is for us in the West. There are historical reasons for this: the concept of society as a unit of discourse is a product of Western nineteenth century history and thought, both the imperialistic European culture from which it arose and the beginnings of attempts to study other cultures that was made possible because of world domination. Most societies in the ancient or traditional world did not encounter societies other than their own, or if they did, regarded them ethnocentrically or condescendingly, or perhaps fearfully. Lacking systematic methods of studying and translating other societies, the very concept of society itself would not have been foregrounded in their thinking and their discourse, and therefore the sense of having a society in which one is embedded—as a fish in water—would not occur.

Some might consider the conception of spirituality I propose in the following as bohemian or anarchistic, and to be honest, I am comfortable with many of the pejorative connotations of those words. Because I am going to argue that transcendence *is* developmental, and therefore not about escaping or doing away with earlier learning, it is about stepping outside of society while simultaneously functioning within it. To be *in* the world, but not *of* it.

And because spirituality is about transcending socialization in the way I shall describe, it is possible that extant spiritual traditions have not entirely escaped their own social determinations. This can be for two reasons: one is that those spiritual traditions are simply not yet spiritual enough themselves, and two, because transcendence is here understood as developmental, it is only natural that even highly evolved spiritual traditions might include aspects of their own socialization as baggage, while nevertheless not weighed down entirely by it. Because of this, we can distinguish between aspects of those spiritual teachings that we can emulate and aspects that we need not follow.

Furthermore, it is understandable how transcendence, and paths to transcendence, may appear to those of a more conventional attitude (or developmental level) to be amoral, or even beyond good and evil. Persons who are developing in spiritual ways are stepping outside of conventional bounds, and may speak and act in ways not acceptable to society. Particularly if these developing people have not yet matured in terms of compassion, wisdom, and egolessless, they may for a time appear to be licentious or morally reprehensible in other ways.

* *

I shall make a distinction between *religion* and *spirituality*. Religion is concerned with molding good citizens into God-fearing souls who adhere to communal and institutional norms, respect private property, and perform their social roles accordingly. Religion is about inculcating conventionality. Spirituality, on the other hand, is about liberating these same souls from fear, guilt, and shame, and breaking them free of institutional roles and communal norms. Spirituality is postconventional, in a truly developmental sense.

Therapy is the new religion. But it can also be the new spirituality. Because of the death of God, and because of the disenchantment of the natural world, people now look to therapy (as a branch of science), particularly to psychology. Therapy can be categorized into two types: those that offer adjustment, coping, and adaptation, and those that exhort transformation, transcendence, development, and maturity. Most behavioral and psychiatric forms of therapy seem to fit within the first category while many forms of cognitive and humanistic forms seem to fit into the second.

While Western approaches reify language and self-talk, Eastern teachings encourage liberation from self-talk. Whether using psychoanalysis or cognitive–behavioral approaches (excepting outright conditioning techniques or psychopharmacology), Western psychological practices often resort to changing the self-talk individuals employ and engage in with others. Language is therefore the principal medium for bringing about change. Within these systems, psychological well-being and positive change can therefore be defined by healthier styles of self-talk. With Eastern approaches, by contrast, self-talk has to be seen through and then let go of. At a certain level, it is our tendency to use self-talk that creates our problems and sustains our samsaric, worldly, realities. Meditation enables the practitioner to expose their self-talk and then let go of it.

When I later more fully describe a scheme of human development, I shall describe therapies emphasizing self-talk as valid for individuals at a particular level of development, but as not appropriate for those at higher levels of development. One limitation of self-talk is that, for all its strengths, it is still discourse-specific. It is always embedded within the discourse practices of a culture. Therefore, its results and its possibilities are prescribed within the language boundaries of the society. Higher development is about going beyond social reality and its boundaries.

SCIENCE

While Eastern philosophies include techniques for spiritual practice and theories for understanding the path to enlightenment, these can be improved by applying a science to understand how to put those practices into effect, a science that takes account of individual differences, among other things. Currently, Eastern philosophies lack a coherent theory of development and a researched body of knowledge regarding human differences, differences that exist with regard to perceptual, cognitive, and personality functioning, and how these vary with development.

Scientific practice, at least as we understand it in the West, did not develop in the East. I shall not go into an analysis of why scientific practices did not evolve in the East. And while I also cannot get into the question of defining precisely what is or what is not *science,* generally speaking I can with some degree of confidence say that science is the process of converting theoretical propositions into some kind of operational form so as to be measured. Once the constructs are operationalized we call them *variables* (that is, things that vary).

The next step is to determine if the variables or measures are reliable and valid. These are fundamentally two different things, although often confused. A measure is *reliable* when the same results can be arrived at over different instances, whether these are instances of time, observation, or measurer. A measure is *valid* if it measures what it is supposed to measure. There are a number of ways of investigating validity and one of the chief ways is to assess the measure's predictive validity: the extent to which knowledge of an individual's score on a measure enables a researcher to predict other things.

Once such measures are made reliable and valid, scores on these measures can be compared to determine what relationships exist between the variables. There are two major types of relationship. One is correlational and the other causal. *Correlational* relationships are the simpler of the two and involve stating that two variables are related in some way, i.e., as one score goes up the other goes up or down. *Causal* relationships occur when you know that correlation exists, and can furthermore assert the precise ordering of the relationship between the two variables, one coming before, and therefore causing, the other. In order to make assertions regarding causal relationships with some degree of confidence, you have to perform experiments.

Researchers do an *experiment* when they manipulate one variable so as to observe its effects on others. This is often done through the assignment of subjects to groups. Most scientific results are reported as differences among groups and not individuals. In the most basic form, one group of subjects receives the treatment and the other does not. Other forms of manipulation involve creating groups that have different levels of the treatment. The manipulated variable is called the *independent variable*. The effects of its variation are assessed by measuring some variable across all groups—this variable is called the *dependent variable.*

To ensure that it is indeed the manipulated variable that is the causal variable, the researchers have to *control* for other possible variables' effects on the dependent variable, that is, the groups (and not the individuals within them) have to differ systematically only with respect to the independent variable, and not other variables which would then be termed *confounds.* This generally takes the form of ensuring that all differences are distributed equally among the groups, and this is achieved by what is called *random assignment.*

None of this could proceed without social structures in place which ensure, on the one hand, that scientists can understand these principles and practice them, and on the other hand, that they can communicate the results of their practice to each other and to the public. Without the printing press, science would never have gotten off the ground. Without resources available to ensure that scientists could maintain laboratories and stay alive while doing so, science would not exist. Without freedom from the pressures of ecclesiastical and political authorities, science would disappear. But even more important, without the perception that scientific practice would lead to social benefits, no one would even care.

Later in this book I shall discuss the importance of simulation to evolutionary adaptation and survival. In the model I propose, science is but one more form of *simulating* or *representing* reality. The process I have outlined, of translating mental constructs into operational form so that they can be tested, is simply a sophisticated form of working with a simulation.

Science is a more rigorous form of testing simulations than the kinds of simulations evolved at the behavioral or species levels. But the characteristic that science shares with other forms of simulation is that it creates an artificial realm on which operations can be performed. These operations are types of tests that are generally conducted in the benign world of the laboratory. The results of these tests enable us to encode descriptions of the external world that make our knowledge structures more successfully predictive of the external world.

Prediction is ultimately about *control*. If you can predict the outcomes of your actions and of aspects of the external world, you can be ahead of things and anticipate things before they actually have to happen. Whether you are a bat evolving a more precise radar-derived mapping of the cave in which you are flying, or a rocket scientist in the cold war manufacturing launching devices that will make your rockets more accurate than the enemies', the ultimate test of the knowledge world, of the simulation, is whether you can predict and control enough of the external world to compete and survive.

In the last century, Western psychology and social science have developed methodologies that can make certain aspects of human behavior more amenable to scientific study. Certain sets of ideas can be tested in systematic fashion. Some ideas that have been studied systematically seem to me to be relevant to spiritual practice. Because I have been trained largely in developmental theory and research I am going to focus largely on propositions deriving from developmental kinds of research. Generally speaking, developmental psychology is about studying psychological phenomenan by investigating how such phenomena vary with time. I believe that certain propositions about the nature of consciousness, ego, and cognition can be asserted that have relevance to those interested in spiritual practice.

A body of research has accumulated that testifies to certain regularities in the development of persons. I believe that the regularity observed in the course of human development suggests also that spiritual development is a part of general human development and that it defines the content of higher development, particularly in adult development. Spiritual development is not for a special type, or subtype, of the species. Spiritual development is a part of the general course of human development. It is, however, a phenomenon specific to the higher reaches of human development, and is, therefore, beyond the reach of many, depending on the various conditions that foster or inhibit human development.

CHAPTER 2

The Nature of Development

AGENCY AND COMMUNION

I would like to propose that we can think of two primary forces that drive the process of development. One is agency and the other is communion (Bakan, 1966). Both are, in effect, responses to separation. In fact, we might see the primary problem of life as one of separation. Separation means, experientially or phenomenologically, that we are cut off from the source of our being. We are living outside of things: abandoned, isolated, castoff, empty, and without succor. One way we can respond is by asserting our mastery or agency: taking control, dominating, subjecting. Another way we can respond is by relating, reaching out, giving, letting go, and loving. These two modes of responding propel us forward through the stages of life. I think that religion, art, philosophy, and love can all be understood as expressions of the human protest at our separation from being.

With the first separation of the child from the mother, there is a panic as the infant tries to reestablish connection. Only when the child is reunited is there peace and fulfillment, then sleep. But consciousness is prodded on by separation and by the psyche's attempts to deal with it. As consciousness of difference is perceived, the infant reacts, alternately by stubbornly asserting its autonomy or, by contrast, craving for reunion. Both of these responses aim to bridge the gap between will and world.

The two drives of agency and communion face their next major transformation in early childhood when the child internalizes social rules by identifying with them. Prior to this time, not possessing the cognitive capacity nor the linguistic ability to represent either other people or itself, the child is limited to obeying commands backed up by external rewards and punishments, or failing that, simply acting out the internal promptings of bodily desires. But with the ability to apprehend him- or herself as an object, the child can exert control over him- or herself as one player in a simulated world of many; thus able to gain approval from the parents, and thereby overcome separation from them, but at the same time alienating the body and its impulses. Some of the energy spent in controlling the external world is directed inside to controlling the internal world—conscience, shame, and guilt are now experienced when the child fails to achieve the image of what the parents desire.

As a mode of agency and mastery—control and domination—self-control paradoxically allows for communion and relating, because such control brings the child closer to the parents, allowing the child to obtain approval, love, and acceptance. The two drives have a dialectical unity. But it is a unity that has a cost in the alienation the child constructs between the mind and the body, and consequently, the natural world. But this dialectical tension, generated by bringing into a unity the agency and communion effects, provides the energetic motivation for the child to insert him- or herself into the mediations that create the ego as a distinct being in a social world. These mediations will be described in more detail later, but for now I will merely outline them.

The self is mediated to the natural world through the social world. This is the basis of the structuring of ego. The social world operates in the currency of agents who *own* their actions, that is, who are responsible. So the self, both cognitively and linguistically, comes to know itself as an object by treating itself as an object, as do others in its social universe. Society has to control its members, and its members are able to control themselves when they can regard themselves as objects. The ego is what can be known of the self cognitively. Society mediates the self to itself by means of the construct of ego. The more developed ego is one that uses the tools of language and of abstract representation to construct itself as having a coherent identity, having an object-nature in a represented social world that is increasingly abstract.

As the child becomes an adolescent, inserting him- or herself into broader and more varied contexts that require higher levels of symbolic processing, the evolving ego is still motivated by the twin desires of agency and communion. The universe is no longer only the one ruled by parents. The universe is a social one, and to know it requires complex symbolic activity. The aim of youth is to capture this world in thought. Separation can be overcome by a conceptual embrace of the world, whether it be in science, religion, political ideology, or philosophy. This is the time of adolescent idealism and utopian fantasy. Relatedness and connection are achieved by mastery of symbolic forms. Later stages of development in adulthood can be defined by the relinquishing of these same attempts at conceptual mastery. The exhaustion of this attempt at mastery is the final protest of the ego, a protest that began with rage at the separation from the mother, with whom it had primal bliss and unity.

Throughout childhood and adolescence, agency and communion have functioned by becoming increasingly differentiated. Mastery and domination became more and more differentiated from connecting, loving, and relating. But with (ideal) maturity, the two begin to work together in a more integrated fashion, overcoming their polar opposition, and functioning to attain the same end: applying attention with the 'right effort,' to bring the mind to rest in the present, into oneness with the world without grasping. A state is possible, and can be achieved, which recalls the preconceptual and preegoic stages in its *unmediated* reality, and therefore *immediate* at-one-ness with life, but which preserves the will and self-control. Such transcendence is rooted developmentally in prior learned structures. Transcendence is not a stripping away of mental structure, but a liberation from the necessity of always dwelling within structure.

Some might think that we have to relinquish agency in favor of communion in maturity. I would like to make the case that both are preserved at each stage in a dialectical unity and tension. While we do surrender our ego in mature development and open ourselves to the transpersonal stages—and thus seem to be allowing more space for communion—we still preserve agency in a number of ways. One of these is in the way we can acquire a deliberate mindfulness, a mindfulness that at this stage has to be deliberate because of the sheer weight of our learned and socialized automatisms.

Rather arbitrarily, I shall call *will* that aspect of our agency that is postegoic or postpersonal. While it is learned and therefore acquired (that is, not innate) it can function in the service of the transcending of the ego. It requires a special kind of effort to achieve effortlessness; perhaps this kind of effort is Buddhist Right Effort, one of the steps of the Eightfold Path. If we surrendered to our spontaneous promptings and desires at this stage, we would only be giving greater scope to our socialized conditioning. We are damaged to the core, and as damaged beings we need to overcome and transcend our conditioning by effortful mindfulness.

I think it is symptomatic of a yearning for transpersonal development to simply want to give up the artifice of ego, with its self-control, its persona of play acting, its feigned politeness, its neurotic productivity, its immersion in roles and conformity and obedience. Eating brownies for breakfast is the epitome of adult regression. The aging male at midlife may have an affair with a younger woman. In milder cases, we might devote more time to simple pleasures. In more extreme cases, we might throw away our careers on a lark or indulge in drinking or substance abuse.

But these paths are hardly the expression of our deepest nature. If self-control and role-playing are relinquished, if we simply let go of our hard-won psychological mechanisms of self-control, we are open to becoming the slaves of the consumer world, the manipulations of the marketplace. These may be as ensnaring as any conformity experienced before. Babylon is perhaps more real now than it ever was, and its charms can ensnare even the most bohemian of us. Witness the lives of such notably frustrated saints as Jack Kerouac and Malcolm Lowry.

Babylon operates by giving us what we think we need to be free, but then it owns us. The market caters and panders to infantile fixations, narcissistic longings for self-absorption, oceanic cravings for more bliss and more sensations. The message at this stage that many refuse to read is that you cannot transcend the ego by means of regression. Regression is to turn backward.

The plight of the protagonist in the film *Leaving Las Vegas* is an illustration of this. He deliberately chooses to throw away his former self, his ego, his identity. Perhaps he is trying to transcend, to develop, to evolve. But what replaces this? The glamour and trappings of Las Vegas, alcohol, prostitutes. He needs a teacher, a method, a wisdom tradition. Without these, he has only the loathing of his former self and an inescapable inner emptiness, a loathing and an emptiness so great he cannot bring himself to share tender feelings with a beautiful woman.

Cognition and perception function as the plaything of attention. This means that we think and perceive as we are motivated to think and perceive. And attention can be awake, aware of the moment and open to being, or it can be driven by programmed lusts and addictions. Unless activated by the perceptual surround, attention and what it makes us aware of, is a *consequent* psychological process of prior learned structures, mostly habits. If attention is not directed by immediate stimuli registering on our transducers, it is an effect of, an outcome of, psychological processing which is in turn activated by plans, goals, desires, biases, habits, fears, and so forth.

Our will is learned. It is the psychological structure that motivates us in our interactions with the social and physical worlds. But at the same time, it is the psychological structure that embodies our higher being, the self that knows and has directly experienced the futility of ego, longing for release from its confines.

A CONCEPTION OF DEVELOPMENT AND THE NATURE OF UNIVERSALITY

A coherent concept of development has emerged from the theories of Freud, Piaget, Kohlberg, Werner, and many others, which can help us to distinguish *development* from *change*. Change is simply anything that occurs whereby we can say that over times t_1 to t_2, A is not the same at t_2 as it was at t_1, and hence that it is different, that it is B. Development is one type of change, but it is a type of change that allows us to say that A is not only different from t_1 to t_2 but also that B is *better* when it has become B.

We can say that development leads to becoming better, but we must keep in mind what we intend by saying *better* and not allow ourselves to commit certain errors.

At a minimum, A at time t_1 is a prerequisite for B at t_2. You cannot get to t_2 without having gone through t_1, nor can you be B without having been A.

While t_2 is not only after t_1 temporally, B is also higher than A. B includes A within itself. This is what some developmentalists mean by *hierarchical integration*. However, A at t_1 does not remain only as it was; it must be somehow suitably reorganized in reaching t_2 to be a part of B.

Existing at t_2 entails being able to perceive or understand what is at t_1, but the reverse is not the case. B can comprehend A but A cannot perceive or understand B.

There is an order or pattern to development such that t_1 leads to t_2 and on to t_3, such that you can never reverse or reorder the sequence to something like t_2, t_1, t_3.

B is more adapted or evolved than A. B answers problems that were posed by A, and in turn will pose problems that will have to be solved by further development in t_n steps.

B has a greater application than A. B encompasses more than A. The domain of application of A is more circumscribed than that of B.

As we evolve from t_1 to t_2, we can say that B is not the same as A, and furthermore, we can say that B differs not only in a merely cumulative sense, but also that B is *qualitatively* different from A, that it is even a different *thing* than A.

Some versions of development include conceptions of development that I will not include in my model. One of these is the notion of *telos*. Telos means that there is a direction to development in the sense that the end or goal is driving the process. We go through t_1 and t_2 and so on to arrive at T_n. The purpose of A is therefore B. Some psychological conceptions of self-actualization seem to imply that humans instinctively strive toward self-actualization.

Another conception is *epigenesis.* This is the view that development is prescribed in the organism as a "blueprint," that development in stages is therefore a necessary unfolding or flowering of what exists in germ form inside of the genome.

Another conception I wish to avoid is that we can understand development in terms of a *plan.* This implies some underlying intentionality, that we go through life to fulfill or actualize some master plot. I do not wish to imply any such notion. We do not suffer because God wants us to ascend a path to salvation requiring penance or purgatory, nor do we evolve higher that we may attain to Godhead, so that the subject can reunite with the object. We do not evolve consciousness as a route for God to wear bifocals.

* *

One of the criticisms leveled at general stage theories is that such theories are merely descriptions of how specific people change, and that such models are only valid for the one culture out of which they have emerged. The patterns are chiefly due to cultural factors, expectations, roles, and conditioning, or else economics or the prevailing *Zeitgeist,* and do not reflect universal tendencies of human nature outside of the society portrayed. When such theories are lifted out of their cultural contexts, and applied to other and different cultures, the latter tend to be judged as less developed. And culture can include more differences than the geographic: racial, sexual, and class cultural differences also require different ways of thinking about development.

The model of development proposed here is based largely on subjects from Western educated literate industrialized societies. And the model reflects the culture in many ways; nevertheless, I do believe that there is something cross-culturally valid about the model. I am proposing that for *all* cultures at *all* times, humans develop from the preconventional to the conventional and to the post-conventional. They also develop from the prepersonal to the personal and to the transpersonal. And they develop from the prerational to the rational and to the postrational.

What I believe is most culture-specific about the following model is the centrality accorded to language and to reflection on language as the catalyst to the transpersonal stages. This in large measure reflects the importance of abstract language in Western educated and industrialized societies. And in other cultures without formal education, without literacy, and without all that is entailed by industrialization, there may be other ways of making the transit from the personal to the transpersonal. For example, in some cultures, such as the Tibetan, the role of the guru–disciple relationship is stressed; in others, such as aboriginal forms of shamanism, the master–apprentice relationship is emphasized.

Another criticism that could be leveled against my model is the exclusive emphasis it places on Buddhist psychology and philosophy to account for higher stage phenomena. While I find many aspects of Buddhism compatible with what I believe to be the case for human maturity, I would like to point out that my use of Buddhism—to the exclusion of Hinduism or Islam or Christianity—is more indicative of my own experiences and preferences, and is not meant to imply that only Buddhists have the last word on the nature of wisdom. I can equally well imagine writing the following account and drawing on other wisdom traditions to do so—perhaps aboriginal shamanism or Celtic paganism. I am simply not well enough versed in these traditions to do them justice.

EGO: BOUNDED SELF AND IDENTITY

For various reasons, we can distinguish ego from self, and I think that this usage accords with much of contemporary psychology. The self is *everything* we are—both the good and the bad, the light and the dark, the social and the asocial, agency and communion, conscious and unconscious, linguistic and prelinguistic—the self as it is before it is fractionated by these very categories and dualities that we employ in our social self-presentations. The ego, on the other hand, is only those aspects of self that have been represented cognitively, to ourselves and to others, represented by largely linguistic means in socially determined and prescribed ways.

The ego is based on coordinating aspects of self that are cognitive with aspects of self that are emotional (e.g., affects, feelings, instincts). While I use the term *coordinate* I could just as well use the term *control*. Both cognitive and emotional aspects are social in that they involve ways of relating our internal lives with those around us. As the ego's processes become more abstracted from specific interpersonal contexts and more connected to broader social realities, and as the ego internalizes the discourses and languages of which it is a part, the ego constructs an *identity*. Our identity is the end product, and one subset, of the coordinations of cognitions, affects, and other-representations into a flexible interrelated set of scripts that provide us with a means of relating our internal lives with social reality. This identity is constituted largely by roles, rules, and norms that are in turn related to our felt internal experience, as structured by projects, goals, values, and ideals. It is this identity that provides the cognitive–affective framework for, and is the product of, our *self-talk,* the internal dialogue we habitually engage ourselves in to confirm our existence as bounded selves in a stable world of objects. And it is also this identity that comes to be the object of mature reflection in what I will call the later "narrative" stage of life.

While it is true that our identity—the abstracted and articulated aspects of our ego—may enable us to participate in diverse social realities, adapt to roles and responsibilities, and while our identity may allow both ourselves and others to predict our behavior and provide a vehicle for self-expression in coherent narratives (as well as many other functions), it is also limiting in that it still only represents a portion of our self. It separates and divides us from ourselves, each other, and the natural world. How to deal with the acute consciousness of this limitation, the one-sidedness and partiality of any constructed or self-structure, presents the main existential task of adulthood, and of the so-called mid-life transition.

It is for this reason that I speak of the ego as a *bounded* self. It is of the nature of ego development that it is based on divisions, separations, hierarchical systems of superordination and subordination, differentiations of self from world, self from others, ego from self, mind from body. Such processes of differentiation eventuate in the autonomous ego, the self-determining agent, the self-authoring identity, the individual soul which we agree is said to possess free will, rational choice, introspective access to the contents of its mind, and control over its emotions and its body.

Abstraction of the ego is required so that the self can adapt to wider domains of experience. As infants we are only required to relate to our primary caregiver. At this level we are only capable of perceiving contingencies of reward and punishment. As young children we are only expected to relate to our families and perhaps a very small peer group (which we do not do very well). In this process we begin to learn about rules. Later in childhood, we learn to relate to a larger peer group and various social agents, such as teachers and recreation supervisors. For this, we begin to construct roles. In adolescence, we begin to learn how to relate to institutions, and for this we require ideologies, values, goals, and the like. In the interpersonal domain, abstraction of ego is necessary for it to adapt to these wider domains of interpersonal functioning. Development requires that we go beyond relating only to concrete relationships and that we begin to enter into broader systems of relationships. Initially, we construct roles that place us within the immediate family and world of peers. But with entry into adolescence and adulthood, the realities to which we adapt have to be more abstract. We therefore construct ideals and values that structure a more abstracted ego capable of negotiating diverse role expectations and contextual demands. But that identity is nevertheless founded in a packaging of roles and expectations that have entirely social origins. To craft such an identity, we draw on language and culture. But abstraction, by its nature, leaves out as well includes, and the abstract identities we possess as we enter adulthood will come to feel inadequate as we try to grasp realities we did not, and could not, consider in our youths.

CHAPTER 3

Evolution

MIND AS SIMULATION

If we apply an evolutionary approach to the study of organisms, we need to ask what role an organ or a faculty plays in the adaptation of the species to its environment. The same approach should be used when we examine the nature of mind, *mind* as a term used in the most general sense. We need to assume that the mind is a faculty or organ just like our lungs or our limbs. Assuming this, the question we ask is: what role does having a mind play in the adaptation of an organism to its physical world? Why is it necessary to have a mind in order to adapt? Any organ or faculty a species evolves consumes metabolic resources, so why have a mind at all?

Selection operates on a species just as it operates on behaviors. We can think of selection as a decision by the environment as to whether something will or will not be. Some species are rewarded in that they survive and are able to reproduce, but many do not. Species survive by being able to leave offspring to the next generation. Reproductive success is the sole defining criterion of evolutionary adaptation. While they may offend our sensibilities, from an evolutionary point of view, cockroaches are very successful.

As well as operating on species, selection operates on the behaviors of individual beings. An environment uses rewards and punishments as methods for sending the message that a target behavior should become a part of the organism's repertoire or that the behavior should be discarded. Behaviors that are rewarded increase in frequency. Behaviors that are punished decrease in frequency.

Both methods of selection, at the species level and at the behavioral level, require some method of trial and error to generate novelty, whether such novelty is a question of a new species or a new behavior. In the case of the species level, a trial might be a mutation originating in the genetic code. An error would be the extinction of the members of the species possessing that mutation. Many mutations make no difference whatsoever to the success of the species. Differential success occurs when certain mutations result in a species leaving more offspring in the next generation, relative to its conspecifics. At the individual level, a trial might be the expression of a new behavior, or as the behaviorists term it, the emitting of a response. An error in this case is having the response punished. Some responses are rewarded, and are therefore selected. Rewarded behaviors have an increased probability of recurring in the future.

The problem with both species and behavioral trial-and-error is that it is costly. To achieve success you have to allow for risk—the chance of failure—whether the members of the species are killed off or whether some behaviors result in damage or pain. Any species that can offset the risk due to failure are going to be more successful at the game of reproduction. And risks have to be taken or trials will not be initiated, and therefore no novel behaviors or species will emerge. If there is no method of generating novelty, there will be no means of adapting to circumstance.

Mind can be understood as an evolutionary adaptation that addresses the need to reduce the cost of trial-and-error selection. Mind is a means of carrying out vicarious trial-and-error selection. Instead of directly acting on the environment, the mind acts first in a *simulated* environment that it creates. Here it can safely test out the probable success or failure of its actions, but they have to be *imagined* actions existing only in a simulated domain, a domain where no real harm to the individual or the species occurs. After a trial is made in the landscape of the imagination, and the organism apprehends the success of that trial, the organism produces the successful behavior in the real world with less fear of loss—whether loss of limb or loss of self. The simulated environment—the landscape of the imagination—is the product of the mind. It is safer to try out behaviors in the mental landscape than it is to try them out in the physical landscape.

The truth of the simulated environment is assessed by the extent to which it reliably simulates aspects of the environment that are relevant to the organism's adaptive actions. Ultimately, it is only simulations that result in changes in the control of behavior that are of significance. The simulation should preserve the relevant isomorphic relations and structures of the environment—that is, map them—but only to the extent necessary to guide subsequent behaviors more adaptively. The test of a simulation is whether it incorporates the factors necessary to compute behavioral adaptation.

Evolution

For instance, it is only necessary from the point of view of evolutionary adaptation that we learn to process, in our simulations, phenomena that exist at a certain level of perceptual grain. We do not need to register the fact of our rotating while standing on our planet, nor do we need to process stimuli pertaining to the various bacterial fauna that work in association with our digestive enzymes. We have evolved our perceptual and cognitive abilities solely for the *value added* in terms of whether such knowing affords us an advantage in terms of reproductive survival.

A species that can simulate its environment successfully will have a better chance of reproducing itself and therefore of passing the test of evolutionary survival than a species that does not simulate itself as an object. But there has to be a *need* to have a simulation. If a species manages to adapt without a simulation mechanism, without a mind, there will be no need to evolve a mind. It is only in those cases where there is differential reproductive success that a simulation mechanism will evolve.

A simulation is not a replication of reality in the sense of being a "true" representation of reality. There is no need for truth in the economics of mind. What is needed is only that there be an adequate *simulation,* and this requires only that there be relevant isomorphisms between the external world and the internal representational world. Structures in the mental have to reflect structures in the physical, so that as the mental is translated into the physical—when thought becomes action—adaptive behaviors ensue. Adaptations are more powerful if the mental can anticipate physical change, that is, provide a measure of prediction and control. You predict and control some process when you can be ahead of it in your simulation, so that you can guide your behaviour more adaptively.

For example, imagine a bird of prey tracking a ground squirrel. This is a hypothetical sketch, as I am not really very knowledgeable of squirrel behaviour. Say it is circling overhead of the squirrel and watching the squirrel's movements. The squirrel is busy searching for nuts for its winter hibernation. It has no idea that a bird of prey is watching it. But when it hears the sound of rushing air or when it sees the shadow cast by the quickly descending bird, it knows to flee to its burrow. Now we can imagine that a bird may or may not have a simulation of where that squirrel might run. One species of bird may be able to mentally compute in its mental landscape which direction the squirrel will run; another may not, and will simply target where the squirrel is at the moment. Which bird is more likely to get its prey?

The squirrel may have evolved behaviors of its own to trick the bird possessing the power of simulation. It may have learned to run in a zigzag fashion, or it may run in the opposite direction from its burrow, deceiving the bird of prey. Or it may evolve a simulation mechanism of its own that instructs it to look up in the sky, periodically updating its ongoing mental map of its world.

It doesn't matter how the relevant computations are performed in the mind of the bird; only that the computations are performed in such a way as to guide behavior more efficiently so as to ensure that the bird is ahead of the squirrel in the eating game. In its mind, for all it matters, the bird could well be juggling pink and purple Ping-Pong balls. It is only important that the Ping-Pong balls be arranged in its mental landscape in such a way as to ensure that the bird is better able to predict where the real squirrel is in the physical landscape.

We can understand Descartes's demon now from a new angle (Descartes, 1998). When Descartes began his examination of the truth of all those things he had come to take for granted, so that he could arrive at certain knowledge once he had excluded all knowledge he could not hold with certainty, he imagined it as entirely feasible that a demon could trick him into believing he was seeing the world, when in fact he was not. The demon could arrange things so that he would believe he was in such a world, when in fact he was in no such world at all. Evolution may not differ all that much from Descartes's demon; at least we have no reason to believe that evolution has to be fair in the game of world-making. Evolution may convince us of the existence of certain phenomena, and it is under no obligation to abide by any of *our* civilized standards for what constitutes ethical or epistemological scruples. As long as we're not dead, evolution is doing its job.

The future—which is a product of mind—is itself an evolutionary invention that enables a species to control the present, but the real future cannot be known. The gamble is that the future will be the same—in evolutionarily important ways—as the past. This is a gamble of the same sort as the gamble in assortative mating that good looks are a sign of good genes or reproductive power. The future cannot be stored and recalled; only the past. Hence the fallible nature of memory. Memory is only one component of the simulation mechanism: it makes sure that there *are* pink and purple Ping-Pong balls to play around with.

In the case of some species, including our own, simulation behaviour was transferred from the physical plane to the social. In addition to organisms constructing models of the physical world, they also constructed models of the social world, simply because the social world was a part of the physical. But in many ways, it was more complex: the social world contained beings that also simulated the world. To adapt to the social plane, your simulation of the world had to contain a simulation of the simulation of the other. And part of that simulation is your own self as it exists in the forever-unknowable mind of the other. This is the evolutionary origin of self-consciousness, of shame, guilt, and of moral and ethical awareness in general.

But the social also acts back on the physical. The social world that evolved over time came to include tools, and one type of tool use that became more predominant with civilization was language. Language was primarily an aspect of the means for coordinating others' behavior with one's own. But its instrumentality was enriched when it could be applied to the simulations of the physical world, simulations that increased their spatiotemporal scope and application.

It is necessary to remember that, like the physical simulation, the social simulation does not require that it be "true." Maybe the Ping-Pong ball in the simulation should "really" be green, but a pink one gets the job done—and so it remains in the repertoire, in the simulation's cast of characters. The mind operates solely in the currency of adaptive anticipation, of prediction and control. What you know of the other is what enables you to anticipate better where the other will be in your internal representation, so that you coordinate your behaviors more adaptively. And ultimately, this gets measured in terms of differential reproductive survival. A lot of what we know of others revolves around sex and children. So much of our treasured knowledge of ourselves and of others, of our social and moral intuition, what we might call our "wisdom," is about having sex and making sure we don't expend energy raising somebody else's child.

The same holds for what we know of ourselves. We do not possess the cognitive machinery to know ourselves with introspective accuracy and clarity. We only know what is necessary to know to be able to update our self-simulation with the simulations others make of us as one object in their representational worlds. Self-knowledge is inherently social. We know ourselves as others know us, or at least, how we *think* others know us.

It appears that there may be some convergence between some of the conclusions of an evolutionary psychology or epistemology and ancient Buddhist psychology. What we know of ourselves is simply *not* true. Indeed, we can never know ourselves, just as a hand can never grasp itself. Self-knowledge is therefore an illusion, an illusion that nevertheless has some social and evolutionary utility. And it is this illusion that underlies ego.

CHILDHOOD AS THE ARTIFICIAL AMNIOTIC ENVIRONMENT

Many have attempted to define precisely how it is that the human species differs from other species: how we are unique, how we are separate from other animals, what makes us *higher* than other animals. Assuming we accept the argument that we are, indeed, a species (and all that this entails), it seems to have been important to thinkers in the past to distinguish humans from their nearest phylogenetic relatives, and psychologists have been no strangers to this enterprise. Perhaps this tendency is indicative of a moral sqeamishness, a squeamishness at being considered related in a familial way to slimy things that crawl on the bottom of the sea, the same kind of squeamishness we experience on a trip to the zoo when we are presented with our obvious morphological resemblance to apes, who turn away from us and flaunt their swollen genitalia in our direction.

Aside from language, or sexual taboo, or tool use, one candidate proposed by psychologists of an ethological orientation that distinguishes us from our primate cousins is the prolonged helplessness of our offspring. In addition to a lengthy gestation period, humans are noted for the extreme helplessness of their progeny over a rather protracted period of time. This is connected to the plasticity of the species in general. Newborn humans are incapable of holding up their heads, let alone of independent feeding, without having to be burped by a caregiver afterwards. Infants cannot walk until at least a full year and, as children, cannot take a trip to the store until well past six or seven years of age. Imagine a child on a trip to the watering hole on the open savanna two hundred thousand years ago. While the slow development of children may present difficulties to anxious parents in the twentieth century, such helplessness would often have been catastrophic in the wilds of our ancestors, when getting food and avoiding predators was much more of a struggle than it is now.

Children require intense surveillance and monitoring on the part of parents, and given how important such surveillance was to survival, certain inborn predispositions toward cementing the parent–child bond would naturally have been selected for. Separation anxiety makes its appearance precisely at the time that infants are first becoming mobile (Cole & Cole, 1996). Separation anxiety is a sign that attachment is developing. Infants attach to their parents, and vice versa. Infant baby gestures, a type of fixed action pattern, seem programmed to elicit nurturing responses from older humans. These processes make it easier to surround the child in an artificial environment for the next few years, a social world that comes to define the entire universe for a child a long time before he or she can venture out into the "real" or natural universe.

By providing a social extension of the amniotic environment for the developing child, a period of development is assured in which the child's brain can continue to grow (for it has not attained its full maturity until well into adolescence). The child requires time to acquire the physical and cognitive skills necessary for survival in the natural world, skills that have to be encoded as synaptic connections in the brain, comparable skills that many other species are born with or learn much more quickly than humans. Human infants also have perhaps the largest heads of any species, relative to body size. And much of this head growth has to occur outside of the womb. If it occurred inside the womb there would be enormous engineering problems at birth.

While the child may be thought of as more "natural" than its parents, in the sense that he or she may be closer to the natural world, the view of the child as a "noble savage" is derived from the romantic philosophy of Rousseau, and is a kind of thinking that ignores the inability of children to cope with or adapt to the natural world using only their own resources, a world that is particularly "red in tooth and claw." Without the incubating protection afforded by the social world, the child would simply not survive. This is one reason why such cases as Victor, the Wild Boy of Aveyron (Itard, 1962), attracted much attention. Although in youth the nurturing provided by the social world is necessary, often benign, and frequently well-intentioned, the same precious world becomes a cage for adults as they attempt to transcend their childhood. In such attempts the soul is felt to be a prison of the body.

The social nature of our species evolved to ensure the unique mode of adaptation that humans practice: we are probably the most plastic of species, and depend on a very sophisticated form of cognitive simulation, requiring an elaborate nervous system to adapt to the greater variety of environments that we confront. But for this adaptation, we require a long period of social "gestation" so that our members achieve viability. Hence, the unique importance of our social world in relation to the status of the social world of other species. And the major adaptation to the social world is the ego.

The child begins life in a state of undifferentiated unity with the world. However, that unity is not something of which the child is conscious. Self and world are originally nondual. But from birth on, society interposes itself between self and world. And this is on a very concrete level. The mother is the child's world, and the mother is society for the child, mediating the child's interactions with the world. The child simply cannot exist without the constant attentions of the mother. As did Erikson (1963), we can understand the development of the child and adolescent as explained by the "widening circle" of social relations into which we enter at successive ages and through which we are mediated to the natural world.

Furthermore, in the human species, society has to mediate between the mother–child union and the natural world. As the female of the species, the mother is vulnerable for extended periods of time. Without the protection afforded by the human band, the mother would not survive on her own. We are not like other species, where the mothers can both nurture their offspring and fend for themselves. Once women entered the childbearing years in the hunting and gathering period, because they were without birth control, women were pregnant and nursing for most of their adult life. And because of the helplessness of the offspring and because of the length of time it took for children to grow up, females required protection by the social band.

* *

For the social world to regulate the child, the child has to construct that social world mentally. This is the essence of what is meant by *psychological constructivism:* the child does not passively reflect reality but must actively create it according to his or her own capacities. The child has to construct a social world in its mind, in its evolving simulation capacity, for that social world to be causally effective, so that the child may be able to control his or her self. In a nutshell, development in the early years consists of the following (Cole & Cole, 1996):

- The child has to know that external objects exist apart from its perceptions (the acquisition of the permanent object).
- The child has to know that one such object is its primary caregiver (the formation of attachment).
- The child has to construct a self or recognize itself.
- The child has to form a conception of the existence of external minds (the child's theory of mind).
- The child has to attain the operative capacity to act on and transform these elements (what is meant by "concrete operations").
- The child has to construct the social roles and rules that constitute social and moral behavior.

This takes approximately seven to ten years. It is significant that Freud (1976) believed that the Oedipus complex was resolved by this age and that the period of latency was in full swing, and it is significant that this is said to be the age of conscience (and not the age of reason, which comes later). This is also the age at which Erikson said that we have the beginnings of initiative and then of industry.

Thus, of necessity, society mediates between the individual and the natural world. There is physical evolution and there is social evolution. One product of social evolution is language. Spoken language is probably millions of years old; written language is only a few thousand years old. Language has an evolutionary course all its own. Language is also a tool of social interaction and allows social interaction to achieve a level of complexity that cannot be approximated by a species without it. And only the human species truly possesses language.

Language arises from society and social interaction, and affects the individual by means of the way it structures cognition. That is, thinking and perception are affected by language. Language, in turn, becomes a tool of thinking. With language, the child is capable of becoming truly social. Prior to language, the child relies on reflexes and can only be reinforced to form operant or classically conditioned behaviors. That is, he or she can only respond to rewards and punishments. However, with language and representational capacity, the child can begin to construct worlds.

Language mediates how the child interacts with the social world and language becomes a tool for the child to enter into interactions with the social world. Language is internalized by the cognitive system as a part of the system's capacity to form and manipulate representations, a capacity that begins to emerge at two years of age. The cognitive system in turn mediates how the child models itself in the social world. Society has to be represented cognitively to be functional, that is, society must be internalized as synaptic connections in order to effectively control behavior.

While internalization takes place, we must remember that the child does not possess the subtle representational capacity of the adult. The child has all kinds of limited representational means that often require that the elements internalized become simplified to fit into the limited informational slots that the child is capable of coordinating. An example is conscience. While in the adult social world, certain moral directives and prescriptions are codified in sophisticated religious and ethical tracts that are transmitted in elaborate rituals, when the young child takes up these same directives and prescriptions they are simplified into the often harsh and punitive vocabulary of the young child's conscience.

One major player in the evolving social simulation, aside from external rules and roles, is the system's model of itself, the ego—self as object to itself, self as role player, self as the controlled and the controller. As we develop, we construct the outward layer first—society as significant others. Society, generally in the form of mother, is interposed between self and world. Language then interposes itself between self and society. Mother employs secondary subjectivity (the tendency of baby to follow mother's gaze toward the external world) and routine scripts or formatted activities (what psycholinguists refer to as "fast-mapping") to slip the child into the semantic world of adults. Cognition then mediates how language is internalized. With representational capacity and language, self establishes ego between itself and society (Cole & Cole, 1996).

We can imagine this process as a series of concentric layers or rings. The self is positioned at the center of a series of rings, rings of mediation that create separation and distance between self and world, rings that protect and nurture the child into adulthood, and rings that also create a prison from which the adult longs for release.

EGO AS MEDIATED BEING

Through a series of mediations created during development, the self is constructed as alien to itself, divided from itself in its attempts to "know" itself, a knowing that consists largely in controlling itself, having itself, grasping itself. First, society is interposed between the self and the natural world. Then the developing mind internalizes that society within its own representational landscape, and by doing so makes an object of itself. By treating itself as object, the mind can better predict and control its behavior, according to societal expectations. And the most significant feature of society to be internalized is language.

The ability to simulate aspects of physical reality, a trait evolved during our evolutionary past, is taken over by the socialization process, which itself also evolved as a result of selection pressures, so that we may effect a simulation of social reality, one's self-simulation being but one facet of the social simulation. And the criterion for judging the truth of social simulations, just like the criterion for judging physical simulations, is the enhancement such simulations afford in our ability to anticipate. Vicarious behavior is constituted in the representational realm, thus saving enormous costs in the physical realm.

One of the products of society is language, which is internalized by the cognitive system. In being internalized, language structures the cognitive system. The cognitive system then becomes capable of representing the organism as one object among others in a representational universe. This is the basis of ego, the purely mental representation of self. The ego is basically the self's representation of its own cognitive–affective processes vis-à-vis others and the external world. The most abstracted and invariant aspects of the ego, those parts that apply across greater time spans and wider domains of experience, we call *identity*.

Society mediates the self to the world, via language's ability to structure the cognitive system to represent the self to itself as an ego. The self becomes mediated to both the world and its self, and hence, alienated. By becoming an object to ourselves, we become divided from our natures.

Both society and cognition have evolved to mediate. Society mediates by ensuring the child's and mother's insulation from the physical world. This is crucial to the human species, whose offspring require such a long external gestation period. Cognition mediates interaction with the world by providing a landscape for simulation, so that vicarious selection can occur in imagination, rather than physical selection in the brute world. We have, as a species, evolved a social life that mediates our interactions with the physical world. We know things primarily through the agency of our mothers, and later, through significant others. We have also evolved a simulation mechanism to effect representational selection, a simulation mechanism that relies heavily on language. These two, society and cognition, acting in conjunction, produce ego. The development *into* ego, and therefore also development *beyond* ego, is therefore entirely contingent on these processes.

Evolution has prepared the infant to enter readily into this artificial social world. Piaget's influence has directed our attention for too long to how the child adapts to the physical world of objects. It is far more important that the infant adapt to the social world. And adapt it does, being prewired for attachment by millions of years of evolution.

The child is prewired to maintain proximity to the mother and to experience anxiety if such proximity is threatened. As the child grows, the nature of this proximity becomes less physical, more emotional, and thereafter, more cognitive. As the child grows, the expectations regarding his or her behavior change. Punishment is the consequence of not fulfilling parental demands (see Kohlberg, Loevinger, and other ego theorists below). Punishment threatens proximity. Thus, the child learns to behave. To maintain emotional and cognitive proximity, the child learns to simulate its own actions in his or her own developing mental landscape, and the motive for doing so is to capitalize on the value of vicarious action in the representational domain. The child learns to control him- or herself to avert parental disapproval and censure.

To achieve control, the child has to regard him- or herself as others do, as one object in a social world. The look of others becomes internalized as the look aimed at oneself as object. Approval is the aim; approval is the more mediated form of proximity the child makes do with as he or she matures. But as approval and the need for it monopolizes consciousness, the ego is increasingly directed by the imperatives of its superego.

With later development, proximity is replaced by approval, and approval is replaced by *identification* (Cole & Cole, 1996). The child substitutes identification for physical proximity. If the child cannot always be *with* the desired parent, she can at least try to be *like* the desired parent. If you want something, you try to become like the object of desire. This is the essence of identification: wanting to be *like* the preferred object, by taking on their qualities and their characteristics. We want to be like those we love, who protect and nurture us. To be like these significant others, we internalize them. Freud (1976) said that conscience is formed when we take over aspects of external authorities and become our own authorities. This is the superego, the internalized voice of prescriptions and injunctions.

* *

If we grant the foregoing, the existence of a state of transcendence, a transcendence which liberates us from ego, is *not* a universal, nor is it part of some direction the universe is striving toward. It is a category error to say that the universe is unfolding as it should, because *shoulds* do not apply when we speak of the universe. Ego is simply a problem for a certain type of social and natural species. If we define transcendence as a solution to the problem of ego, to what is a contingent problem to a certain type of social species, then we cannot be the species toward which all of evolution aims, if we think that evolution aims toward *our* particular transcendence or enlightenment. Evolution, whether physical or social, does not *aim* toward anything. The conception of a hierarchy of life forms is only relevant if we accept the medieval notion of a Great Chain of Being, but it is not germane to our evolutionary framework. From the point of view of evolution, things simply happen. Species arise and they pass away, each adapted, for however brief a time, to the ecological niche from which they arise. Any purpose we might wish to see in natural selection is a projection of our human desire, a desire that is itself a result of the same forces of evolution.

"Enlightenment" would not exist were it not for the existence of *samsara*. And samsara, as humans experience it, is contingent on processes of physical and social evolution. Evolutionary pressures have evolved brains that are sophisticated enough to adequately simulate our physical worlds, "adequately," that is, only to the extent that we are alive. Evolution has also made us a social species. The interaction of these two factors brings the samsaric world into being into which children develop. This same samsaric realm is what we inherit as adults.

The purpose of the universe is not the transcendence of the human ego. The farthest galaxies care not one iota whether any of us escapes the wheel of birth and death. Our evolution is a product of contingency and of circumstance. Evolution has created the conditions for our current state of suffering and misery, as well as of our survival and of our reproductive success. And it will be up to history, and the manner in which we, as humans, make that history, to determine whether we can act back on and alter the nature of our determined being. Enlightenment occurs in specific social and historical circumstances. And these circumstances are something that can be made.

CHAPTER 4

Impulse Control and Repression

REPRESSION AND HAPPINESS

Perhaps, as was demonstrated in an earlier section, the prolonged state of helplessness in infancy and childhood uniquely differentiates us as a species in comparison to other species. Or perhaps it is our next subject that uniquely characterizes us. One may say we are unique as a species in being *rational* or *social*; however, both of these characteristics may be observed on some level in certain other species. More to the point may be that we are the *neurotic* animal. And, by neurotic, I mean *repressed.* Humans are the species that adapt by repressing. While it may be possible that other species adapt in some limited ways by employing some kind of repressive measures, surely it is humans who exclusively employ repression in such a large-scale fashion.

As much as we may lament the effects of a strict socialization—the process resulting in repression—it seems as if some degree of repression is necessary to civilization, at least as we know it. Children *have* to adapt to social reality. They have to substitute the *reality principle* for the *pleasure principle,* in Freud's terms. Impulses have to be controlled, and the ego (and superego) is the psychological mechanism that evolves to bring about this control.

Freud argued in *Civilization and Its Discontents* (1975) that repression, and hence also unhappiness, was necessary to civilization, and that it was therefore adaptive. The chaotic and amoral world of the instincts—both sexual and aggressive—has to be controlled by an ego so that the social order can be maintained and transmitted over the generations. The infant's unsublimated libidinal desires are first controlled by the parents, but with development through the psychosexual stages of Freud or the psychosocial stages of Erikson (1963), the child learns to control impulses without the need of external reinforcement, by means of the internal mediation of self-knowledge structures.

Part of my thesis is to accept Freud's view that repression is necessary for civilization, and therefore that unhappiness is the result of civilizing pressures. But we must be clear what we mean by "civilized." It is not just certain neurotics or psychotics who suffer at the hands of the warring factions of ego, id, and superego. We all do, and our individual differences in personality or character structure (ego) situate us along a continuum that varies in terms of pathology, and therefore that varies also in terms of the degree of unhappiness caused by the repression born within.

This thesis also concurs with that of Buddhism: *Life is suffering.* The universality and unavoidability of *dukkha*, or suffering, is the first of the Four Noble Truths. As long as we dwell within *samsara*, trying to attain happiness within a "worldly" framework, we cannot escape suffering, we cannot escape the frustration of our desires. Buddhism assumes that suffering is inherent to samsaric existence and posits that suffering is overcome only when the samsaric realm is transcended in nirvana. This book will show precisely how samsara has a developmental dimension to it, reflecting the vicissitudes of human biological and social existence.

Just because repression is necessary to civilization, it does not follow that repression has to be maintained throughout the entire life span. Repression, as defined here, is a psychological response that assists adaptation to society at a certain level of consciousness development. As the development of consciousness progresses, such a means of adaptation may no longer be required. With increased intelligence, with better ego functioning, with more reality adaptation—whatever we call it—some of the pressures to adapt to the social world become less pressing, at least psychologically.

In maturity, although we may no longer necessarily have to repress so as to adapt, repression still lives on in what we retain from our past in our memory and in our character structure. Our egos and our memories are outfitted in such a way as to ensure the perpetuation of the past into the present, including past repressions. Even if the more mature ego does not employ the same overtly repressive measures against itself that it did as a child in accommodating to the external world, the effects of these repressions nevertheless live on in the psyche and in the body, controlling attention and affect and thinking in ways that replicate the past.

The path of spiritual development and the road to more mature adult consciousness requires, in part, an awareness of how past automatisms control present consciousness. This is part of the Buddhist practice of mindfulness. It may also be part of what Christianity teaches when it asserts that we cannot escape sinning, and must therefore forgive and be forgiven. And it is also an aspect of what Eastern philosophies, such as Hinduism and Buddhism, teach regarding *karma,* or the ubiquity of conditioned existence.

In spite of the prevalence of conditioned habits and automatisms, there are ways to liberate and unburden consciousness from the control of the past. Some of these ways have social sanction and some do not. Some ways of unburdening us from the past only replicate the bondage effected by other forms of conditioning: one cognitive–affective script is replaced with another. Often the individual does not know who is really "running the show" of their own mind—and this is why an analyst may be necessary, as in the case of psychoanalysis, or that a master or guru may be necessary, as in the case of Buddhism.

Whereas Freud summarized the goal of psychoanalysis as being "Where id was, there shall ego be," it is my opinion that his position perpetuates the status quo of ego's control of id and consciousness. Freud may have argued this for a number of reasons. One reason was his picturing of the unconscious as a garbage can of discarded impulses (a view criticized by Jung and Reich, among others). Another was his professional identification with mainstream scientific thinking and rationality (both embracing positivism and mechanism). Another might have been his own developmental level.

Freud often wrote as if happiness were unobtainable. In this, he might be said to agree with some of an evolutionary orientation who argue that we really are not "wired" for happiness at all, and that, from an evolutionary perspective, it makes no sense for a species to be happy *all* the time. If a species were in a state of relatively permanent quiescence or satiation, it would not be motivated to engage in adaptive behaviors. A happy species is lunch. Even the short experience of postcoital pleasure is an evolutionary risk that is gambled for the sake of pair bonding and gene exchange. Happiness is only adaptive from an evolutionary point of view when it functions as the proverbial carrot at the end of the stick, that is, when it is *out* of reach. I agree with both the evolutionary and psychodynamic perspectives that happiness is not a quality we possess because of our birthright or nature.

Happiness cannot be "obtained." Happiness cannot be "grasped." From the perspective of Buddhism, our experience of unhappiness is a result of our *grasping* for happiness. Furthermore, the word *happiness* does not refer to an obvious event or object existing in the external world. For one thing, the experience of happiness is relative to the experiencer. And one of the dimensions that make happiness relative to the experiencer is developmental. Happiness is experienced relative to the level of an individual's development. With each evolution in development, happiness is experienced differently.

From a transpersonal perspective, Freud's conception of development was indeed limited. He believed that character was fixed very early in development, and that the task of analysis was to provide a more effective fit between the personality of the analysand and the social world. Freud's theory of human potential was circumscribed. Consequently, his statements regarding the possibilities for human happiness are similarly limited, situated as they were in a truncated conception of human development.

As will be seen in the following, there is a broader conception of human development emerging that can allow us to redefine the nature of happiness and of human potential accordingly. And the task of analysis, or therapy, or of spiritual teaching, is to bring the individual nearer his or her "potential." This allows for a glimpse of happiness that does not require that it be grasped at so desperately.

Freud seems to have felt that, ultimately, happiness was measured with reference to the bliss of uterine existence. For Freud, the *nirvana principle* defined the *pleasure principle,* and this was conceived of primarily in terms of reduction or elimination of libidinal tension. Civilized life, which at best requires sublimation, or at worst, outright repression, affords only a modicum of tension reduction. We are constantly tense, and from an evolutionary perspective, it pays to be tense.

Of course, our physiological mechanisms for discharging tension evolved for a different set of ecological circumstances than we currently find ourselves in. We are consequently burdened with a tension system that is no longer adaptive, but that has not had the opportunity to evolve to our changed circumstances—on this point, see Selye on the Stress of Life and the General Adaptation Syndrome (GAS) (reviewed in Cole & Cole, 1996).

We can, however, reintroduce the nirvana principle into our conception of happiness, and do so by incorporating both Buddhist teachings and a broader conception of human development. Nirvana, and therefore happiness, *can* be pursued by one of two paths: by regressive means or progressive means. *Regressive means* indicate means that are essentially infantile, reactive, and constrictive, and that might be said to characterize psychotic, borderline, or preoedipal disorders. It is regressive to define fulfillment strictly within the terms of an energy/economy model that posits pleasure solely in terms of the reduction of tension, as Freud described it. *Progressive means* include methods, paths, and techniques that facilitate consciousness expansion and development. By these means, happiness or nirvana is approached, not only by the elimination of tension or by the dissolving of the subject–object split, but by virtue of practices and paths that include and embrace the structure of ego while at the same time transcending it.

To bring this section to a conclusion, then, we can agree with Freud in *Civilization and Its Discontents* that unhappiness *is* the general human lot, that civilization and society *do* require a surrender of the possibilities of fulfillment, and that children *do* have an arduous task ahead of them of adapting to the exigencies of the social world, having to give up infantile fixations as to what constitutes pleasure. But, this necessary evil, an evil that requires that society mediate the natural world psychologically by means of the internalization of its directives in the form of ego, is an evil that can be transcended with maturity. Ego, with its curtailed restrictions on experience and its stifling of our bodies and our affects, is also a steppingstone to transcendence. And this transcendence can be achieved because of qualities unique to the cognitive system, particularly its architecture of consciousness and attention, which I describe below.

REPRESSION AND CHILDHOOD COPING

The developments of early childhood as described by psychoanalysis have generally been overlooked by many because so much controversy was generated by Freud's claims about the Oedipus complex. Because Freud seemed to place such emphasis on the boy's desire to have his mother sexually and the young girl's desire to have a penis, claims that mortified his contemporaries and that baffle and outrage many still today, the more important aspects of his theory regarding socialization and identification have been overlooked. I shall sketch an account of early childhood socialization that avoids the more "colorful" claims of psychoanalysis and that also allows us to situate ego in its rightful place in the psychological economy.

It is in the years from two to five that socialization per se occurs. Socialization consists of two complementary processes. One is internalization; the other is personality. Internalization is "taking in" from the environment, *taking in* so as to be *like* significant aspects of the environment. Personality is the way that unique aspects of cognitive and affective functioning get laid down in the brain, in spite of the tendency of the internalization process to orient toward imitation or replication. I shall focus here on internalization and, for the moment, leave out personality development, as the latter concerns individual differences. My aim here is to explicate what is most general or common.

Internalization requires the capability of representing or simulating. Our native endowment of raw simulation capability is somewhat limited, but when scaffolded by language and symbolic thought, is capable of building internal representations of significant aspects of the world. Once children possess the tools of constructive thought, they begin to create forms of mental life that reflect significant aspects of their social world.

But the child must have the motivation to do this psychological work. And the most effective motivation is reward and punishment. At two to three years of age, the child is acutely conscious of the contingent nature of the social and physical world, that he or she is at the mercy of both circumstance and powerful others.

If the child could somehow anticipate the consequences of his or her behaviors, he or she could avoid punishment, obtain rewards, and—perhaps more importantly—win the approval of significant others. The child gains this control by taking over into her or his self objects from the external world. These "objects" are put in place psychologically to enable the child to develop from *external* to *internal* control. Once these objects are internalized, the child is divided within, internally conflicted, but now capable of self-observation, self-guidance, and self-punishment.

The child uses these identifications to be able to regulate the self. Once able to regulate the self, the child is spared the necessity of having to be regulated by the external world, and this affords a measure of autonomy and freedom from external control, as well as ensuring approval from others. A key factor in self-regulation is the ability to *inhibit* (probably localized neurophysiologically in the frontal lobes). Several studies have shown how this ability to inhibit responses develops in these early years (Cole & Cole, 1996).

The ability to simulate, enhanced by symbolic representation, creates the psychological capacity for internalization. Internalization ensures that key elements of the world reside in some form within the mind. Once constructed within, the elements of the external world are in a better place to control the child by enabling the child to control his or her self. Self-control and inhibition might seem adaptive, but they do have negative ramifications because of having been developed in the early years. The elements of the world that are internalized or imitated are simplified representations of the external world, assimilated by newly evolving representational capacities that scale the subtleties of the social world down to the comprehension of a three-year-old. And the increase in the capacity for inhibition often results in repression, especially when the child experiences anything intimidating, threatening, or even worse, traumatic.

By five to six years, the child has the key elements of a socialized personality. Piaget described the child's morality in these years as a *heteronomous* morality (Gruber & Voneche, 1977). A heteronomous morality is one that is based on obeying the rules of more powerful authorities, no matter what; where the letter of the rule, and not the spirit, rules; and where all that counts is the action and not the intention.

This is the period where the child develops a conscience, which Freud termed a *superego*. The superego was said to be the outcome of the Oedipus complex. Overlooking the details of what Freud claimed was the genesis of the superego, we can agree with him that a conscience or a superego coheres when key objects in the external world are taken in and become a part of the internal world. This internalized agency assumes the role performed by parents: observing the self, giving it orders, judging it, cajoling it, threatening it, and punishing it.

Erikson (1963) situated early childhood in the second and third psychosocial stages of *Autonomy* versus *Shame and Doubt,* and of *Initiative* versus *Guilt.* He focused on the conative components of this period, when the child acquires will and self-direction, respectively. Erikson frames his stages as a series of crises or choices, and in the second and third stages, the negative side of the coin is Shame/Doubt and Guilt, the outcomes of failures to develop Autonomy and Initiative. His theory highlights another aspect of the important changes occurring in this period, a period when the child acquires self-control and self-regulation, capacities that are not givens, but have to be constructed in social interaction.

Kohlberg's (1976) Stage One is described as *Heteronomous* morality. The child begins the path to reflective judgment and morality by simple adherence to rules, largely in order to obey authority. Kohlberg's theory begins with Piaget's description of a heteronomous morality and differentiates it into three stages in the acquisition of conventional morality. Stage Two is called the *Instrumental* stage: following rules only when it is to one's interest, meeting one's own needs, and letting others do the same. Right is defined by what is fair, which is in turn defined as an equal exchange, a deal, or an agreement.

Kohlberg situates the acquisition of conventional morality and conscience at a somewhat higher age than either Freud or Piaget. This is because his focus was on *reflective judgment,* and not simple *behavior.* Stage Three is when conventional moral reasoning is obtained. It consists of living up to what is expected of you by people close to you or what is expected of you in your role as son, daughter, brother, sister, friend, and so on. "Being good" means having good motives, showing concern, and keeping mutual relationships by trust and respect.

Moral development begins with the consciousness of punishment and rewards, the awareness that there are consequences to one's actions. Only later is the mechanism of reward and punishment internalized. To act according to social rules requires that such rules control libidinal impulses from within, and not only from without. Children do not really obey, and do not possess a conscience, until they have internalized the rules. When they can behave without the surveillance of their parents, they have become their own controllers. Delay of gratification and self-control are necessary if a child is going to win the approval of peers and parents. But because the child has limited cognitive capacities, to conform to internalized social rules they learn to exclude aspects of their experience and of their natures. Consequently, they learn to symbolize only what is accepted by convention.

Cognitively, young children are not capable of ambivalence, or the toleration of contradiction. For children, morality is a matter of "tit for tat." Children insist on ritual, on strict conformity to stereotypes, that an individual be simply "bad" or "good" without qualification. They even have difficulty applying more than one adjective to a noun or in seeing that objects or persons can be multiply classified.

Besides being cognitively underequipped to cope with the demands of adult reality, children are physically powerless and dependent. They are powerless in terms of size, in terms of strength, and in terms of physical competence. Part of the resistance to evolving beyond the earlier state of primal narcissism is the dawning and undeniable awareness that the world will simply not conform to infantile wishes. The world is infinitely larger than anything toddlers can hope to placate. At times, children are overwhelmed with anxiety, helplessness, and fear of the loss of love. Consequently they develop coping and defense mechanisms to control impulses that are not acceptable, to allay fears that cannot be explained, to stop dreams that terrify, and to inhibit feelings that threaten to overwhelm. These defenses are carried over into adulthood as neurotic defenses and character armoring (Washburn, 1994).

All of us carry into adulthood repressions and defenses in our psyches, processes that have been overlearned and made habitual via automatization. We no longer have conscious control of these processes, yet they continue to regulate our cognitions, our feelings, and our behaviors. Because of them, we operate in our day-to-day lives with a dual unconsciousness: there are affects, thoughts, and sensations that we are not allowed to experience, and, in turn, we are not conscious of how we do *not* experience them by our active defenses. This is because these are automatized, controlling experience from behind the scenes.

Repression, self-control, and delay of gratification are at first hard-won achievements. They require constant surveillance and monitoring by a caregiver to be successful. But through the process of identification or internalization, the child learns to take over some of the function of surveillance on his or her self. Children desire to be like their caregiver ("identification") and so take an objectifying stance toward their own body and feelings, thus becoming divided from their being. The body becomes an object under the control of the emerging "self." Conscience begins to develop, and with it, shame and guilt. And the process is made more expedient by the use of language, which enables the child to understand his or her self and others by the means afforded by language (and *only* in the terms afforded by that language).

In this process, children can be even more censorious and more condemning than adults. They do not possess a sophisticated vocabulary for the description of internal processes and states. They label simplistically and categorically. They cannot tolerate ambivalence or contradiction. They cannot mentally attend to more than a few dimensions at once. Consequently, when they find themselves in situations where internal feelings or desires conflict with the social order, they judge their feelings and desires categorically, resorting to primitive defense mechanisms to ensure that those feelings and desires are not experienced. They repress their feelings and desires, and call them "bad" or "evil." The easiest way to control desires that are not acceptable is to deny them altogether.

The problem is that these repressions go "underground" and become, with time, part of the personality of the child: as part of the defense mechanisms of the ego's adaptation to social reality and as part of the character armor that controls and suppresses feelings. These repressions are not experienced consciously, but are only experienced in terms of their effects as muscular tension, constricted breathing, and a chronically low level of energy (Lowen, 1975). These repressions are carried over into adulthood and continue to determine the course of our habitual cognitive–affective functioning, at a time when it is no longer necessary to cope by means of such strategies (Gould, 1978).

The cognitive and linguistic processes necessary for social adaptation are based on children's ability to represent their self as an object to themselves. That objectification is achieved early on by a cognitive and linguistic being who can only process his or her experiences in simplified terms and categories. This objectification is fraught with overgeneralizations, dualities, and rigid polarities. While representations include aspects of lived experience, they also exclude more subtle aspects of experience, banishing them into unconsciousness. But self-objectification does enable the child to obtain the approval of significant others. With time, the child constructs an ego ideal that becomes not just the objectified self, but also the projected self, a self crafted to win approval, an approval largely based on a denial of nature.

As children, we are forced to evolve personalities that fit us as objects into our social worlds. We are the "good boy" and the "nice girl"; we are not the "bad" child down the street who is shunned. We craft a self-presentation that emphasizes our conformity within a larger social order we only dimly understand. As children, we are literal and judgmental, and the stories by which we script our lives are riddled with the damage we innocently do to our bodies. The problem later is that the childhood scripts so imperfectly constructed still drive us in adulthood into self-defeating paths of neurosis and unreality. While as adults we may live in a larger, wider, more sophisticated and abstract social universe, we still possess script lines inherited from childhood. These script lines often portray us as ridiculous and absurd little beings in a drama constructed out of entirely limited cognitive tools; a drama that is no longer taking place except in the realm of imagination.

Much of our waking state, what we attend to, what we think about, and what we feel, is determined by unconscious forces whose origins we do not know consciously. Some might argue that this was the chief insight bequeathed to us by Freud. We can only experience the effects of these forces. Certain of these effects are recurring and habitual: for instance, habitual ways of responding to authority figures or habitual ways of responding to members of the opposite sex. These effects are often what we refer to when we say of somebody that they have this or that kind of *personality*. These complexes push our thinking, feeling, and behavior into coercive and habitual patterns.

This kind of self-determination is very agreeable to the social powers that would have us be predictable and rule-governed. Our cognitive adaptations to social reality enable us to function in larger social orders. Conscience doth make cowards of us all. We readily transfer our expectations and attitudes deriving from parental authorities to social authorities. For a limited processing organism it makes sense to have automated some processes so as to free attention for other more energy-demanding tasks. But for many, by later adulthood, it dawns on us that almost all of our conscious lives are based on these automated conditionings.

The process of repression and the internalization of cultural dictates continues well into adolescence. Only now it is enriched by the full cognitive capabilities supplied by language. Able to engage in the widest abstraction afforded by the culture, able to decenter from the immediate interpersonal collectives in that they live, and able to entertain propositions that span enormous space/time intervals, adolescents evolve an identity that is connected to goals, projects, and values that derive from their ego ideal, an ideal that has its origins in the denials and repudiations of early childhood.

While the identity achieved may appear to be decoupled from the interpersonal collective by virtue of abstraction and increased self-directedness, its direction is still oriented by the internalization of prohibitions and prescriptions evolved at a relatively primitive state of development. The adolescent is not freed from obedience or conformity. Rather, he or she has evolved to greater feats of conformity that can function over wider and broader domains of interpersonal life, across contexts and situations that transcend the immediate demands of circumscribed childhood realities.

The repressions, defenses, and rigidities we develop are carried with us into adulthood as postures and holding patterns: character armor. We adapt to stress by constantly mobilizing ourselves for it. Because our egos are ever vigilant of the external world and ever surveillant of the internal one, we are in a state of siege. The garrison mentality is often normal for the well-adjusted ego. Balancing on a tightrope between anxiety and depression, we are never in our bodies, in our bellies, or in our breath.

A COMPARISON WITH OBJECT-RELATIONS THEORY

I would now like to compare my theory of ego development with that of object-relations theory (Cole & Cole, 1996; Washburn, 1994; Wilber, 1986a, b, c). The latter is a particular branch of psychoanalysis that understands development more in terms of relations with others than in terms of reorganizations of intrapsychic structures. Object-relations theory proposes what I call a "family drama" explanation of ego development, where the principal caregivers in the child's environment are conceptualized in largely mythic and narrative terms.

According to object-relations theory, the child begins in an *autistic* state where no differentiations between self and other or self and world are possible. In Freud's terms, the child is in a primary oceanic state of oneness. The next stage is called *symbiotic*: the child knows its physical self but only as related or fused with the mother. Between the symbiotic stage and the *oedipal* stage, about which traditional Freudians have written so much, is the *separation-individuation* period, which object-relations theorists characterize as centering around experiences with the mother.

The first phase of the separation-individuation stage is the *hatching* phase: the child "hatches" out physically from its embeddedness in the mother's protective embrace. This is followed by the *practicing* phase: the child is predominately narcissistic at this phase. The world is its oyster. The mother exists as a stable home base to which the child can return at any time. But with further separation, the child enters the *rapprochement* phase: the mother, in the child's consciousness, attains full object permanence: she can exist apart from the child's perceptions of her, and can therefore *not* be available. This precipitates abandonment anxiety. The child knows the mother as all-good, loving, nurturing, warm, soothing, blissful, *or* as all-bad, engulfing, withholding, punishing. The representations of the mother are split. And so is the child's representation of his or her self: all-good partial selves and all-bad partial selves. The child cannot coordinate these representations into a stable form of object constancy in the rapprochement stage.

For the child to achieve a stable and integrated object representation of the mother, and a stable and integrated representation of his or her self, as the child enters the Oedipal stage the child represses the intensity of affects activated by the partial selves and others, and thereby achieves a more integrated representation of self and mother. The child distances his or her self from its mother and its own feelings, and begins to identify with the father, both as a model of ego-based independence and as a rival for the mother's affections. This is termed *primal repression* and *primal alienation*. The child distances his or her self from affects that come from within and from intimacy with others, although the child does not consciously differentiate these as we do. At the Oedipal stage, the father serves as the basis for the internalization of parental directives. But this precipitates depression and mourning for the lost object of love: the mother. But as the Oedipal stage is surpassed these feelings are swept aside and the latency stage is entered.

With latency the child is ready to enter what Erikson calls the *industry* stage, the child is ready to learn how to perform; in Kohlberg's sense, the child is ready to learn how to think in a conventional moral fashion. The body is now an object and an instrument for the subject, which is now identified with a mental-egoic self. Dualism is attained: ego is separated from the nonegoic core. The nonegoic core is known by the child and conceptualized by Freudian thinkers as the id. As the self is divided into ego, id, and superego, the spontaneity and polymorphous perversity of the preOedipal child is transformed into the inhibited and sexually dormant child of the latency stage. The child begins to develop tensions and constrictions in its lower body.

This account of psychosexual development, from preOedipal to Oedipal to latency, is compatible with my own theory, but seems to include elements that are unresearchable and not testable by any empirical means. Yet it seems to explain so much that is observed in a clinical context. When all things are equal, and it is not possible to choose among competing theories, traditional philosophy of science indicates that we should opt for that theory which is more parsimonious. I believe my own account is both simpler and more parsimonious.

The child is born as an entirely natural being, an organismic and polymorphously uninhibited little creature that, to survive, must become a social being. We, as a species, are a social species. We survive because we bond together, because we allow society to mediate our interactions with the natural world. We learn to live in a social world and not a natural world. We are also a species that is dependent for a long period of time on our caregivers. We have an unusually long period of physical and then psychological gestation. The long period of psychological gestation allows for the development of ego and the first mechanisms of self-control, among other things.

Now, the instincts for becoming social are innate; these are instincts for affiliation, security, need for love, communion, and so on. But the means for becoming cognitively social are in large measure *not* innate; they must be learned. It would be too much of a digression from our discussion to explain why this is so. The chief means for becoming cognitively social is the development of ego. Be that as it may, children have to enter into the social world by coming to know themselves as an object in the social world. They have to develop a representation of themselves that they can use to insert themselves into the social world of caregivers and peers. And so children have to know themselves as object. They have to adapt to the demands of the social world by learning to control themselves as members of the social world so the caregivers in their milieu do not have to.

The problem, and the origin of repression and dualism, is that as children conceive of themselves as an object, and as they learn the first means of self-control, they have limited cognitive capacities. Thy repress themselves, not to please the father or to distance themselves from the mother (these means seem to be too deliberate). To put it in plain and simple terms, children repress because they are "stupid." They can only learn very limited and therefore constricting representations of themselves. Children have few learned structures with which to assimilate their world: they have very simple language and very limited processing resources. And they use a very crude technique of self-control: repression. With the cognitive architecture we have, this means of self-control becomes ingrained in the brain and directs consciousness in the form of habits and automatisms. Later in adulthood we learn more sophisticated techniques of self-control, such as sublimation and suppression. Even as adults, our consciousness, or our child-consciousness, is still automatically activated by eliciting circumstances. We react before we even see.

The difference between this account and that of object-relations theory is really only that this one is simpler. And in the absence of researchable methods of testing the competing propositions, the law of parsimony dictates that we should opt for the simpler theory. Indeed, I would like to suggest that the "family drama" account is motivated by mythic and narrative impulses that are reflective of the stories theorists feel compelled to entertain when they are at the narrative stage of life (see below).

TRANSCENDENCE AS DEREPRESSION

Because we do not experience the present in adulthood, relying as we do on our representations, we may come to feel a sense of staleness, a lack of richness and vividness. This is because we are stuck in our concepts of how things are, which are the ego's attempts to duplicate old experiences. We try to be happy by holding on to how things were. Memory contains nothing but the past; memory is constructed from the remains of the dead. Thus, we are "sickled o'er by the pale cast of thought."

Because we occupy most of our time in our thoughts of how we and others are or ought to be, we may feel we have already been here before, and that we can all too easily predict what we are going to do. This state characterizes normal neurosis. This same lack of present-centeredness may become pathological as *depression,* where the present is seen through the jaundiced pessimism of the defeated ego of the past, or this lack of present-centeredness may become pathological as *anxiety,* where experience is constantly framed against the impending catastrophe that looms on our every horizon.

Part of spiritual development, or the evolution of consciousness, is about breaking those mental circuits that force us to live in thoughts of what we cannot have or have lost or hope to win. According to Eastern philosophy, the way to weaken and eventually sever the hold the past and future have over our consciousness is to be mindful in the present, to allow a gap in the cascading and ceaseless sequencing of thoughts and feelings that play themselves out in states of conditioned reality.

In the language of Eastern thinking, the weight of the past and its hold on the present is termed *karma* and the reality it binds us to is termed *samsara*. This is a reality that is constructed—in the East they tend to say that it is constructed by our minds, but in the West we tend to say it is constructed by society. Samsara binds us because of our ignorance. And ignorance is simply lack of awareness, an inability to experience the moment as it presents itself: naked, raw, sharp and penetrating, without filters, without reference points, without smokescreens and games.

While our culture celebrates "the pangs of conscience" and exhorts self-consciousness as that which distinguishes us from animals and children, making us more than mere brutes and babies, these same faculties hinder our spiritual consciousness from evolving. Spiritual consciousness is, in part, about letting go of the habit of taking the self as object. Spiritual consciousness is about turning off the chatter and commentary we ceaselessly make to ourselves as we monitor our behaviour.

By taking ourselves as objects, we are never really ourselves. We are only ourselves observing ourselves, monitoring ourselves, comparing our selves with images of how we would like to be and how we want to be seen by others. We are thus divided from ourselves and not authentic to our selves. When we have some really good ice cream we are more concerned with how it compares to the other ice cream we have eaten, or what ice cream we will eat in the future, or the ice cream the person next to us is eating. At the point of orgasm we immediately bring ourselves back into our little identity and begin planning ahead for what we will have for lunch or who we have to phone in the afternoon.

Constantly tense, constantly under stress, we constrict our breathing so that we may freeze the moment solidly in the time frame of our minds, afraid of a free consciousness abandoned to the phenomenal world. It is our breath that connects us most obviously to our worlds and it is our breath that is the barometer of our soul. With our breath we can let ourselves go as well as let the world inside, surrender our grasping and give ourselves away. With our breath we can let the world into the pit of our belly and open ourselves to things as they are, grounding ourselves in the present. And it is with our breath that we begin meditation.

When we allow ourselves to exist in the moment without interrupting ourselves, without monitoring, without the incessant chatter of our conversations with our selves and imagined others, we allow space for our "selves" to emerge. We relax our self-judgments and give ourselves permission to be what we are. From this, we learn to experience a warmth toward ourselves, an openness to all aspects of our being. In childhood and youth, we had to learn how *not* to trust ourselves so that we could become what we imagined others wanted us to be, so that we could win their approval. With transpersonal development, we let go of the need for approval, and from this arises true tenderness and compassion, first toward the self and then toward the world.

CHAPTER 5

Cognition

FIXATION OF BELIEF

Cognition evolved to serve the tribe, and by means of the tribe, the purposes of evolution, which are simply survival and reproduction. Evolution dictated to cognition that it be an obedient instrument of adaptation. It was only much later in the scheme of things that humankind, in an act of *hubris,* required that cognition should fulfill the epistemological requirements set forth by *our* canons of culture, themselves really just the epiphenomenal steam of other more important cognitive operations. Cognition was shaped and defined by the pragmatic necessities of survival and reproduction, i.e., know where a good hunting ground was, know how to make a good arrow, know how to coordinate others to carry out a hunt. There was evolutionary pressure to simulate only those aspects of the world that were relevant to the species's survival.

And for the human species, the most important aspect of the world was the social world. This was because the human species took the gambit at some time in the past that social cooperation would best perpetuate the species. There was evolutionary pressure to understand others and oneself only in such a way as to ensure cooperation, and a large portion of cooperation consists of how to give and receive orders. There were evolutionary pressures to shape cognition to serve specific purposes; there were no particular evolutionary pressures to develop mathematical or poetic or scientific faculties.

We can distinguish between cognition about the physical world and cognition about the social world. Our cognitive architecture is inadequate when applied to the subatomic realm, and barely adequate to follow basic scientific reasoning (witness the paucity of demonstrated formal operational thinking ability). However, as far as the physical world and the business of life is concerned, our cognitive processes are quite successful at the following sorts of things: identifying and remembering where objects in a scene are, how to assemble tools, where certain plants can be harvested, how to find a source of drinking water.

Similarly, when it comes to social cognition, we are not naturally endowed with the insights of wise or compassionate people. We are, however, quite capable of identifying where we may position ourselves in a pecking order (dominance and submission), when our mates are showing signs of sexual attraction to conspecifics other than ourselves (jealousy and insecurity), when our progeny are distressed (care and pity), who our relatives are (who we will treat with love), and who we will treat as the out-group (that is, who we will treat with indifference or hatred).

In the case of both physical and social cognition, I will make the point throughout the following that we possess a cognitive apparatus that is designed for the fixation of belief, and not the testing of these beliefs in a systematically logical or scientific fashion. For most purposes, the efficiency and quickness with which we can stamp the imprint of beliefs into our minds is more important than patiently forcing our minds to pursue a steady accumulation of information by applying systematic procedures (which requires the coordination of thousands of others in elaborate technical and social communities to be useful—scientists working alone accomplish little). For the purposes of evolution, we need only to learn what is relevant and to learn it quickly. To escape from drowning we do not need to perform a chemical analysis of the composition of water; we need only an instantaneous perception to get out of water that is over our head.

We are believers by nature: we take in what we perceive from the environment to be true, and we take in what we learn from our immediate reference group (the family) to be true (this is one factor that allows us to learn language so rapidly in childhood). For most purposes, it does not make evolutionary sense to bracket our cognitions about reality as probable or tentative, constructed or relative, so that later we may systematically evaluate knowledge claims dispassionately. In the heat of the evolutionary moment, when the receptive female presents herself or the fearsome predator appears, it is imperative that we ascribe truth value to our representations so quickly that we do not even for a moment regard them as representations. We are wired to make the evolutionary gamble that our simulation of the world *is* the world.

Because we have evolved a complex and elaborate social order (much more so than other species) we have evolved a complex mode of simulating that order, and ourselves within it. But just because we can have representations of ourselves (within that order) it does not follow that those representations are accurate, that is, valid with reference to our "true" self. We are wired to develop certain representations of ourselves and of others to enable social coordination and interaction, and that is all. We are not wired to develop other kinds of representations. We can consider ourselves as related to others through roles, rules, prescriptions, reciprocities, affirmations, and so on. We have evolved so as to take these structures as real, i.e., that we are what we construe ourselves to be, that we are our ego, our socially constructed and bounded self. We come to accept that simulation of our self, inserted into the social order, as our "real" self, and not to see it as a fiction or fabrication.

Because we have to coordinate our actions with others we have to learn how to control those actions. We have to represent ourselves within the social order so that we can monitor and control ourselves. Actions are monitored best when the actor has an internal ("cognitive") means of self-surveillance, so that others do not have to monitor and control him or her behaviorally, as is the case for children. Surveillance is more efficient when it can be carried out in a simulated environment rather than the behavioral one, a simulated environment that nevertheless maps isomorphically with the external world in important respects, germane only to evolutionary demands. This frees the organism from the more costly and direct behavioral forms of surveillance. Children require direct behavioral forms of surveillance before they can develop to the point of being free from external rewards and punishments. But the freedom won has a cost in terms of the pangs of conscience children learn to endure, pangs that arise within, without the mediation of external prompting.

THE PRIMACY OF THE SOCIAL

While cognition is sometimes studied as a form of higher logical functioning, as in the case of the Piagetian tradition, or as sophisticated problem solving applied to abstract tasks in the cognitive psychology and computer simulation tradition, or whether it is studied as abstract reasoning skills in the intelligence testing traditions, the picture that has emerged is one of the reasoner as a scientist or a chess player or a mathematician (Anderson, 1980). By contrast, in the social psychology tradition there has been a tendency to construe cognition as conformist and compliant, reflecting group norms and opinions rather than initiating original thought or testing propositions systematically.

Early work in social psychology has reminded us of the power of the social situation to dictate beliefs. Cognition, to the extent that it reveals itself in social behaviors, has been shown to function to reflect group-achieved norms, to be a consensus maker and not a consensus breaker.

Asch's experiments showed that people's perceptions of line lengths could be made to conform to group norms even if those group perceptions conflicted with accurate perceptions. Milgram's famous experiments on obedience to authority revealed the extent to which people will inflict pain on others simply because they are told to do so. And Zimbardo's prison simulation studies at Stanford indicated that normal college students, without any apparent psychopathology, can be induced to behave in both passive-dependent or authoritarian-aggressive ways, assuming the roles required by their costumes and their environment, roles dictated by the situation. These studies, and others like them, reveal the readiness with which people will adapt to a social situation and mirror its expectations (Zimbardo, 1999).

Religion is simply one type of belief system, founded in social interactions. Bertrand Russell once commented that religious beliefs had nothing whatsoever to do with rationality, and the simple reason he adduced for this was that the major determinant of the content of people's religious beliefs was not the reasonableness of the beliefs or their fit with experience, but rather the particular neighborhood or place on the planet where people happened to grow up. Russell is citing an obvious fact: religions are distributed geographically. The major determinant of the content of what people believe is where they happen to live, and this indicates that people will tend to believe whatever it is that their neighbors believe. No rational process of comparison or evaluation intervenes.

We are a species that believes. Belief ensures group conformity. With shared beliefs we can coordinate our expectations of each other and behave according to group-accepted norms. Shared beliefs assume that we all can refer to commonly accepted images and patterns of conduct. Shared beliefs ensure that we are enculturated in commonly accepted stories on which we can model our behaviors so that we can understand each other's behaviors. Without a corpus of myths and stories to draw on, we would fail to recognize our own humanity in each other.

For rules, roles, and norms to function effectively in guiding behavior, they have to be embedded in larger narrative frameworks that provide the overarching meaning for how we learn to situate our behaviors with reference to others and coordinate our actions. To adapt to the drama that is our social lives, we have to be able to take on the scripts of identity and meaning our culture has transmitted to us. Our cognitive architecture is proficient at ensuring that we adopt scripts and routines, but it is not as well evolved to allow us to reason reflectively and critically about the content of such scripts. Once such scripts are learned and practiced, once they have become automatic and ingrained into the flow of control in our brains, it is even harder to stop them.

Many of the world's problems can be traced to the fact that we are primarily a believing sort of species. Nationalism, racism, religious and political intolerance of all kinds occur because of a failure of groups to share and conform to the same creeds. As a species, when we were still foragers, hunters, or early agrarians, we did not encounter dissimilar cultures and societies, and if we did, they were treated as the enemy, as the competitor, as the out-group, because they threatened our resources, because they wanted our women, and because they might kill our children.

Furthermore, once our cognitions begin to hold that such and such a state of affairs exists, such and such a state of affairs actually does come to exist. Social reality is more produced and plastic than we conventionally allow (Berger & Luckman, 1967). Common sense holds that we acquire our beliefs about the world from the way things are; the job of our cognitive processing is to mirror that way things are—accurately. The causal relationship is unidimensional.

But experiments in social psychology have demonstrated that the causal relation can often be bidirectional. We do not simply perceive ourselves as we are. We make certain observations of ourselves and then attempt to construct theories to explain to ourselves what it is we are doing. Social psychologists call this *self-perception theory.*

Once we have these theories in place, regarding ourselves and others, we go about constructing the world in our own image, whether we view this constructing as a creative transformation of reality or as a procrustean endeavor. And this is what is meant by *the social construction of reality.* A variety of phenomena attest to the power of beliefs in shaping reality. The social categories we develop and project on others actually do divide the world into in-groups and out-groups. When we project these beliefs onto ourselves we engage in *self-fulfilling prophecies*; we behave in ways consistent with our beliefs about ourselves. Even our level of optimism can modulate our immunological functioning. When we project our beliefs onto others, we create behavioral confirmations; our expectations can cause others to conform to our thinking about them.

BIOLOGICAL ARCHITECTURE

As fallible and very limited in the amount of information that they can process, our cognitive abilities can be understood better if we have some idea of the architecture of the system. By *architecture* I mean those biologically determined and relatively fixed characteristics of our brains that have evolved to serve evolutionary goals. Our brains have certain characteristics that cannot be modified by experience. Just as our stomachs can only digest certain nutrients or our eyes absorb certain wavelengths of light, so can our brains only perform certain operations within certain constraints.

What we are conscious of is a function of what has a sufficient activation level in regions of the brain, whether the source is actively determined processes or passively determined processes. Activation level is the product of the brain's biochemical and physical properties. Consciousness is the result of the interplay of two processes: one a relatively active process of *centration* and the other a more receptive process of *awareness*. Memory is generally the source of knowledge structures that determine what gets centrated; awareness is generally the result of sensation arising from the environment. Both the active and receptive processes have strict limits in terms of processing load. Each requires a sufficient activation level before their contents enter consciousness.

Two sources of stimulation compete for access to consciousness. One source is the internal world, which is stored as memory, consisting largely of learned elements, which serve as internal stimuli. The other source is the external world in the form of sensations, perceptions, or feelings that are activated or aroused as a result of stimuli affecting the organism. When memory predominates we speak of *top-down processing*; when sensations predominate we speak of *bottom-up processing.*

Memory, or what some cognitive psychologists call *long-term memory*, is very large and apparently inexhaustible. It enables us to store the millions of details of one or more languages, it allows us to recognize thousands of different persons in a mere fraction of a second, it has the ability to be able to recall detail about perceptual arrays that rivals most AI (artificial intelligence) machines. While retrieval capacity may be variable, storage capability seems to have no upper limit. Retrieval is about providing the most effective cues that will activate the relevant parts of our memory repertoire, and this part of memory is modifiable via learned strategies.

Both the active and the passive aspects of consciousness have serious processing limits. Sensation and perception can only channel a limited number of elements into our focal attention. If you are attending to elements of a visual display, you cannot process the left field as well if you have to attend to the right field at the same time. And if you are engaged in visual processing, you cannot attend to auditory stimuli as well, nor pick up as much detail proprioceptively. And if you are processing elements of the right visual field and you receive a sharp pain in the arm (from bumping it against a desk, for example), you will not be able to perceive changes in the visual field because of the stimuli imploding from the proprioceptive senses.

Similarly, the active aspect of consciousness, *centration,* can only hold a certain number of elements in attention. If you introduce new elements into the span, old elements are pushed out. If you try to hold one telephone number in mind and somebody asks you to remember another, if you try to remember the second, the first will be lost. The span's actual size is disputed, but it does operate within a very narrow window, influenced by such factors as arousal, fatigue, interest, and so on.

Evolution has provided us with several means of overcoming the size of the span of centration. Of course, one means of overcoming the span's limit is the organism's ever-present option of relying on perception. If the environment can serve as the source of activation of a stimulus element, then there is no need to rely on internal sources of activation for that element. But another means of overcoming the size of the span of centration is based on a biologically evolved and ubiquitous architectural feature—*automatization.* (There are other methods of overcoming limits to consciousness that are not directly attributable to evolution, but are rather due to cultural factors.)

Because there are only a certain number of elements that can be centrated at a time, one strategy we have evolved to get around this limit is to "chunk" the elements that compete for centration. Whereas earlier, two elements would occupy the span, now these same two elements can be combined to become one, and thereby occupy only one space in the span. It is chunking that explains some of the efficacy of practice. Practice builds automaticity. As you repeat thinking strategies, motor behaviors, or ways of processing the world, you chunk the elements you attend to so that they occupy less processing space. Once these elements are automatized, they can perform without consuming the resources needed for centration.

One way of thinking about the cognitive system adopted from computer science is a way of seeing learning as taking as its object its own processing, that is, to be self-referential. Elements of a program are called by statements. Elements can exist in a system independently or be brought into play in a coordinated fashion. In programming, you can make one statement stand for several other coordinated statements. Calling the former invokes the latter. With a limited centration capacity you can only bring a fixed number of statements to the foreground of processing. But if statements can invoke other groups of statements, you can effectively get several statements going at once while only having to centrate the one superordinate statement, which invokes the other substatements.

However, we must not think that centration operates in a vacuum. The cognitive processing that is a result of centration itself has its own determinants. Centration is an effortful and limited resource that has to be activated by other elements in the cognitive system. Affects, personality sets, prior learning, perceptual inputs—all these acting separately or in conjunction via top-down processing can activate centration by eliciting goals that direct the processing resources of the system in certain ways and not others.

Furthermore, the processes that have been automatized, and are therefore no longer accessible to consciousness, may be so automatized that they no longer operate in a conscious fashion at all, but their effects will. This way, these automatized processes will not consume as much of the central processing resources. Habitual routines, scripted performances, and mental sets may be so automatic as to be unavailable to conscious awareness, but we can be conscious of the effects of these structures. They become activated in our long-term memory store as a result of experience and direct our conscious processing in an unconscious fashion.

You become aware while driving that your engine makes an unusual sound. This activates a cascade of thoughts and feelings: you haven't taken the car to the garage for a long time, visits to the mechanic are always expensive, you haven't put aside money this month to handle car expenses, you have other bills to pay, you haven't made much money this year, your boss is a cheapskate, you haven't asked him for a raise, you have doubts about your competence on the job, your father always made you doubt your manhood, you hate your father, the older guy in the car in front of you slams on his breaks, you blare your horn at him and yell an obscenity, a cat runs out from in front of his car, you feel like an ass and you are red in the face.

Much of this train of associations is not available to habitual consciousness. But the effects certainly are in our actions and in our habitual affective reactions to things. We are conscious only of the effects of these patterns but not of the many interconnected processes that bring them about. Similarly, once we have learned how to ride a bicycle we no longer have access to the many motor coordinations that we originally had to learn as children.

The problem, then, is that while attention is thereby freed from the requirement to process elements that have been overlearned and automatized, the elements that are automatized can then no longer be the distinct focus of attention and awareness. We do not notice all the details of how we tie our shoes or brush our teeth or how we perform certain social rituals or bodily functions, except at a gross level. We learn to be conscious of aspects of our world that are problematic, novel, or disequilibrating, and we learn by not noticing or not being mindful of experiences that are habitual or routine.

We have a cognitive system or architecture that is biased to operating as a signal-detection mechanism, a system on the alert for anxiety-provoking signals or signals that indicate the probable satisfaction of biological needs. When the present environment does not provide the organism with threats or gratifications, it begins to look for new problems or desires in its simulation, via scanning its long-term memory store. We invent things to worry about or fantasy worlds that gratify our desires. Attention is the servant of learned and predetermined biases toward detecting stimuli that indicate rewarding or aversive experiences. Attention is seldom deployed to the everyday or prosaic. Yet most of our lives consist of events that have no direct relevance to avoiding anxiety or obtaining need gratification. So we don't pay attention to these events, and fail to live in the present moment. We are biologically and socially programmed *not* to be mindful of our environments or ourselves. And as a result, we may come to a point where we may feel empty.

As we learn more and as we get older, more of our conscious lives are determined by top-down processing. Memory directs the span of attention and constitutes a good portion of what the span of attention is deployed in activating. Perception and sensation, or bottom-up processing, may initiate a chain of thoughts or images, but in no time the contents of memory take over with an almost infinite cascading of associations, and become the content of what we pay attention to. We notice a novel sensation—a sunset as it casts a unique shadow over the skyline; we watch the drops of water that bead down on our study window in never-before-seen branching patterns—and in seconds our minds switch on the machine, processing thoughts and images of that sensation—no longer the sensation itself.

One portion of memory is devoted to storing elements relevant to processing our cognitive, affective, and social lives. This portion requires that we have knowledge of our selves as objects situated in a social universe. This portion of memory is *ego*. As we mature into adolescence and early adulthood, more of our consciousness is occupied by its imperatives. The ego often directs what will be centrated, and what is centrated is more and more often the very contents of ego. We therefore live in a reflection of our worlds, a reflection that is socially constructed.

One of the principal guides determining what gets automatized is the language and thinking patterns prevalent in a society. If a mode of social practice and discourse causes you to attend repeatedly to phenomena, you are more likely to overlearn or automatize those phenomena and not others. If words referring to aspects of experience direct your attention more to that experience, you will more likely develop habitual ways of responding to that experience. Such learning, in a sense, then goes "underground," it tends to become subconscious, and begins to control conscious attention by means of processes that are not themselves subject to voluntary control. Large proportions of those processes that determine what is consciously perceived are not consciously perceived. As a result, language and social discourse cause us to perceive in socially acceptable and habitual ways. Certain aspects of our perceived world become the focus of our attention by means of processes that we cannot normally centrate.

It makes both evolutionary and social good sense for us *not* to habitually perceive aspects of our worlds. Each of these realms possesses criteria for determining relevance, and thus large domains of experience get condemned to irrelevance. With adult maturity, many aspects of our modes of responding to our lived world are conditioned and automatic. While we are relating to our world we may not therefore be *in* it because we are processing via overlearned schemata. Top-down cognitive processing may allow us to adapt to natural selective pressures and social expectations, but it does so by making us the slaves of our memories, that is, slaves of the past, blind to the present. Thus we are creatures of the mediated worlds of our peers rather than the world afforded us by natural perceptions.

Because we can automatize, we can pay attention to novel aspects of our worlds and still have mental resources available, which can be directed to relevant phenomena. We centrate things that are relevant to our affects, our goals, and our needs, and we make routine those things that are habitual and no longer require active processing. As we mature, more and more of our experienced world becomes automatized. This enhances our ability to adapt to the natural and social world, but we do so at the expense of not being conscious of most of that same world. Most of our automatized patterns for adapting to the social world are encoded in those repertoires of our personality we call *ego.*

Just as we can learn bad habits as well as good, so can we automatize unhealthy routines as well as healthy routines. Because many of the things we learned that became parts of our ego or personality were things we learned while we were young, it is easy to see why many of these are based on distortions, confusions, simplifications, and arbitrary directives. On the one hand, as children we possessed very limited cognitive abilities and strategies, and had to assimilate experience to very limited schemata. On the other hand, we may have had parents, teachers, older peers and siblings who treated us in an authoritarian fashion, forcing us to accept prescriptions and injunctions that only served their own interests. Either way, we acquired habits of thinking, feeling, and behaving reflective of primitive stages in the development of consciousness. These are still, in adult life, capable of controlling the contents of our consciousness.

It is our *karma* to experience things in the present according to the habit tendencies of our past lives. But the effects of our karma are not inescapable. While much of our lives are lived like those of programmed robots because so much of our brain's circuitry is automatized, we still possess an active centration process and a flexible awareness process. And with changes in consciousness over the span of development, significant changes in centration and in awareness can occur, changes that can make us more open to and appreciative of the contents of centration and awareness. And with practiced mindfulness as well, we can reduce the powerful effects of our conditioning, to become more fresh, open, and spontaneously alive to the moment.

COGNITIONS ABOUT SELF

For evolutionary reasons, we can see that cognition is not about achieving a state of "knowing reality." Religion has defined its set of beliefs as revelation, and it has done this to ensure its power. The scientific revolution was instigated by those who sought to displace the power of the church, and it did so by holding that its propositions were more "real" than those of the church.

If cognition does not display, reveal, or "mirror" reality, if cognition only processes functional representations, then when we consider cognition about the self, we are led to the conclusion that such cognitions are, by their nature, not true. Cognitive representations, by their very nature, cannot capture the self. And, if this is true, then the ego—defined as cognition about the self—is an illusion.

Social cognition is about conformity to the tribe. It is cognition about how to fit one's behaviors into the group-accepted norms of regulation and reciprocity. Social cognition is a process of representing the self as an object in a world of other objects, and thereby controlling itself. As argued earlier, spiritual development in adulthood is concerned with the transcending of ego. Ego is constructed to insert the self into the social order. The self is inserted into the social order via the construction of ego. The focus of spiritual development, then, is transcending social cognition and the ego. And the message of spirituality, in contrast to social constructionism and social and linguistic determinism, is that we are *not* only our socially constructed selves.

A cognitive system endows its possessor with a unique survival advantage. Instead of employing behaviors as fodder for trial-and-error selection, the possessor of a cognitive system can use its simulations of the external world as a landscape in which it can perform vicarious trial- and-error selections, saving costs in terms of lost limbs and damaged tissues.

Language takes over the cognitive system and piggybacks on the system's ability to represent physical entities and itself as one such entity in a simulated world. In addition to representing itself as a physical object among other physical objects in a largley "natural" world, language structures how that same system represents itself in more abstract categories as one role vis-a-vis that of others in complex social systems.

COGNITION AS REPRESENTATION OF SENSATION, PERCEPTION, AND ACTION

If we grant that cognition evolved to serve the purpose of simulation, then we have to remember that simulation, in addition to not being a pure "reflecting" of things, is entirely structured and constrained by the properties of the systems that produce them. On the one hand, we have to consider that there is no evolutionary requirement to be "true"—only functional. On the other hand, even what has to be simulated is not itself the way things are. Even before we get to the level of cognitive representation or cognitive transformation (further up in the information-processing hierarchy), we need to acknowledge that the elements on which cognition is operating are structured by our nervous systems in specific ways. The systems that cognition is meant to reflect are sensations, perceptions, and actions. And sensations, perceptions, and actions are biologically constrained and programmed methods of extracting data or information from the environment in narrow and predetermined ways.

Even if cognition somehow were to evolve to some pristine level where it could simply capture whatever was offered to its processing systems in some kind of "pure" form, still we would be stuck in our biological life worlds just as much as the salamander or frog is, unable to see beyond the mud and algae of our sensoria, immersed as we are in our biologically constrained *umwelt*. Perception, sensation, and action are all tied to properties of the organs they are based on. These organs do not "transmit" information from the external world in some kind of unadulterated fashion. For example, at the level of sensation, signals are transduced into neural firings. These firings reflect some of the properties of the signals they transmit, but they also equally reflect properties of the nervous system transmitting them. Furthermore, not all possible signals are picked up, only those the system is prewired to pick up.

Cognition does not simply "reflect," it also acts on objects that are received, and it acts on objects, or transforms them, in ways that are designed to enable the system to better "anticipate" what will happen best. Just as there are only certain properties that can be "reflected," so are there only certain actions or transformations that can be enacted. For example, cognition can only simulate properties of the visual system such as which section of the electromagnetic spectrum the eye is responsive to. Similarly, transformations or actions can only be modeled or simulated that are possible in some analogue form in the behavioral or action capacities of the organism. Classification and seriation are the standard such transformations studied by Piagetians (Gruber & Voneche, 1977). Both of these are mental operations that have close analogue forms in the behavioral repertoire of the human species, a repertoire that is determined by our functioning within three-dimensional space by means of the hands, arms, and legs our species happens to be born with. Piaget claimed that such operations are interiorized actions. If they are interiorized actions, they can only reflect properties of the actions interiorized.

Perhaps too much has been made by developmental psychologists of the powers and potentials of mental operations. As part of the backlash against behaviorist theorizing, psychologists since the 1960s have been investigating how the organism acts on its environment as well as how it is receives from its environment. Characteristics may have been attributed to these actions that somehow endow the possessor of such actions with transcendent qualities that do not really exist, at least as a result of the possession of such actions. Our mental repertoire of mental operations and transformations is as much rooted in our biological natures as is our repertoire of perceptual and sensorial capabilities. We are just as strictly a species possessed of certain organs of knowledge in the operative as in the figurative domains of cognition.

In conclusion, I have argued in the foregoing that cognition is very limited and constrained, and that this should serve a cautionary note when we reflect on what exactly it is we are doing when we say we are thinking or reflecting or knowing. However, in addition to the biologically based means of overcoming cognitive constraints, we have also evolved a tool for transcending the cognitive limitations I have been discussing, and that tool is language. Language enables the information-processing system to go beyond faulty reflection and clunky transformation, and to construct worlds unavailable to other species. With language, you have the possibility of science, of history, of mathematics, and of art and the storied narrative of our being.

CHAPTER 6

Language

LANGUAGE AS A CULTURAL PROSTHESIS

Language enables its users to overcome the limitations of the cognitive architecture. This includes: the outsourcing of the long-term memory store, the increase in temporary attention span, the preservation of the thought trace in physical form, the creation of a public domain of discourse, and so on. By amplifying and expanding the cognitive architecture, I wish to show how language increases a species's power of simulation, and therefore enhances its evolutionary success rate. In the next section on language, I shall describe how language provides another simulation domain not dependent on individual processing capacity, and how language creates a new domain of selection that creates new principles of fitness. In the third section on language, I describe the ways in which language affects cognition and how we can understand both social constructionism and linguistic determinism.

With the evolution of language, humans acquired a better capacity for simulation of the external world, a capacity that enhanced their adaptive capabilities and contributed to their reproductive success. Language could be used as a tool to extend the cognitive simulation capability of the brain. Many of the limitations and constraints imposed by the cognitive architecture discussed in previous chapters could be overcome by the use of language. Principles of natural selection ensured that those members of the human species who possessed language survived better than those members of the species who did not.

However, it should be kept in mind that hominids survived with only spoken language for millions of years. Written language evolved quite recently and has not evolved at all for many societies. Because of this, the evolution of written language has not affected the human species as an *organism,* that is, the evolution of written language has not affected humans at a species or genetic level because such changes require hundreds of thousands of years to take effect. But written language has had enormous effects on the evolution of language per se.

Language enhances evolutionary success by extending and enriching the species' powers of simulation. One of the major ways it improves the powers of simulation is by conferring the ability to communicate: to share cognitions. Once cognitions are shared they can be operated on in many more ways than they would if kept private. If a thought can exist beyond the particular circumstance of one thinker, it can then be developed and extended, added on to and elaborated, in ways beyond the capacity of that one thinker. When cognitions are more readily shared, they have longer duration, greater reach, and more chance of being called on for future processing. Furthermore, when the originator of a thought dies off, the thought itself can carry on in the memory of the collective.

When a thought is not shared it can only be operated on in ways conceivable to the one individual. But when a thought is shared, it can be operated on in ways beyond what is conceivable to that individual, and it can therefore become something other than one individual can imagine. Once a thought exists in the collective domain, it achieves a life of its own and can become something greater than anything conceived privately.

Part of the sharing of thoughts, the communication of thinking, is the externalization of ideas. When ideas are externalized, they take on a reality and a life of their own. Given the limited processing span of the human cognitive architecture, there is a limit on what can be processed at one time. But if an idea can be externalized, it can enter into the apperception of thought without having to occupy a "slot" in the limited span of attention. Because an external source serves for the activation of the thought or idea, an internal source of activation is not required.

Thoughts are wispy things. In the middle of a conversation it is common to lose your thought if your partner does not give you space or time to express your thinking. People will often rush to record their thoughts on paper so as not to lose them. Of course, if some thoughts are reinforced by the environment, they stand a better chance of occurring again. But for every thought reinforced by the world, there are countless others that are not reinforced and are lost for all time. Some thoughts cannot be readily expressed as words; perhaps they occur more readily as images. If not given verbal form, there is a chance the thought will be lost.

Once a thought is able to enter the vernacular of a tribe or a society, it will be repeated—by oneself and others. Once a thought is shared, others have a certain probability of using it that increases the overall probability of its being repeated in any individual's attention. If a thinker can grasp a word or string of words from the repertoire available in a culture, they will more likely activate the thought carried by the words. Of course, the thoughts each person activates in conjunction with a series of word forms are not all shared in identical ways.

But with the evolution of *orthography*, that is, written language, the preservation of thought entered an entirely new domain. An entire society and all of its practices, its traditions, its rituals, and its myths, could be preserved and transmitted or re-discovered at a later time.

With the evolution of language and the development of written communication, thinking could in turn be used as a simulation world in itself. In other words, language extended cognitive processing, functioning as a prosthesis, and it eventually created a new domain of simulation altogether. More specifically, language extended, enriched, and multiplied the processing capability of the cognitive architecture by affording and facilitating greater working memory space. Language also created an autonomous domain of simulation that acquired a degree of independence from individual thinkers. A form of long-term memory could now function autonomously of the physical medium of brains. And since, with orthography, language could be preserved in various symbol systems apart from that of neurological coding, language could grow in a world of its own making. Symbol systems and the products of such symbol systems were not subject to the same processes of death and decay that humans are subject to. Memories could now last beyond two generations. Thus, history was constructed. Knowledge could become a reality apart from its having to be instantiated consciously in the brains of individual thinkers.

LANGUAGE AS AN AUTONOMOUS DOMAIN OF SIMULATION

As language gets preserved in various ways, it becomes an autonomous domain that begins to manifest its own laws of selection, functioning as an alternate simulation domain above and beyond the cognitive, behavioral, and species's domains. Examples of language domains are symbol systems.

Because language could function in a largely autonomous domain of its own, its evolutionary benchmark was no longer solely what it could contribute to the enhancement of individual survival and reproductive success. While it is true that language is an organ of the species, as are our lungs or our heart or our brain, unlike these physiological adaptations, the forms of language came to outlive the individual users of those forms. This meant that language could produce forms that became subject to evolutionary pressures not contingent on individual reproductive success. Whether a given language form contributed to individual survival and reproduction was no longer the sole criterion for whether it would be preserved in the next generation.

While initially this domain evolved because it enhanced the evolutionary survival of humans, language soon acquired its own laws of evolution, whereby ideas could themselves evolve over time, requiring humans only as temporary carriers of meaning. And this world began then to act back on the thinkers who constituted it. History, memory, and narrative began to constitute the individual. Collective structures began to determine organisms.

With language, more mechanisms of social evolution came into play. Language forms now had a universe in which to propagate that transcended the limited life spans of each member of the species. Language could evolve in tandem with social evolution and survival. If a language could piggyback on a viable set of social practices that had a differential survival rate in comparison to others, those language forms could be propagated. As social practices evolved, some outliving others, languages that attached themselves to and transformed social practices and institutions had a differential survival rate relative to other language forms. This process can be seen today: languages die off that are attached to societies that cannot compete in the survival arena. And the English language is clearly the winner in the language survival game because it is attached to Western capitalism.

Biologists such as Dawkins (Dawkins, 1990) speak of the evolution of "memes" as occurring in parallel with the evolution of genes. Memes are cultural entities that propagate much like genes. But they exist largely in the minds of human carriers, and in more advanced cases in the artifacts of a society. Memes are ideas, values, practices, habits, anything that can be called "culture." Some memes have propagated over long periods of time and some have had a very short existence. Memes evolved out of the natural selection process, but have acquired an evolutionary trajectory of their own. While somewhat different than genetic evolution, memes, like genes, replicate, compete for survival, sire offspring, have differential reproductive success, mutate, produce novelty, and die out.

The philosopher of science Karl Popper (Popper, 1963) sketches a theory of three worlds: the natural world, the world of mind, and the world of culture, and discusses how the third world of culture is acquiring a greater degree of autonomy as science and knowledge progress. The third world begins to evolve in ways that are distinct from the other two worlds, and as it becomes more elaborate and sophisticated, acts back on and transforms the other two worlds.

Written language is necessary for cognition to function in more abstract and de-contextualized ways. Written language is a symbol system that affects and transforms the user of that system, enabling and facilitating modes of thinking that an unassisted cognitive system could not produce with its own resources. Written language also allows history to enter the individual's thought processes, because language contains the imprint of history; consequently, the individual, by virtue of the possession and use of language, becomes, in turn, possessed and used by language and its history.

LANGUAGE AS CULTURAL DETERMINATION

The adaptive power of language lay in how it enabled a processing system, instantiated in a physical organism, to simulate its world more effectively: to predict and control it. And the curious thing about language is that it eventually gave its users the ability to predict and control more effectively than ever before because of the way it creates the world it supposedly only reflects. Language not only reflects cognitions about the world; language structures cognitions about the world. The world becomes known in linguistic ways, thus affording a more effective mechanism for the prediction and control of social beings.

What can be learned and chunked inside the brain is a function of what is apprehended simultaneously in the span of centration. What is held before the span is largely a function of whatever is presented by the environment, whatever is facilitated or afforded by the circumstances of life, as well as what can be added by the thinker's own cognitive resources. Language makes it possible for much more material to make it into the span of attention.

With language, the possibilities for adding to the elements in the span are increased enormously. On the one hand, people using language can thereby represent elements in thought that they otherwise would not have at their disposal. Language can scaffold and support strategies of thinking that can ensure that new elements are centrated with old elements or elements elicited by the environment (Bruner, 1990; Vygotsky, 1978). Once centrated, the elements can be learned and chunked, making it easier to subsequently bring these elements back into the span now that they occupy less space.

Language makes it enormously easier to teach, that is, to transmit information socially. Elders teach primarily by the ways that they arrange circumstances to ensure that important aspects of the environment are attended to (Bruner, 1990). The elders use their experience to make it more likely that evolutionarily important aspects of the world are centrated. With elders providing a structured environment, there is therefore less reliance on chance. The natural world, the world "red in tooth and claw," is a much harsher teacher than the social world, if we consider "harshness" strictly from the perspective of physical consequences. Therefore, with teaching by means of language, the young can benefit from the experience of the old. This is another aspect of the power of simulation. If some older individual produces the trial behavior, it can then serve vicariously as a trial for the younger members of the tribe without the younger having to take the same physical risks.

When the tribal elder wants to teach the young the dangers of traveling to the forbidden valley, a place of danger because of predators, the young do not have to actually go to the valley. A word or several words can refer to the place beyond the hills to the east. Of course, this can lead to abuse if nobody ever goes to the valley to learn that the predators no longer exist or that a new crop of fruit trees has grown there.

The old teach the young with language. But with maturity, some individuals can become capable of using language to teach themselves. This is what is referred to today in the adult education literature as "self-directed learning" (Brookfield, 1986; Knowles, 1980; Merriam & Cunningham, 1989). Learners can achieve sufficient mastery over the structures of language, and thereby use it to support and scaffold their thinking processes, thinking processes they would not otherwise entertain. This is a part of what the scientific method is. This also explains the efficacy of using writing to think. In the process of arranging bits of language as scribbles on a sheet of papyrus, or in the process of orchestrating mellifluous sounds as temporal tones, thoughts occur that would not occur otherwise.

Language informs and structures cognition so that we become socialized into the semantic and narrative forms of culture. This is a part of what writers mean when they refer to *social constructionism* (Berger & Luckman, 1967). Social reality creates itself through individual thought as well as external institutions and practices. Language is one medium, a very important one, for the creation and transmission of social reality. Language exists across time and generations and ensures its transmission by the way in which cognition can mirrors its structures. Later, I describe how structures pertaining to individual identity and narrative are two such forms of cultural determination.

* *

It is said that language is "stringy" (Miller, 1991). By "stringy," I mean that language is a matter of stringing bits of things together according to rules, like beads on a string. The smallest bit is the phoneme: the basic sound pattern. *Phonology* is the study of how sounds are made. The next smallest level of bit is the morpheme, the smallest element of meaning in a language. *Morphology* is the study of how words and meanings are built up from morphemes. The next level is *syntax*: how words may be arranged to form grammatically correct sentences. *Pragmatics* is the study of how purely linguistic bits get lawfully connected to behaviors in the social world, how linguistic constructions become a part of behavioral scripts that allow us to understand how behaviors may be coordinated.

Each of these areas of study investigates how the elements are combined together in ways to produce meaningful language. And the ways of combining are always sequential and linear. One thing is placed *after* another. Language was spoken for thousands of years before it was written down. And it still retains the property that it inherits from the biological substrate from which it evolved: temporality or time. The auditory system and the vocal apparatus operate sequentially. The temporal lobes operate sequentially (Luria, 1973).

Language structures its elements according to sequential rules. This structuring gets mapped, via learning and development, into the ways the cognitive system performs. Language scaffolds a sequence of words, which ensure that the paths down which cognition travels are rule-bound as well. And with social reinforcement and repetition, these rules soon ensure that cognition regularly does reflect the habitual routes carved out by language. Cognition lends the power of automatization to the rule-governed functionality of language. While language provides the rules, the brain provides the power by means of cognitive chunking and attention. Language provides the steppingstones of thought; but by habit and repetition, cognition provides the banks for the flow of consciousness.

But syntax, morphology, and phonology are not exhaustive of language. Language also comes in the form of scripts and stories. These higher-level structuring principles contain rules for the stringing together of their elements. The elements of scripts are behavioral role expectations and sequences. And the elements for narrative structures (see below) are the elements commonly ascribed to fiction: character, plot, scene, conflict, resolution, and so on. Each of these is constituted of complex language structures. As scripts and narratives are internalized and as they gain control over the cognitive landscape, they provide the structuring for the sequencing of events into experiences, the stringing together of actions into past, present, and future meanings.

By all these sequencing principles, each a product of language, consciousness is made to flow in step-by-step, one-moment-after-the-other, structured, lawful, and predictable fashion. Moments in a person's life never simply exist in themselves as still depths in a shaded pond: each moment is an occasion for a cascading of thoughts within the brain, a cascading that leaps over spans of space and time, spans charted and laid down in a rule-governed fashion by language. We can never perceive a sensation or engage in an action without it becoming framed by language into syntactical, semantic, pragmatic, and narrative structures, all of which direct the flow of consciousness in linguistically and socially determined ways.

With the increasing complexity of language, and particularly with the full-scale use of systems of orthography, the stringy sequentiality of language was transformed with time into a more spatial kind of reality. Thoughts occurred as part of larger systems of meaning that were apprehended spatially rather than temporally. Meaning is a relation of elements within a system. Once you assert one element, the others are implied. Words imply, as part of their meaning, other words, and using them inserts the user in multiple overdetermined meanings that go beyond the specifics of the here-and-now context. This makes it more likely that we can come to live in a fully constituted world extending over both time and space. As we think, the structure of language and the speed and associative properties of cognition weave wider worlds for us to dwell within. We dwell within a historical world more than a world of intimacy with others, we perceive a world made more by science than by our sense organs, and we live in our personal identities or story lines more than we do our bodies.

This makes good biological sense. Because language makes thoughts transit from one to another with a certain degree of regularity, and because cognition registers these sequences by mechanisms of learning and automaticity, our minds are impelled to simulate more aspects of our worlds and to do so more efficiently and automatically than they would otherwise. Given the auspicious interweaving of language and cognition that has occurred in the evolution of humans as a social species, we have become perhaps the only world-inventing species (Bruner,

1986). And we invent worlds in a way never before possible, worlds that carry us away with their apparent reality.

And because we invent, and consequently live in, worlds of greater and greater complexity, we can predict, control, and conquer the natural world unlike any other species, as well as predict and control each other. But as we invest more and more of our attention and awareness in these invented worlds, we have less and less time for the *uninvented* world, the world of sensation and perception unstructured by linguistically-determined cognitions. And I believe it is this desire for an uninvented world, an immediate world, that prompts the first glimmerings of a quest for a spiritual life.

While it is reasonable to discuss how technology affects language practices, we should not go too far in separating language from technology. From a certain perspective, language *is* technology. Language is a tool created in society that is used by individuals to achieve results. From an evolutionary perspective, language has extended the cognitive powers of simulation. Language is not manufactured in a factory, nor is it the product of the invention of a singular individual, patented with the government. Nevertheless, language is socially constructed and created. And language is a tool that has evolved with time in identifiable ways that have affected how we think and how we comport ourselves in our culture.

One of the ways we know how language affects thinking is by studying changes in language technology. When we do so, we can see that changes in thinking have historically paralleled changes in language technology. The major revolutions in language technology have instigated revolutions in thinking as well. Language has evolved from a spoken form of communication to a written form. This was the first major revolution. Once language became written, it could be preserved. Once preserved, it could develop a degree of autonomy from its human bearers.

Written language evolved at the same time as large-scale social transformations were taking place. Social reality had consisted of concrete encounters in clans, tribes, and other communal structures. Now social reality became organized around systems of hierarchy based on elaborate divisions of power, stratifying people into different roles with reciprocal responsibilities and rights. Social control came to be defined by adherence to abstractions and less on direct physical rewards and punishments. This required a process of socialization whereby the conscience of the individual provided the psychological foundation of an autonomous agent internalizing the symbol systems of the social order.

Such a social order classified, categorized, constituted, and reified individuals within it. As they were socialized into these orders, they became better instruments of such orders by cognitively constituting themselves—*representing* themselves—as persons of such and such types who were related to such-and-such types of other people, possessing certain internal traits, and defined as entities within an overall coherent reality. Once persons internalized the forms required of the social order, they became better instruments of that order.

Children require rewards and punishments and are motivated by pleasure and pain. As they mature, they develop conscience and self-consciousness, that is, they define themselves as objects over which they develop internal methods of control. Ego becomes separated from id and in turn regulated by superego. Sublimated pain comes to be experienced as shame and then guilt. Pleasure becomes defined as living according to the dictates and prescriptions of ego ideals. These psychological structures are internalizations of social control processes. Once they are internalized, society can function more efficiently, albeit at a certain psychological cost.

It should not be forgotten that throughout most of the history of written language, only a few possessed the ability to read and write: scribes, priests, and only some of the nobility. The audience for the Homeric epics listened to recitations. Even Jesus did not write down his teachings, nor the Buddha. Even for those who were able to acquire written language, most of the learning of it consisted of memorization. Often there were only a few copies of essential texts and their access was restricted. Only with the invention of the printing press did more people have access to the texts that defined culture.

The next major revolution in language occurred with the invention of the printing press. Language could be better preserved, passed around, and operated on once made so readily "copyable." With the technological change in information production, profound changes in thinking and culture occurred. We cannot understand the scientific revolution nor all of the momentous changes associated with the Reformation and the evolution of a capitalist economy without acknowledging the importance of the printing press and the production of books. And the next major revolution in language technology is the computer revolution, that is, information technology, involving hypertext, the World Wide Web, and multimedia. These will bring about enormous changes in how we learn, how we think, and how we will interact with others in producing knowledge.

If we cannot observe changes in language technology, we will not have the frame of reference to see that the ways we think are shaped by our time and place. But with a sense of historical linguistics we can indeed see that thinking is affected by technology. This sense of historical and linguistic relativism was not present in ancient cultures to the extent that it is now. Because changes in technology and thinking are occurring more rapidly, it is easier to consider the effects technology has on language and the effects of language on thinking.

Prior to written language, thinking was mythic and participatory, concrete and embedded in communal and social life, and expressive of psychological and intuitive truths. With the advent of written language, meaning was able to transcend concrete determinations and retain abstract meaning in spite of change. Written language enabled its users to access meaning across specific interpersonal situations and communicate in ways that transcended face-to-face realities. Realities could be invented, constructed, and transmitted across space-time boundaries, realities that became increasingly decontextualized.

The reality of a psyche that is so linguistically constituted is that it is also historically determined. Language and its various technologies construct us as social beings. But the social beings we are constructed as have changed over time. The kind of socially constituted personalities we are at this juncture in history has not occurred before in the history of the species. We are more abstract, more alienated from our bodily selves, and more distant from a nature that has been rendered disenchanted by our conceptual attempts to order and control it.

Because language creates its own domain of selective principles, it is possible to preserve and replicate simulations that are not adaptive or functional from a biological point of view. Because language can evolve in its own domain of selection, it can constitute and order realities that are even deleterious to the species as an organism. These ideas and values may be transmitted from one generation to the next because they are interconnected to social practices that enable their users to be more powerful. But these ideas and values may themselves be harmful to the experiential life worlds of those entities that transmit them.

We can point to both positive and negative consequences for spiritual consciousness brought about by changes in language practices. While the invention of orthography freed the individual from the primacy of the immediate surround in terms of what could be thought about, it also acted to subordinate the individual to social abstractions and culturally constituted realities. With the information age we can observe changes in cognition that will probably have an impact in terms of the evolution of spiritual consciousness: the building of a global village, the democratization of the flow of information, the greater accessibility of information, and enriched individual autonomy and self-directedness in learning. A discussion of such changes more properly belongs in another work.

PART II

On the Threshold of the Spirit

CHAPTER 7

Identity

IDENTITY AS DEVELOPMENT AND AS ACHIEVEMENT

In the following, I shall describe "identity" less glowingly than other developmental psychologists might. I take a perspective on the formation of identity from the point of view of the entire life span and of higher stages of consciousness. While identity *is* an achievement and *is* a break from earlier more conventional and less differentiated stages, it is at the same time very limited when viewed from the perspectives made possible at higher levels of development. One of the ways I shall describe identity as limited is in the way in which it is still very much conventional, differing from earlier ego structures only to the degree to which it is more abstract and less bound to interpersonal context.

I use the term *identity* to refer to a psychological organization that grows out of the ego's adaptation to a broader social world than the exclusively interpersonal world of the child. It is an organization that is more sophisticated than earlier forms of control, yet still based on the same need for control and predictability that both the superego and ego are grounded in. In spite of being associated with individuality and nonconformity, identity is nevertheless a higher-level adjustment or accommodation of the ego to the demands of the social world.

As young children, we relate to our parents, our siblings, our extended families, our immediate peers, and a few representatives of the social order—teachers, doctors, ministers and priests. But we generally have very limited interactions with the social order per se. Rather, we interact with others in a direct and interpersonal fashion, and the psychological mechanisms of ego and superego are sufficient for this purpose. But as our social universe expands, as we enter the widening circle (Erikson, 1963), and as we are required to relate to more varied contexts, more abstract rules, and more generalized others, we construct an identity, an internal universe, made up of appropriate roles that are largely socially sanctioned.

Identity cannot be internalized from the immediate world surrounding us. It must be "put together," it must be crafted and constructed out of the available roles and rules that society presents to us as viable options, options that we internalize and reconfigure. Once internalized, these roles become identifications. As identifications, they must be coordinated with our desires and feelings, and, in turn, related to our social world.

The internalizations that make up identity differ from earlier internalizations in that they have characteristics that allow us to relate to the larger social world: not just in terms of personal others, immediate contexts, and direct objects and events, but also in terms of generalized others, abstract contexts, and generic objects and events. Language is essential for this. An adolescent has to possess a certain level of linguistic competence to be able to construct an identity.

One of the ways we may distinguish ego from identity is in the nature of the internal monitor we sometimes call *conscience*. In childhood, according to Freud (1975), we are monitored by our *superego*. The superego is the internalization of parental interdictions and prescriptions (Pascual-Leone, 1990a, b). It operates by mobilizing the affects of guilt and shame. These affects take over the control function that had been performed by external reinforcement as scheduled by parents. The early conscience is absolutist and severe, often more severe than the parents, on whom it is modeled. But as an internal monitor, it is too limited and too literal to ensure accommodation to the larger social world of adults. We need an internal monitor that is more generalizable and flexible to coordinate our lives with the more diverse and abstract roles and rules of adult life. In psychoanalytic circles, this internal monitor is called the *ego ideal.*

Cote and Levine (1987, 1988a, b) have postulated three value orientation stages: the moral, the ideological, and the ethical. These are the stages in how the adolescent supplants the superego with the ego-ideal. While the superego is considered necessary for a child to cope at an early, less cognitively sophisticated stage of development, the superego must later be supplanted by the ego-ideal, which replaces and counterbalances the dictates of the superego with its own less stringent and more subtle voice. While the *moral orientation stage* is characterized by the predominance of the superego, the *ideological stage* is characterized by overly simplified ethical precepts that allow the adolescent to experiment and role play in the expanded universe of discourse, the social order. At the *ethical orientation stage,* the simplifications of ideology are replaced with the complexities of mature ethical judgments, which are less categorical, less stereotyped, and less egocentric than the ideological stage, and more tolerant of contradiction.

As the ego ideal develops, the superego is not eliminated; it is only superseded in terms of its functioning in the economics of personality. Mental circuits are seldom erased directly from the brain; but they do become less connected to habitual routes of processing, and therefore have less of a chance of becoming activated as we process our worlds. Such circuits are left to languish in the corridors of long-term memory. But the superego continues to exist behind day-to-day adult consciousness, often controlling the show beneath our conscious awareness.

* *

We may understand conscience as one of the theaters of the mind where we play out the vicissitudes of self-esteem and guilt. The following comments require an understanding of what has been discussed earlier regarding mind as *simulation*. When we speak of self-esteem, part of self-esteem is an image or picture we hold of ourselves that has strong associations with powerful affects. One such affect is guilt. It helps as we navigate the social world to hold such an image before the mind's eye, because we can do things within the world of that image we could not do in the actual world, allowing us to test things out before actually carrying them out in behavior.

We can use the images of self-esteem as a predictor of the outcomes of our actions. We are better able to guide and monitor our actions if we can refer to a representation of our self in our social simulation. We frequently resort to thoughts about successes that have enhanced our self-esteem when feedback from the real world is infrequent or unreliable. When we are uncertain about how our actions are going to impact the world, we frequently look to our self-image to assess how our fortunes fare. And while we may speak of certain propositional facts about self-esteem as adding form to its substance, the texture and felt quality of self-esteem is due to the affects that color its appearance: guilt and pride, shame and vanity.

Michael Lewis (1993) distinguishes primary from secondary emotions in early childhood. Primary emotions are those that are present before the child is capable of self-recognition: joy, fear, anger, surprise, sadness, and disgust. Once the child is capable of self-recognition, the secondary emotions appear: pride, embarrassment, shame, guilt, and envy.

Self-recognition is necessary for self-esteem. Guilt is intimately connected to self-esteem. It is a negative affect that causes self-esteem to become depressed if the image of self is not equal to our internal directives. The social advantage of mobilizing the affect of guilt is that it provides an early warning system that signals that aversive events might follow, i.e., withdrawal of love, or even punishment. Guilt is a way of making you feel bad before you *really* feel bad, because of others. If you can learn to activate guilt appropriately, you will feel better in the long run. In childhood, obedience and the avoidance of guilt ensure that love is not withdrawn or that punishment is not suffered.

Some have noted how early ego development can lead to the construction of a false self or false self-system (Laing, 1979). The notion of a false self can be understood in relation to the comments regarding simulation of self. The false self is said to be constructed as a way of enabling the child to interact with caregivers who do not provide love, nurturance, or security. The ego is said to become rigid and overly self-contained as a means of avoiding disappointment. In the process, the ego becomes overly disassociated from the body and its feelings, exclusively identified with what goes on in the head.

But psychoanalysts describe these processes as characteristic only of the neurotic. Buddhism, on the other hand, points out that we are *all* neurotic, we are all mentally *diseased,* not only those whom we label as mentally ill. We all suffer from a false self invented to avoid guilt, censure, loss of approval, rejection, withdrawal of affection, and, often, the infliction of abuse. And the theory of mind I am elaborating agrees that the self we construct is a *simulation,* a simulation the rudiments of which are programmed by evolution and which are marshaled to negotiate the vicissitudes of socialization.

We grow up consciously and unconsciously elaborating a false self that we use for commerce with the external world. And many of us later in life become increasingly aware that this false self is empty, and that it serves as the basis for both primal repression and primal alienation. Primal *repression* leads to separation from the body and primal *alienation* to separation from others (Washburn, 1994). But aspects of this false self are necessary to assume conventional moral behavior.

* *

When people do not seem to adhere to the conventions of morality, we say they are without a conscience. That is, they do not seem to have developed either a mechanism of self-esteem or a barometer for its modulation, such as guilt or shame. Consequently, if we are going to get such people to behave morally, we as a society have to subject them

Identity

to concrete rewards and punishments. Such is the case with sociopaths. And when the rewards or punishments are withdrawn, or in the absence of an observing agent who can administer a schedule of reinforcement, individuals without a conscience can be expected to return to prior immoral behaviors. When they have internalized the elements of conscience and are able to act morally, we say they are doing so out of "free will," i.e., they are no longer acting only to avoid external compulsion. But when they act morally as a result of reward and punishment, we say that they are doing so only because their environment expects it of them.

Of course, the mechanism of conscience can backfire, and in cases of pathology, unhealthy levels of depression and guilt result, immobilizing the person. But social convention and conformity require some moderate level of guilt and depression to figure as a constant in our psyches, to function as a backdrop to our lives, so as to keep us "on track." One of the changes that happen with higher stages of development is the refiguring of the role that guilt and self-esteem play in consciousness.

* *

Identity can be understood as part of the process by which we become less dependent on others for maintaining our self-esteem. As young children we are entirely at the mercy of our parents and of others to reward and punish us, but we soon take over this process for ourselves and internalize it so that we become our own instruments of reward and punishment. At first, morality and control operate via external reinforcements. Later, we rely on guilt, activated internally. In adulthood, we rely on ideological self-esteem and self-definition to serve as barometers of control. More and more of the social world becomes internalized to the point that the whole court and jury, both the police and the priesthood, resides in the mind.

Some accounts of adolescent identity grant the superego a new role in the emerging economics of the mind. The superego, as the directive force of conscience, gets tethered to the ego ideal, and within the integration of a new project, a new identity, provides the motive power and psychic force directing the ego in its life construction, the forging of a path into the social order.

Identity is about individuation, and individuation is largely about distancing ourselves from the censure and control of parents (note that this kind of individuation is quite different from the process of individuation described by Jung). One factor that catalyzes the break with parents at puberty is the upheaval of libido. If there is one thing that will jolt young people into a sense of themselves as *distinct* from their parents, it is the awakening of sexual desire in puberty. And this is triggered by the genes, by the pituitary gland signaling to the hypothalamus that it is time to wake up the hormones. The temporary truce between children and society that Freud described as the latency period is destroyed.

Sex is a force opposed to both the superego and opposed to society. As we enter the Eriksonian periods of identity and intimacy, the task of adolescents and young adults is to channel sexuality into socially sanctioned and socially sublimated forms. But until they do, adolescents threaten the social order. Parents, educators, and moral authorities everywhere sound the alarm when the young brazenly flaunt their sexuality. Witness the early reactions to rock'n'roll: television had to edit out Elvis Presley's lower torso. Witness the debate every spring over dress codes in public schools: as the sun warms and the flowers bloom, the display of bare midriffs and bare thighs has both school officials and parents up in arms. What do you think incited the Warsaw Pact authorities more in 1968: Dry political propaganda written by university professors? Or Mick Jagger flaunting his hips on stage in front of Warsaw's screaming youth? Adolescent sexuality destroys the reprieve achieved in the latency period, which, in Erikson's terms, consists of the periods of initiative and industry, times when the child inserts her- or himself into socially acceptable roles.

You cannot be a good girl or a good boy in the eyes of your parents while you are engaging in premarital sex. Sex helps free the ego from the dominance of the superego and helps to precipitate the construction of the ego ideal, a necessary factor in identity formation.

We as a culture force adolescents to engage in illicit sex. We have no acceptable means of channeling or sublimating adolescent sexual behavior into appropriate expressions. Our sporting activities, our church socials, and our schools provide no genuine outlet for sexual behavior. Instead, we officially uphold the sanctity of marriage and monogamy, pretend our young boys and girls are not brimming with hormones, and then get up in arms at the rates of adolescent pregnancy and AIDS. We have culturally constructed a phase of life between childhood and adulthood, and then have made the rules function to ensure that the sexually maturing in this phase are not allowed legitimate expression.

The adolescent must nevertheless express sexuality in some way, and so, of course, guilt results. The emerging identity must develop the capacity to tolerate guilt: it must endure the ambivalence of guilt and the accusations of guilt before a successful identity can be formed. This is true for the females in Josselson's (1987) longitudinal study: only the Identity Achieved, of the four identity statuses (see below), were found to be able to handle guilt, and in some sense, go beyond it. The Foreclosures seemed not to experience guilt, perhaps because of the extent of their denial and repression. The Diffusions seem not to experience guilt, perhaps because of their weak superegos. The Moratoriums, by contrast, were suspended in the grip of guilt, unable to work out the contradictions experienced.

Once the superego is weakened, once puberty is completed, once young adults construct ideals and dreams of their own that possess some autonomy from those of their parents, in other words, once they achieve some semblance of identity (however flawed), the time for social rebellion abates, and another period of adaptation to the tribe ensues. For most young adults, in contrast to adolescence, young adulthood is characterized by marriage, career, and childrearing, all activities that are socially sanctioned and that require the sublimation of energies into appropriate channels. Little energy remains for interests or passions outside of socially circumscribed domains. Young adulthood, by contrast to adolescence, is largely a period of adjustment and conformity to the demands of adult life. But it too is a period of limited duration, and the adjustment and conformity achieved are threatened later by the second eruption of psychic disobedience—the midlife crisis.

IDENTITY AS FICTION AND AS CONSTRAINT

Many who write about adolescent identity write that *identity* can be understood by contrasting it with *role*. *Role* is what society expects of you when you assume a position in society. Roles are defined and determined before the individual enters into them; roles are therefore said to have a social and institutional reality *prior* to that of individuals. But *identity* is considered to be a self-chosen synthesis of internal motives integrated with social roles. Identity is therefore more highly differentiated than role. Nevertheless, roles, some of which make up the content of the ego ideal, have their origins in the traditions and expectations of one's society, or as I shall explain in the next section, the myths and stories of the larger narrative fabric.

Interestingly, when James Marcia (1980) began to research identity in young people, he asked them about their *occupation* and their *ideology,* the latter consisting of both religious and political orientations. Marcia developed his content analysis of interview material based on these issues, yielding the coding scheme for the four identity statuses: Identity Diffusion, Foreclosure, Moratorium, and Identity Achieved.

Identity statuses, according to Marcia, can be understood as the outcome of two changes: whether there has been a *crisis* of identity, that is, whether the adolescent has had to break from conventional embeddedness, and whether there has been a *commitment* to a chosen path. If there has been neither a crisis nor a commitment, Marcia called the status *Diffuse*; if there has been no crisis and only commitment, Marcia called it *Foreclosed*; if there has been a crisis but no commitment, you have *Moratorium*; and if there is both crisis and resulting commitment, you have *Identity Achieved*.

Only when the last of these, Identity Achieved, is clearly present, can we say that the individual has successfully negotiated the identity crisis. The other three statuses—Foreclosure, Identity Diffusion, and Moratorium—are essentially failures to effect a successful resolution of the identity crisis. Only about 25% of subjects have generally been found to be in the Identity Achieved status (Balk, 1995).

Occupation and ideology consist of one's work and one's belief systems. Work and belief systems are both ways of accommodating to the adult world and the social order: what you do to make money and what creed you believe in with respect to the church and the state (i.e., ethics). While the church and state have many functions, their main sociological function is the legitimation of rules and morality—how to act.

It is unprofitable to try to ascribe truth value to the words and images that guide people in their day-to-day work and their daily interactions with each other, to ascribe truth to their *character* or their *ethics*. In the modern world, or even the postmodern, the realms of character or ethics do not possess criteria that can be evaluated scientifically for their truth value. This is why contemporary philosophers of science have labored to demarcate hermeneutics from science.

Rules and morality prescribe the means of self-control and self-monitoring that define how we are to behave as virtuous citizens. Their content is relative to the society of which they are a part. Rules and morality provide the form, as it were, for the functioning substance of obedience. Self-esteem and guilt provide the motivating or affective power for rules and morality to work, so that rules and morality are embodied as self-control and self-monitoring. With the ego ideal firmly ensconced in the complex of identity at the end of adolescence, we set out on the path of adulthood: knowing who we are, where we have been, and what we want to become.

But there is a downside to this; for explanation we shall move out of developmental research and draw on some insights from other areas of psychology, the first being narrative psychology. To quote Howard:

> Habits at first are silken threads—then they become cables. The same could be said of stories. Thus, a paraphrase of Shakespeare's more dire warnings becomes appropriate, Beware of the stories you tell yourself—for you will surely be lived by them. (Howard, 1991, p. 196)

Somehow, as we grow older, the story line or the story script, which is invented or assembled from elements of the cultural milieu, becomes less available to conscious scrutiny. In the brain, these scripts become neurologically denser, more compacted as dendritic fusions that are activated whenever the relevant area of the brain is turned on. Situations encoded as input from the external world activate schemata, which in turn trigger the activation of scripts and routines, and much of this encoding process is neither conscious nor changeable. We become lived by the stories encoded in our brains.

To understand why silken threads become cables, we have to turn to cognitive and neural science. By virtue of the architecture of the mind, we know that activation pathways become more closely associated and more chunked together the more they are used. Learned schemes become routine habits that no longer require deliberate attention to become activated.

Turning from neural science to social psychology, we can make the following observations:

When we are presented with a discrepancy between our actions and our beliefs, we tend to change our beliefs to accord with our actions. We actively seek to maintain consistency, to avoid contradiction, even at the risk of distortion and self-deception. Leon Festinger (1957) called this phenomena *cognitive dissonance.*

When situations are ambiguous, when we cannot readily observe the true causes of our actions, we freely infer or even invent causes that make sense to us, that accord with our beliefs about ourselves.

One of the tenets of *attribution theory* (Zimbardo, 1999) is called the Fundamental Attributional Error (FAE). When we observe actions, we tend to infer that the causes of the actions are other people's dispositions or traits. We tend not to pay attention to either situational or environmental determinants, except in the case of ourselves. This tendency to "intrapychic determinism," regarding others, accounts for human biases in our attempts to explain the social world.

Once we tend to believe something of either ourselves or other people, we tend to make those beliefs come true by our actions (Zimbardo, 1999). If we think that the students in our class have higher IQs (when in fact they do not), we will grade them higher; if we think the rats we are training in our laboratory are "maze-bright" (when in fact they are not), we will tend to record their learning as faster. This is known as the *self-fulfilling prophesy.* We tend to *make* true what we believe *is* true.

From this we can see that self-perception is *not* an act by which we apprehend the interiors of our minds with uncontaminated access. We have to *infer* what is going on, and to infer what is going on we have to project hypotheses. And sometimes we make things up.

In the history of psychology, introspective methods of observation were commonly used before the turn of the century (Fancher, 1979). It was believed that if you had the proper training in how to avoid biases, and if you were trained in a neutral (theory-free) language of description, you could have uncontaminated access to the contents of the mind, the elemental components that make up consciousness. But it was soon noted that the so-called theory-free observations made in one laboratory were not the same as the theory-free observations made in another. What was observed in the mind seemed to have a lot to do with the training the observer had been subjected to. The behaviorists, particularly Watson, reacted to this by banishing all methods of introspection.

This is related to the human propensity to construct explanations, causal accounts of what is going on, and the equally important propensity to impute these descriptions or theories to "persons," persons who behave like objects in a mechanical universe composed of "things." This imputation is essential to prediction and control: knowing the causes of our own and others' behavior puts us securely in the pilot seat of life. Human knowledge is instrumental; it seldom consists of an empathic insight into the heart of another. Human knowledge is an exclusively cognitive structuring of independent and dependent variable relationships that are organized as cause–effect sequences. These stipulate what the input and output is of any object or animal, machine or human. A close examination of these input–output relations yields nothing when we zoom in on the exact and elusive space where input becomes output. When it comes to "knowing" the soul of another, we face the black box of the mind.

But there *is* a mode of being not predicated on this style of relating, a mode of dialogue, of playfulness, of open receptivity, what Labouvie-Vief (1994) calls *mythos,* as opposed to *logos*, all of which is now part of a cultural shift from modern to postmodern consciousness, and part of a new personality dynamic, a spiritual change, that emerges as we shift from the autonomous, institutional, and agentic to the postautonomous, interindividual, and communal.

Michael Washburn (1994) believes that identity is, in part, a response to the social threat posed by adolescent sexuality. Identity in this respect parallels the superego of earlier childhood in that it is a social mechanism that is both an internalization *and* an identification. The energy of newly released libidinal energy is channeled by the structure of identity into roles and rules, roles and rules that are at a higher and more flexible level of representation that the strict roles and rules of the superego. But identity is still a means of self-control and of self-monitoring. And it is based on a choice of what we are to be, and perhaps, more importantly, a choice of what we are *not* going to be. This is why the road not taken beckons, and it truly beckons for many in midlife.

This perspective on identity can be better appreciated when we examine the course of identity in midlife. For it is only later that maturing individuals sense the insufficiency of what they have become as a result of the choices made in youth. From the point of view of the young, the *dream* (which is an aspect of the ego ideal) can motivate us to greater heights; from a more mature point of view, the dream is also what keeps us trotting contentedly around the race track of life with blinders on.

In the more specifically adult models we will discuss later, the descriptions of adolescent identity take on new aspects when considered as part of the entire life span. In Kegan's (1982) model, identity is negotiated and completed at the stage he terms the *Institutional*. And when this stage is contrasted to the one that follows it, the limits are more apparent. The Institutional is described as imprisoned within its own self-possession. The Institutional treats emotions and feelings as administrative problems. Closeness and intimacy are often experienced as threats. Any experience of loosening up may also be experienced as boundary loss or impulse flooding. Change may be avoided because of the fear of not knowing.

In Loevinger's model, the stage that most closely matches the identity stage is the *Conscientious*. It is based on the earlier *Self-Aware Stage's* apprehension of the conventional embeddedness of the *Conformist Stage*. The Conscientious Stage holds to long-term self-evaluated goals and ideals; it is based on a sense of owing responsibility and obligations as well as of expecting privileges, rights, and fairness. Achievements are measured by self-chosen standards. The Conscientious is able to see its self from the other's point of view, and operates from a longer time perspective and a broader consideration of social context than the Conformist. The major elements of conscience are in place (the ego ideal); the internalization of rules is completed. In other words, society has completely taken up residence in the psyche. The growing self has inserted its soul into the social order—indeed, it possesses a soul only by virtue of its socialization.

* *

Just as we may see the Eriksonian stages of initiative and industry as preparation for societal roles, so may we see the stage of intimacy versus isolation as a further channeling or sublimation into social expectations. The onset of puberty and the release of hormones signal a break with conformity and conventionality, a break with the relatively quiescent phase Freud termed *latency*. For society to function, and for the individual to avoid punishment or ostracism, this biological eruption must be redirected into ego-based accommodations. Maturing adolescents or young adults must consolidate an identity to ensure that they find productive work and a meaningful identification—both ideological and moral—within some acceptable niche in society. And they must direct their sexuality into nonthreatening and reproductively viable expressions: in our society's case, into marriage and monogamy. Intimacy generally ensures that libido stays on the tried and true course of exclusively "straight" genital sexuality, and away from any resurgence of polymorphous perversity. We let our dyed orange hair grow out, we remove our tattoos and our nipple piercings, and we give up our androgenous flirtations, all so that we may put on our aprons, take spatula in hand, and make barbeques in the suburbs.

Erikson never claimed that any identity structure was permanent, but the more recent work of Levinson (Levinson, Darrow, Klein, Levinson, & McKee, 1978) clearly shows the transience of achieved identity. A casual inspection of divorce statistics or a brief conversation with a marriage counselor will quickly assure you that intimacy is not lasting either. As a species, we are probably not *permanently* monogamous, but for us to have become conditioned into believing that we are has required centuries of church and state persuasion. One aspect of the Judeo-Christian heritage is the assumption that we have a distinct and permanent *soul* that we can bequeath to another in marriage, a soul whose essence does not change from birth to death. This assumption, and many others, are connected to a whole constellation of ideas—a mythology—that is being questioned in a new postmodern world that is only now dialoguing with other traditions, such as those of the East.

Research in anthropology (Fisher, 1995) suggests that monogamy is not the rule for humans as a species; rather, we seem to be designed for *serial monogamy*. We get together temporarily with the opposite sex to produce offspring, and then the male moves on once the female is no longer as helpless, leaving her to raise the child and find another suitor. Because of this evolutionary heritage, and the way it predisposes us, our monogamous arrangements require that we be under constant surveillance to uphold cultural standards of sexual conduct, this in spite of the many years of internalizing social scripts. We shave the heads of women who consort with the wrong men, we stone adulterers, we marginalize homosexuals, we ostracize those who espouse lifestyles that threaten "family values." But no matter how much energy is directed to upholding the Judeo-Christian ethic, we always seem to have prostitutes, men still take mistresses, wives have sex with their tennis instructors, middle-aged professors ditch their aging wives for younger students, and Presidents accept oral favors in the White House.

One of the traditional religious institutions established for the purpose of transcending identity is the monastery. In Buddhism, meditation and study of the scriptures are not the sole and sufficient routes to enlightenment. Monasteries are an ideal environment for stripping away identity, for purging away the conventional self. All individuating clothing, hair, and affectations are removed. Attributes of sex, race, property, nation, class, and caste are all set aside. Among the vows of practice is celibacy. Until a few short years ago, there was no birth control, which meant that for the majority, sexual behavior invariably led to children, and to all the associated attachments and responsibilities children entail. Parenting serves to anchor and reinforce adults securely in their identity, an anchoring that the practice of dharma attempts to undo.

Before Siddhartha Gautama embarked on the path of the Dharma, he left his wife and children. Traditional Hinduism structured life so that after men had fulfilled their duties as householders, they took up the spiritual life. In Chinese society, during the Sung and Tang, older men gave up their Confucian roles as government functionaries and took up the path of the Tao in the misty mountains.

* *

Building on the biologically evolved capacity for simulation, for mental representation, based on the cognitive architecture of self-monitoring and self-reinforcement, we create and then maintain an identity that directs our actions and our thoughts. With the identity structure firmly in place, we become our own regulators of affect, our own arbiters of self-esteem. And for the greater good of society, this is desirable.

This means that society does not have to provide the external rewards and punishments that kept us moral when we were children. Society does not have to keep the towers of surveillance in place with their revolving searchlights penetrating into every aspect of our waking and sleeping days—because we ourselves do it. This frees up societal resources for other things, such as childrearing and the conquest of the natural world.

As society has evolved over the centuries, as it has come to rely on more abstract, decontextualized, and more codified forms of organization, and as it relies less on concrete and interpersonal forms of regulation and control, people have gotten better at constructing abstract identities. The mechanisms of reward and punishment, of surveillance and monitoring, are more and more internalized, and therefore harder to see. This is how we can understand Protestantism, the reduction in the need for corporeal punishment, enlightenment rationality, and the individual quest for life, liberty, and the pursuit of happiness within the circumscribed universe of capitalist restraint.

But correlative to this internalized identity is an increase in the incidence of both depression and anxiety. Both the range and variety of mental illnesses have changed throughout history. Illnesses that once were common are no longer with us as new mental problems appear. But if there are any illnesses that most uniquely plague twentieth century Western society, these illnesses are depression and anxiety. And both of these are rooted in the ego, and more particularly in the structure of identity.

Depression is rooted in the mechanisms of self-esteem. Standards of self-monitoring are established somewhere very high up in the ego ideal, such that the ideals cannot possibly be lived up to. Because of the enormous gap between expectation and actuality, paralysis ensues. The weight of perfectionism and of idealized pressures fault the lowly self at every turn until stalemate ensues. Depression is rooted in self-loathing, the squelching of affect, the sense of self-strangulation, and a pervasive sense of worthlessness. Furthermore, these thoughts and these feelings are permanent, pervasive and personal (Seligman, 1990).

Anxiety is rooted in a pervasive and free-floating sense of constant *threat* to self, identity, and project. On every side loom both the named and unnamed fears that eat away at identity's composure. One's actions are always in danger of being undone, one's stability is always threatening to dissolve, some object of paranoia is always looming large on the horizon. The individual is convinced that someone or something will most certainly pull the rug out from under each enterprise. The result of this is a tension, a continual holding of the body in bands of muscular tension, as well as an incessant and subtle stifling of the breath.

As some of us mature, the structures of identity seem to weaken their hold on our perceptions, our feelings, and our actions. Once our identity has secured us a place in the larger social nexus and once we have played out our role or our script to some adequate level of adaptation, consciousness seems to allow for a gap in the routine, as it were, a glimpse of possibilities not contained within our structures of self-knowing. Perhaps this can be related to the architecture of mind I have alluded to earlier. Consciousness is the way that our learned structures control attention and therefore what it is that we are habitually aware of. And it is the nature of cognition to streamline the processing of its elements by chunking and by automatization, so that cognitive components are more densely associated, more tightly packed in the economics of a limited-resource processing machine.

And this means that some attention, some awareness may be left over for less automatic kinds of processing. At some point in development, we come to see some light through the chinks in the armor of our soul, a "soul" that may be weary of the weight of its suit of mail. This is a soul ready to risk nakedness and vulnerability, ready to let go of all the protective coverings assumed for the battle of life. This is a soul ready to take a stance of nonviolence toward life, to let the banners drop, to toss away all the shields, and stand barefoot in the grass, the wind caressing the skin, the rays of the sun warming the bruised and battered shoulders.

This is a soul ready for meditation, ready for its own transformation, ready for treading a path that leads to its own undoing. Meditation succeeds because it takes advantage of the economics of consciousness and attention. Let the thoughts arise and pass, let them bubble out of the mind, but always return to the breath, to the still point of awareness at the tips of your nostrils. And silently wait for that gap, the gap in the chatter of consciousness, a consciousness still trying to maintain itself as some solid *thing,* some solid thing that begins to glimpse that it is only "empty phenomena rolling on" (Goldstein, 1976).

CHAPTER 8

Narrative

INTRODUCTION: THE TRANSITION TO THE POSTCONVENTIONAL VIA LANGUAGE

If you recall my earlier considerations regarding the mind as evolving as a result of natural selection, we can then see identity as the product of the need for prediction and control in the social world of adults. The psychological structuring provided by identity creates, among other things, stable and predictable adults who can autonomously fulfill behavioral expectations at all kinds of mentally abstract levels, not requiring concrete rewards and punishments. Not only do we need to predict others and society, but society and others need to predict us. By becoming our own monitors we reduce the need for society to monitor us directly.

Social order requires prediction and control. We can see the legal system, religious institutions, and educational systems as consisting of mechanisms that shape young identities, and when those young identities are securely in place, these same systems are geared to maintaining and reinforcing those identities. These institutions consist of many components, a subset of which are ideologies and creeds. These provide the narrative cement in which to hold the story lines of our lives. These are like the master stories society provides and the context or backdrop in which persons construct their individual life stories. And these same systems or institutions, in which ideologies and creeds are embedded, are called on when the psychological structuring fails, that is, when the individual fails to adapt to the social order.

Identity may fail to develop sufficiently for some individuals. At worst, those individuals who do not develop become a burden to society and require the guidance of the more socialized or developed. But for most, identity does develop successfully enough. If it did not, we would soon not be able to function as a society and as a culture.

Although society requires identity, it need not dominate the landscape of our consciousness for the entirety of our lives. We are not only what we have been made to be to fulfill the objectives of the social order. We are not simply that individual who pays the parking ticket on time, who provides the bank with the monthly mortgage payment, who gets the kids ready for school at the same time each day, who has dinner on the table reliably, and who performs on the job in ways that are useful to our co-workers and the powers that be.

After the dishes are done, after the bills have been paid, and after the lawn is cut, after the phone calls are returned and the kids are put to bed, there are still currents in our lives that seek out new courses. However successful our careers or however exhilarating our accomplishments, for some there is more that needs to be experienced. After fulfilling our roles and performing in respected ways, there is still more to our selves than what is required by our identities. And so the middle-aged male may retire to the garage to work on his yacht, the accountant may take up her piano in the front room, the blue-collar worker may retire to the pub down the street where the young girls bring a glimmer to his eyes.

There are parts to our selves not confined to our identities. Another imperative exists other than the imperative to be in control. There are aspects of our beings that are not subsumed by the necessity of good behavior. We are not *only* our roles or our scripts. This other imperative transcends the social one and the moral one: it is perhaps an *aesthetic* imperative that transcends obligation and duty. It speaks to the intuited aspects of our lives not granted a voice by the ordinary and mundane. This more aesthetic imperative is called the *narrative*.

We construct stories of ourselves first to fit ourselves within the social order. Our first identities are ways of adapting to occupations, maintaining relationships, being good citizens. But as the impulse to restorying and rescripting ourselves transcends the banal and the predictable, we incorporate other criteria by which to invent ourselves. These criteria are aesthetic, existential, and more authentic. The narrative impulse requires that we build more comprehensive, cohesive, and integrative personal structures.

* *

Narrative psychology is a way of practicing psychology that adopts a different metaphor for describing human beings from the metaphors adopted by, for instance, behaviorist or cognitive psychology, which each seem to have adopted metaphors from the physical sciences

(Bruner, 1986, 1990; Freeman, 1993, Polkinghorne, 1988, Sarbin, 1986, White & Epston, 1990). The central metaphor of narrative approaches is derived from the arts—specifically literary criticism and hermeneutics. It is a metaphor that suggests that people are the writers of the stories of their lives. This means that lives can be understood as constructed out of elements much like those of fiction. These elements may be identified as plot, action, sequentiality, perspective, scene, character, goal, instrument, trouble, resolution, and so forth. While to some extent invented, stories also have varying degrees of canonicity in that they incorporate elements from tradition.

Stories have a beginning, middle, and end. People make sense of their lives by "emplotting" the actions and the events that make up their lives in stories. Stories are sequences of experiences that structure events. These stories become the frameworks by which lives have meaning and purpose. It follows then that when we try to understand the actions of others we should function as hermeneuticists, treating actions as *texts* of possible meaning. This means that when we try to understand others we should not work like scientists, aiming only to accurately map objective reality.

A narrative approach is a more desirable metaphor than the metaphors that have traditionally been used by social scientists, such as the metaphor of mind as a conditioned reflex or the metaphor of mind as machine. A narrative approach sensitizes us more to the role of metaphor in our understanding. Thinking through the lens of a narrative approach implies that the goals and purposes of both mental health professionals and social scientists have to be reevaluated. The objective will not be prediction and control nor the charting of a flow diagram as a criterion for understanding lives.

Bruner (1986) made the distinction between *narrative* and *paradigmatic* modes of understanding. Psychology has traditionally emphasized the paradigmatic, but he argues that it is now time for psychology to advance the narrative. The paradigmatic approach works with generalities and universals; the narrative approach works with experiences and particulars. The paradigmatic aspires toward causal explanation whereas the narrative strives toward interpretive understanding. Knowledge is objective for the paradigmatic while knowledge is infused with the subjective for the narrative.

Narrative approaches have been defined in a number of ways. I would like to convey a sense of the meaning of narrative by discussing it under the following aspects: freedom; temporality; cognitive structures; culture, stories, and symbols; lives as texts; the nature of reality; the nature of breaches and ruptures; and therapy as narrative repair.

FREEDOM AS REWRITING

We can reinvent the stories that structure our lives once we become aware—but only when we become aware—of their storied nature. We can transform our species-specific genetic inheritance and we can alter our prescriptive and often repressive social programming. We can rewrite the inheritance of our culture and see through the one-sidedness of its values and the arbitrariness of the perspectives it has foisted on us. We can become aware that we are the authors of our futures rather than the players of social scripts.

The metaphor of life as narrative means that lives are constructed as stories we tell both ourselves and others. Our lives are known only as interpreted through the means of a text we have creatively fashioned: our memory, our past, our circumstance, our waking and sleeping states, what we choose to know and what we choose not to know, who we choose as friends and who we exclude, what societies we identify with. These stories can be composed deliberately. But throughout much of our lives, particularly in childhood and early adulthood, we often are forced to take up stories in anything but a deliberate manner, pressed as we so often are to get along, to get things done, to gain approval, and to avoid censure.

What uniquely characterizes adulthood is the opportunity to rewrite our selves, to redesign our identities. Adulthood is the period when we are on "the threshold of story," as Randall (1995) puts it. We become capable of *having* our stories rather than simply *being* our stories. Once we *have* our stories, we can take a perspective on them as stories and begin rewriting them according to more internal criteria, criteria that are often more aesthetic than conventional. Before we are able to rewrite our selves, we operate according to criteria set for us by society. The reason for this is that we still identify ourselves with society and its requirements. We cannot get a perspective on ourselves outside of the social. We are like fish that cannot see the water we are swimming in. In the early stages of development we are identified with social evaluations; we live out the stories that have been scripted for us by others because we cannot see any self separate from stories.

Freeman (1993) notes, citing Bakhtin, that we need to understand first how we are externally determined before we can be free. For Freeman this understanding is the beginning of the possibility of a rewriting of the self. It is the act of rewriting the self that creates the conditions necessary for interpretation. Interpretation leads to reinterpretation, hence rewriting. Interpretation is a creative act, but something created is always created out of something given. It is in the act of rewriting that we freely choose ourselves: who we will be and who we will become. But we do not create ourselves from a blank canvas. We work with the materials at hand.

Kegan (1994) writes that authority and freedom have a changing dialectical relationship with development. Authority is earlier that which is defined by others. It consists of external voices, prescriptions, interdictions, and absolutes. With development of agency (his fourth-order Institutional self, see below), authority becomes that which comes from within. We speak then of being self-authoring.

Rewriting the self does not mean that we create our identities from nothing. We work as artists with the materials at hand, including our genetic programming and our social conditioning, and the latter includes what we have inherited from authorities. When rewriting ourselves, the materials are essentially language—the forms and structures it possesses—and our experiential and social worlds, as well as our bodily selves. The authority of tradition, our lived world, and our bodies serve as the basis for constructing self-authority. Authority is first that which we have to accept and which we identify with. Only later can the self make an object of and make external its internalized contents, and thereby come to develop its own forms of self-authority.

TEMPORALITY

A narrative approach sees our lives as stories that are invented, not objects that can be analyzed either causally or mechanistically. Because the future is open, and because our stories have as one of their elements a projection into the future, nothing regarding our "essence" or "real self" can be known, because our essence is not a "thing." A stone can be known in all its aspects because it is simply *there*. But no human being is simply *there*: we always escape ourselves and "reality" by projecting future possibilities. And with the positing of futures, the past and the present can both be reconfigured. There can always be a reworking of the plot to open up a new course of action or, indeed, a new self. Because the future is inextricably connected to the rewriting of stories, our lives therefore cannot be apprehended as objects. Any given totalization or configuration can always be transcended by imagining a new future.

Our lives as stories consist of past, present, and future. The past is rooted in our sifted, selected, and continuously reconstructed memories, our continuously reconstructed histories. The present is now, but is at the same time ungraspable except as a confluence of past and future. The future is an imaginative projection based on our purposes, goals, and fictions.

Because humans are intentional, projecting toward invented futures, a narrative psychology requires a hermeneutic approach. Hermeneutics is a method that works by projecting totalizations or meanings onto the "data" of experience, totalizations that are always underdetermined by the available data. Such totalizations require a configuring of meanings that go beyond the present and yet which are nevertheless based in the present. Hermeneutics arose from textual exegesis: how to translate between different texts or how to interpret a different culture's texts in terms of one's own culture. Hermeneutics is necessary for understanding to occur because we cannot understand any thing outside of the meanings supplied by our culture. The *hermeneutic circle* describes how understanding relates to things, not by trying to reflect what exists out there—because such objectivity is impossible—but in how understanding occurs in the fusion of horizons, where what is known is understood in the attempts to project a whole that will bring together and cohere all the separate parts. We cannot understand the parts except in terms of the whole, but we cannot see the whole until we have grasped the parts.

For example, one of the ways we understand something is to ask questions. Whether we do this casually in our day-to-day interactions with others or whether we do this rigorously by a scientific method, what we are doing is asking questions of our objects of inquiry. We can only formulate questions from within our present interpretative framework. Such questions set the stage and prepare the way for what answers can be heard.

Likewise, as we attempt to understand all the pieces of a person's life, we are forced to project narrative totalities, which are always underdetermined by the data of our observations. This is true whether we speak of coming to understand others or coming to understand ourselves. And part of the totality that composes a person's life is the future. Because it is sown into all the threads of our life, the future as part of a narrative fabric of meaning creatively reconfigures both the past and the present. As we imagine new futures, the narrative totality, in which and by which we interpret our own lives and those of others, is altered. Any event, from either our past or our present, can be seen in a new way when it is viewed as a beginning to a different future. The loss of an old friend or the end of a relationship can be interpreted either as the demise of wished-for hopes or the opening up of new horizons.

COGNITIVE STRUCTURING

Behaviorism reached its peak in the 1950s. Because it espoused positivism, it focused only on what could be reliably observed. Inferences regarding unobservable mental entities were avoided. The "doing" of psychology was limited to what was measurable either as stimuli or as behavior. With observation restricted to observable stimuli and behaviors, speculation regarding the contents of the "black box"— what was in the mind mediating between stimuli and response—was avoided.

With the cognitive revolution, which really got under way in the 1960s, arguments were made that a science of psychology could make inferences regarding the contents of the black box, provided that by the use of such statements more exact statements of prediction regarding observables could be achieved. Within the area of information processing, a subdiscipline of cognitive psychology that treats the mind like a computer, a distinction was often drawn between bottom-up and top-down processing. Bottom-up processing was when the stimulus features present in the environment determined behavior. Top-down processing was when central cognitive structures residing within the mind or the black box determined behavior. These cognitive structures were studied by cognitive psychology. Traditional examples of cognitive structures studied include Chomsky's generative grammar and Piaget's stages of growth in cognitive structures.

It is significant that an early exponent of the cognitive revolution was Jerome Bruner (1986, 1990). He helped popularize the cognitive approach in the 1960s and helped introduce the perspectives of both Chomsky and Piaget to many readers, particularly in the United States. But he has more recently been critical of the cognitive perspective, and particularly the information-processing perspective. He has argued that it is too reductive and too restrictive in its application of scientific method. Contrasting the *paradigmatic* approach of cognitivism with the *narrative* approach he proposes, he has nevertheless retained the emphasis on cognitive structures in the making of a science of human behavior. It is just that these structures are now so much more sophisticated and therefore harder to describe.

Many cognitive structures are related to language and discourse forms; some deriving from syntax (e.g., subject and predicate), others deriving from narrative forms. These schemata provide the structures by which we interpret events and by which we pattern and organize our thinking about actions. We cannot perceive events solely on the basis of the "bare data" of our perceptions. We cannot help but frame "data" within structures. Actions are invariably assimilated into discourse events that are, in turn, part of larger units of meaning making.

In a manner similar to how Gestalt psychologists demonstrated how perceptions are organized into good forms (*pragnanz*) by the properties of the nervous system, so too are people's actions organized into sequences of events the larger units of which are stories. It should be noted that Gestalt psychologists are considered the forerunners of the cognitive revolution. Both the Gestalt and the narrative perspectives suggest that we do not make observations of objective units of behavior; rather, we impose our narrative sense of what constitutes "good form" on the flow of perceptions and actions around us. Furthermore, this imposing of form creates what will be the units of observation in our realities. Observations become data when they are fitted into a story that we impose on events.

However, in contrast to perceptual gestalt, which are innate, the forms of narrative are not, although Bruner (1986) suggests that our earlier *capacity* for narrative in childhood may be innate. These narrative forms are acquired as a result of participation in the culture's symbol systems and social practices. Language as semantics and syntax provides the lower-level structures and forms as well as the higher-level pragmatic forms of discourse and narrative. By the time we are adolescents or adults, we cannot describe events outside of the possibilities of description made possible by language practices.

Cognitive science has demonstrated that we filter information selectively in top-down fashion and also that we have a limited attentional capacity. Because of these and other hardwired constraints, we process information by imposing structure. If we were passive perceivers who simply absorbed or "picked up" information, we would not have to structure it. Narrative psychology persuades us that one way we structure perception is to "story" it; we interpret and transform reality by inventing stories with the forms of language and discourse.

In Freeman's (1993) account of Sartre's Roquentin in *Nausea*, Freeman criticizes the narrator's attempt to pierce the veil of fiction and tell things as they are, on the grounds that this cannot be done. Writers on narrative take the postmodern point of view that the bond between *word* and *world* is broken. Understanding never escapes the worlds constructed from language. By necessity, human understanding works from *within* language. Anything we know, any event we *tell*, any act of communication, occurs entirely within language. A popular term is *intertextuality*. This term describes how knowing is always about relating words to other words, but that in the endless weaving of word relationships, we never map *words* onto *things*. When we speak of things, we are speaking, and when we speak, we are speaking of words and of words alone.

The narrative perspective endorses this view and holds that both linguistic determinism and cognitive structuring are universals. Our lives are written from within the house of imagination, a house we dwell in of necessity, a house we cannot leave. Indeed, some of the various depictions of life outside the house of language suggest that it is a life to be avoided. William James's description of the newborn infant existing within a "blooming, buzzing confusion," and Roquentin's apprehension of a void, of a random and chaotic nothingness, seem to indicate that a world outside the categories of language is threatening.

Freeman shows how the modern view that self is prior to and creator of meaning—a perspective he identifies with romanticism—has been superseded by a postmodern view that holds that meaning is prior to self. Self is a product of language and discourse. Without a house of language, without a fiction-making domain, there would be no self.

CULTURES, STORIES, AND SYMBOLS

In addition to being situated temporally, our stories are situated spatially among a cast of characters to whom we relate and with whom we share a body of cultural myths by which we interpret ourselves and others. Through plots, stories structure events. Many plots are canonical, rooted in tradition. "Emplotting," the act of plotting, requires characters and settings, as well as other ingredients. We configure each other into roles and personae—heroes, mentors, villains, helpers, and so forth. We tend to see situations as tragic or as romantic. The cultural repertoire on which we draw for the material of our constructions—plots, characters, settings, and the like—is embedded in practices and systems of meaning making we are not conscious of in our earlier years. Nevertheless, these systems of meaning making constrain the roles we model and enrich the available personae we adopt.

Canonical stories can structure our lives in many ways. Life imitates art. Could this be only because art imitates life so well? The media on which we draw for the shaping of our stories are changing. In ancient times, epics and myths were spoken. In the Middle Ages, the major fund of stories was the Bible. Because most people were illiterate, the stories were often conveyed in graphical forms. Stories were often played out on the stage, but it was probably uncommon to actually read the plays. The novel, as we know it, appeared in the eighteenth century and was generally accepted as a form of literature at the same time as literacy spread, with women reading at least as much as men, if not more. Christian stories were now not the only ones used in the schools or in the media available. Because literacy only became the norm by the turn of the century in Western cultures, it is relatively recent that books and texts have been the main transmitters of story. At the same time as literacy became the norm, other means were introduced to convey stories: radio, cinema, television, and now multimedia.

There have always been ways of conveying stories and people have always listened to or read stories. But I would like to emphasize that while we might agree that the stock of stories on which we draw does influence how we script our lives, we should not assume that only straightforwardly fictional stories are the sole kinds of stories to influence us. Stories are transmitted in other ways than simply by means of fictions. As we grow up we learn roles. Roles are acceptable patterns of behaviors, a type of story. These roles are part of character. And character is the personae we project as we interact in social circles. At first, our characters require confirmation and reinforcement from others to function. Our social circles expand in larger concentric circles as we develop. First, we learn roles in the immediate context of family. Then we learn appropriate roles within our circumscribed circle of peers. As we go to school and church, as we take up sports and jobs, we learn to craft richer and more abstract characters. With maturity, we eventually construct an identity that firmly connects us to our relationships and our careers. And identity allows us to not require constant confirmation and reinforcement from others so as to regulate our behaviors in predictable ways.

These characters do not stand alone. They are part of the way reality *is,* according to society. Things are a certain way and the way we fit meaningfully into the way things are is to play roles. These roles ensure that we interact sensibly and meaningfully with others. We learn how to be a son or daughter, a buddy or chum, a good student, a regular churchgoer, a reliable paperboy or baseball player, a trusted employee, a good parent. And the ways these roles constrain behavior is part of the larger scene of how social reality constructs what will come to be. Roles, characters, and identities are the mechanisms by which we learn to play our part in the play. And if we don't play, we are left out in the cold.

That these roles are indeed *roles,* and do not reflect inner *essences,* can be seen most easily if we adopt a cross-cultural and historical perspective, something that has been more easy to do over the course of the last century or two. What we understand by the nature of childhood or adolescence has radically changed over time. Likewise, the roles considered respectable for women have changed drastically over the last generation. And, because roles are a part of larger plays, larger stories, which we might call ideologies, so too will the roles of men change as well. Definitions are now changing drastically for what is considered appropriate for the aged. And are these ideologies really all that different from myth?

Psychologists are as prone to taking on and assuming prevailing stories and myths as anybody. The ways in which they conceive of how we move through the life span have been shaped by the predominant stories available: for example, adolescence as the period of *Sturm und Drang,* or aging as a period of contemplative withdrawal and wisdom. These prototypical story lines can be both constraining and facilitating. Even the types of mental illness reported change with time and history. Hysteria (now termed conversion disorder) is seldom reported anymore whereas multiple personality disorder is more prevalent. Depression has been on the rise since the Second World War. Perhaps the frequency and types of mental illness that occur are influenced as much by the available stories and themes predominant at any given time as by specifically medical determinants or socio-economic trends.

LIVES AS TEXTS

Events are the stuff of our lives. Events involve an integration of cognition, affect, and action with the world. Events become experiences when they can be read as texts where we alternate in our roles; we can play at being hermeneutic interpreters or creative authors or involved actors. When we interpret actions we are behaving like literary interpreters or hermeneuticists. This is true of our interpretations of ourselves as well; we take our actions and thoughts and feelings as texts to the extent that we regard them as *other* from us and in need of interpretation. Consciousness of experience is not direct; it always involves an interpretation, and interpretation is inextricably rooted in language.

When we invent or rewrite our selves or our scripts, we are functioning as authors, as creators of meaning. The object created is our lives entire, and our lives are a text of meaning, of words and expressions. We craft our relations with others. We initiate *actions* that are more than *reactions*; they are gestures of writing on the pages of our future, lives that exist in a future that may never be achieved as we conceive it, but that nevertheless informs who we are in the present.

When we take action, we act somewhat less reflectively, but we are invented nevertheless, involved as we are in our stories or projects.

Doing is both utterance and objectification (Packer, 1991). As such, our actions can be interpreted and appropriated from different perspectives, our own and those of others. Our actions cannot be observed objectively, or readily analyzed into units that can be measured, quantified, and described in scientific value-free language.

It is particularly in our capacity as actors, but also as authors and interpreters, that the story can take over, that a fiction can develop a life of its own, a momentum that impels us to act, that draws us with its allure, and that eventually spins us more than we spin it. While this can signify a fulfilling life and a creative engagement with the world, it can also spell the end of creative invention and, in the worst cases, a limitation of freedom.

NATURE OF REALITY

Adopting a narrative approach, the clear-cut distinction between fiction and reality becomes more problematic. Stories, which are all that we may know of our lives, cannot be said to be about "real" persons or events—they are fictions. We cannot describe a reality that can be known apart from interpretation; answers provided by interpretations presuppose questions and questions entail theoretical baggage, baggage that cannot be left behind regardless of the trip taken. Interpretation is always about "storying," that is, fitting a series of actions into a sequence that makes some kind of narrative sense.

As we seek to story our lives, we actively change what we observe. The Heisenberg uncertainty principle, part of which holds that the act of observation affects the object observed, applies in psychological description perhaps more so than in other kinds of description. The hard duality of subject and object is broken, a duality that so much of positivist thinking maintains. We do not find psychological traits or entities as a botanist might find a rare species in a tropical forest. By entering the forest, by trying to describe or model what we see in it, we affect and even create what we find.

Therapy or self-discovery is not so much an excavation or an archaeology, but a collaborative construction, aesthetic and existential, between therapist and client of what is willed, on the basis of what has been interpreted, according to a story invented in the present. There is no pure level of observation uncontaminated by "prejudice." The psychological universe is as silent as the celestial until we set questions to it; these questions are necessarily structured by our preunderstandings.

And there is no question without a theory; theory itself, when applied to persons, is really a kind of story.

If our selves cannot be known in the ways we know physical objects, then we can invent ourselves more freely and aesthetically than we might have, given more conventional ways of thinking. Perhaps we can see more of the "play" in the play to which our roles have constrained us to adopt. There is less need to find out how things *have* to be if part of the way things *are* is how we make them out to be. The Delphic dictum to "know thyself" is less a matter of finding how things are than of creating what we will be with the powers of imagination.

BREACHES AND RUPTURES

Packer (1991) and Bruner (1990) both draw attention to the importance of narrative in addressing ruptures or breaks in the storied fabric of our shared being. By "break" or "rupture," I mean a failure or breakdown in shared communication that affects how interactions are negotiated. When communication and interaction flow smoothly, relationships can be taken for granted. The narrative assumptions each party shares in the interaction need not be questioned; indeed, the narrative assumptions shared may not even be conscious. But break or rupture in shared assumptions and communication inaugurates a period of exceptionality.

Bruner notes how narrative has elements of both *canonicity* and *exceptionality*, and states that it is the latter that must be negotiated by means of interpretive procedures, procedures that are a part of the culture's toolkit of prosthetic devices for thinking. It is during such phases of exceptionality or rupture that the implicit narratives by which people regulate their lives can become explicit. It is only during times of conflict that the narratives we instantiate and the procedures for negotiating them become foregrounded in our day-to-day lives.

It would seem that the experience of breach or rupture is becoming the norm in our postmodern era. As Randall (1995) puts it, the master narratives that had brought together and made our cultures coherent are available no more. Consequently, the demand for narrative is no longer the exception but the rule. When one lives in a small town and never leaves the provincialism of that small town, one never becomes reflexively aware of the codes and norms that regulate one's behavior in that small town. But step out of that town and then return, and its network of implicit and regulative controls become obvious—perhaps intolerable. With today's technological developments, most of us can no longer maintain the insularity of the proverbial small town; more of us are in the state of negotiating meaning with dissimilar others now than at any other time in history. This means that now more than ever, more of us are "in over our heads" (Kegan, 1994) and may not be developmentally up to the task presented by contemporary society of negotiating narrative identities in the midst of such uncertainty.

While Bruner (1990) argues that the interpretative procedures or resources for negotiating breaches in the narrative ground of our lives reside with the culture, I would argue that these procedures have to be cognitively represented in the brain and used effectively within the cognitive architecture so as to make a difference. Such representation and use requires developmental maturity, maturity both in cognition and in consciousness.

While it would seem that Bruner's account of the role of cultural traditions in shaping our narrative structures optimistically assumes that such traditions tend to be benign, accounts such as those of White and Epston (1990) imply that such traditions are not so favorable to personal development. For White and Epston, cultural tradition is based on maintaining a tight connection between knowledge and power. Individual initiatives toward breach and rupture may be fought or resisted by the status quo, and therefore need to be more radical, often instigated by those most repressed. Stories have a practical socioeconomic dimension: discourses are not only about language, but also about how language maintains relationships of power. Many cultural traditions actively oppose individual initiatives toward break and rupture. And part of the role of therapists (and educators and clergy and spiritual teachers) is to provide cultural support for individuals to make such radical moves. And this brings me to the topic of therapy.

THERAPY AS NARRATIVE REPAIR

Howard (1991) has described life as the stories we live by, psychopathology as stories gone mad, and psychotherapy as exercises in story repair (p. 194). Quoting Mair,

> Stories are habituations. We live in and through stories. They conjure worlds. We do not know the world other than as story world. Stories inform life. They hold us together and keep us apart. We inhabit the great stories of our culture. We live through stories. We are lived by the stories of our race and place. It is this enveloping and constituting function of stories that is especially important to sense more fully. We are, each of us,

locations where the stories of our place and time become partially tellable. (p. 192)

While I share the sentiment expressed, the following quote provides the key point with which I take issue:

> A life becomes meaningful when ones sees himself or herself as an actor within the context of a story—be it a cultural tale, a religious narrative, a family saga, the march of science, a political movement, and so forth. Early in life we are free to choose what life story we will inhabit—and later we find we are lived by that story. The eternal conflict of freedom versus destiny is revealed in the old Spanish proverb: Habits at first are silken threads—Then they become cables. The same could be said of stories. Thus, a paraphrase of one of Shakespeare's more dire warnings becomes appropriate, Beware of the stories you tell yourself—for you will surely be lived by them. (Howard, 1991, p. 196)

In childhood we are never "free" to choose our stories in the way Howard writes. Stories are something we are socialized into—in fact, *forced* into—however enlightened the despotism of the enculturating agents. We have no choice but to make narrative inferences within the "envelope" of cultural scripts; only later can we begin to engage in *conscious* narrative reasoning. We are first written by our scripts; it is only with maturity that we have an opportunity to have a *perspective* on our stories, even to be aware that they are stories and that they need not have the taken-for-granted reality status conferred on them since childhood. This is part of the task for therapy: to show people how to be more reflective and creative storytellers. But, as will be argued, in trying to apply this in therapy, we need to recognize differences in developmental capacity or readiness for narrative thinking.

The task of a therapist or teacher is to actively listen to the stories of their clients. It is largely the habitual expectations, the automatic thoughts, the asking of certain questions and not others, "the narrative core" that causes people to suffer in the ways they do and to engage in confirmatory biases that reinforce their beliefs. This makes the task of therapy one of "narrative repair."

Seligman (1990) makes the focus of his cognitive–behavioral approach one of making the client actively dispute habitual cognitions, which cause them to engage in personal, pervasive, and permanent explanations of internal events. These kinds of attributions result in pessimistic evaluations of the client's own capacities, leading to learned helplessness and depression. What is important is the type of story the client is habitually telling him- or herself. We cannot figure out what the "true story" of events is apart from the client's construction. Therapy is a matter of getting the client to write a more adequate or preferred story so that he or she has the possibility of breaking the cycle of depression.

Pursuing Howard's suggestion that we see psychopathology as stories gone mad, we may view depression as a pessimistic explanatory style or story. Keen (1986) has written that we may conceptualize paranoia as a cataclysmic and tragic story style. Other pathologies may be understood as the client's living out stories gone mad. If the therapist's role is one of helping to get clients to distance themselves from their story, and to thereby rewrite their stories, difficulties will arise in treating those patients who cannot construct a self separate from their story. Such cognitive interventions may only assist clients in coping with the current story but cannot aim at story reconstruction.

If, as the quote from Howard cited earlier indicates, stories are habituations, then they can be seen as having dominating and subjugating consequences as well as liberating and enlightening effects. White and Epston (1990) write that the presented problems in therapy can be worked with when the problem can be *externalized.* Once externalized, the client is assisted to see how the problem affects him- or herself and others, and then to consider how they, in turn, affect the problem. This can lead to the perception of what are termed "unique outcomes": facts that might not have been experienced were the client only perceiving under the influence of dominant discourses. The client is encouraged to perform new meanings and construct alternative stories. While therapy can provide an "artificial" environment for the externalizing of problems, later in development the capacity for this externalization becomes more self-directed.

The perception of unique outcomes entails that the therapist engage in counterpractices undermining the pervasive influence of dominant discourses that subjugate the client as an individual, objectified and "thingified" within a power/knowledge matrix. Stories as constitutive of individuals have their basis in systems of control of which we are a part. Psychoanalytically, we can see these systems of control as internalized with development into superegos or ego ideals. The stories we first come to write of ourselves are, indeed, a function of socialization, and the prime objective of socialization is *control.*

As Vygotsky (1978) wrote, a child has to learn how to go from being controlled by others to being controlled by him- or herself. White and Epston, borrowing heavily from Foucault, interpret this to mean that the gaze of others must come from within. With socialization into the human community we have to become our own regulators. The panopticon functions best when it is internalized—and even best when it cannot be seen at all. However, we need not always be docile creatures; we can turn against these internal voices, by means such as the kind of therapy Gould (1978) writes of when he speaks of the steps for contradicting childhood consciousness, for disputing childhood fears and childish beliefs. But these kinds of therapy cannot be practiced with anybody at any stage in their life; individuals have to be ready.

TRANSCENDING NARRATIVE

At whatever level of analysis we choose, the human species is prewired to construct worlds. At the level of sensation, whether we examine the cones and rods of the eye's retina or whether we examine the nerve endings of the ear's cochlear membrane, we find no objects, no space, no time, no world of any sort. At the level of perception—higher up in the information-processing "ladder" of the brain—we can say that there *are* objects, space, time, and the rudiments of a world. Many computational processes enable a processing system to construct a world from the paltry input provided by the senses, a world that is then imputed or projected to the external world. This is the study of *perception* in psychology. The success of this world-creating process is judged by the crucible of evolutionary success.

As we grow through the conventional levels of development, with language and culture we are able to transcend the perceptual world of the infant and live within a social or cultural world. This is a world constituted by language, based on symbols, and later, concepts. It is a world with all of the elements required of a life: objects, places, people, history, norms, roles, and rules. This constituted world is then projected onto the external world and lived in as if it were the real and only world. The child or adolescent imputes this constituted world to the world "out there." That is how the individual adapts to the outer world. It is only with higher stages of development that the nature of the projection as *projection* is glimpsed.

Within this constructed world, each repertoire of symbols and concepts that make up individual persons becomes packaged into bundles of behavioral expectations that we call *roles*. These roles are interrelated with others by means of *rules* that are defined with reference to *contexts*. How roles are instantiated in a given context is determined by *scripts* (Pascual-Leone & Irwin, 1994a, b). With increasing development, various series of scripts are coordinated into more encompassing narratives by which higher-level roles are packaged as *identities*. Interpretation of these identities is necessary to investigate how it is that people construct meaning in their day-to-day lives.

Up until the conventional levels of development, the social world afforded us by our use of language is taken as the world in itself, because we have no means of separating or distancing ourselves from this world. At conventional levels, it is more accurate to say that we *are* our stories rather than that we *have* our stories. Although it is due to the powers of mind and language that the world is made, it is really more a matter of the individual being *made* by the world rather than the individual *making* the world. It is only with more developed intellectual powers that we become reflexively aware of the constructed nature of the world we dwell in.

With maturity, which may come for some generally later in adulthood, and which may never come for some at all, we apprehend the multiplicity of both our own and other's worlds and begin to appreciate our ability to operate on, and even transform, such worlds. Furthermore, we begin to intuit a world apart from our symbolically constructed world, a world beyond language. The repeated failures to achieve full closure in our cognitive grasping, the continued contradictions thrust on us by our unruly emotions, the failures to predict both ourselves and others, create the ground for repeated experiences of a "liminal" nature. We begin to notice and acknowledge a new power, a transformative and transcending power to act on our world, to change it, and even to step outside of it and walk into totally different and other worlds not of our society's making.

The symbolically constructed world of our identity is contradicted on numerous levels. It must negotiate the competing claims of others and other cultures, it must acknowledge its own multiplicity in having contrived different worlds for different folks, and it must grant the reality of worlds of feeling and experience not accounted for in its version of things as they are.

In childhood and adolescence, and further onward into young adulthood, development is clearly in the direction of greater adaptation to the social world: first, adaptation to the immediate family, then peers, then other social groups, and finally, adaptation to society in the most general sense by means of abstracted ego structures, what I am calling *identity*. In effect, adaptation does go on well into maturity. But later in adulthood, we adapt no longer only to social processes. We come to adapt to the natural world without and to the psychological world within, an adaptation that is no longer really "adaptation" at all—that is, adjustment of something within to something without—but rather an opening to what is within and an opening to what is without.

While adaptation as a kind of development can proceed well into adulthood (particularly in the cases of career change or switching of roles), the development that is *unique* in adulthood, and distinguishes development in adulthood from development in childhood and adolescence, is a form of development that is the opposite of adaptation to the social world.

Levinson (Levinson et al., 1978) wrote of a reduced concern in adulthood for making it in the "tribe." Making it in the tribe is the function of ego. While it may strike some as odd that contemporary society can be seen as a tribe, that is precisely the way to see it from a postconventional perspective: it is parochial, biased, conditioning, and constricting. Referring to Jung's account of individuation in adulthood, Labouvie-Vief (1990) wrote,

> A major task is to give up identification with the conscious ego and to open oneself to the more organismic self-processes in which the ego is embedded ... the self is this more inclusive embedding and regulating process, and the major task of midlife is to give up the egoic, idealized definition of self and open oneself up to this broader organismic structure. (p. 74)

The ego is the structure that the self constructed to cope with the demands society placed on it. In childhood, the self had to be mediated to the natural world by the social world and the product of this mediation was a rudimentary ego. Ego, in turn, mediated how the self related to the social world via its self-representations. To develop more effective self-representations, the cognitive system employed language to build a more abstract and context-free set of representations. According to such a system, reality becomes what can be described within such a system. Aspects of experience not conforming to such a system are not attended to or are repressed.

For some individuals at later stages of life, as pressures to adapt decrease, as coping requires less attention, and as less effort has to be expended in presenting a viable persona to the public world, the ego can afford to relax and allow experiences to occur without continuously having to monitor them. Control processes can be relinquished; surveillance mechanisms switched off. We can spend less time watching ourselves.

In maturity, adults face more contradictions to their idealized conceptions of what they are and what can be expected from others. These idealized conceptions or ego-ideals are no longer taken so seriously. The adult begins to notice that different circumstances trigger different ego ideals and that these ideals are in contradiction with each other. Time and again, experience shows that life is always much greater than any conception of it allows and that our self is infinitely more complex than any simple conception of it affords.

With time, the adult experiences more obstacles to the fulfillment of expectations, expectations that are a function of the ways we project possible worlds. This piles up more frustrations and more disappointments. More threats to self-esteem cause us to question the rudiments of what constitutes self-esteem. Loss can be avoided or defended against in youth but cannot be so easily avoided in adulthood. In youth there is always a vast tomorrow to make up for what is not fulfilled today. In adulthood that tomorrow becomes more restricted in both time and place. Dreams have to be reevaluated when it becomes obvious that they will never be achieved.

The combination of increased age, enhanced competence, breadth of experience, and the increased probability of disillusionment with the promises and claims of others brings about a reduction in the youthful respect for authorities, whether these authorities be older or more privileged. Because one is often treated now as an authority by those much younger or because one has worked closely with those held in authority by others, the shiny appeal of prestige and power wears off. It is not really the youngest who can see that the emperor has no clothes; it is really the older among us who have seen so many more claims to status and the trappings of power evaporate.

* *

As children and adolescents grow, more and more of the world becomes embraced and captured in their more sophisticated cognitive structures. Failures to understand are met with more determined efforts to achieve abstraction, precision, and control by means of more efficient cognitive structures. But with maturity, the trajectory of increasing cognitive adaptation meets up with more limitations, limitations that cannot be surmounted by greater abstraction or reason. The relativity of judgments, the linguistic-embeddedness of thinking, the inescapability of interpretative horizons, the correlativity of opposed conceptions, all interact to force each thinker to grant that reality cannot be captured within purely intellectual conceptions, and that such conceptions contain within themselves their own limits by virtue of their nature.

In youth, cognitive representations of oneself and of others were constructed to enhance the ability to predict both one's own behavior and that of others, thus reducing anxiety and insecurity by affording greater control over the world and oneself. As these representations become more successful at predicting and controlling our lives, they also become self-fulfilling in the prophecies they make, which is the other side of the coin of closure and security. With prediction and control, come predictability and being controlled. And then there are those stubborn things that can never be predicted and that well up from within us in our moments of fatigue or that flicker in the periphery of our vision in the gray light of a restless dawn.

Adolescents and young people seem to believe that they can live forever. With the deaths of parents and peers, the illnesses of close ones and the pervasive sense that one's own mortality is looming, the verities of youth are weakened. Every look in a mirror reminds us of the passing of days, the weakening of our faculties, and the diminishing of our strengths. When we get together with our family or friends, often after increasingly longer absences, we face what seems like speeded-up time-lapse photography—thinning hair, creases around the eyes, bulges about the thighs and waists, brown speckles on the hands.

Because we have seen more people and have been more places, our present experiences are more likely to evoke memories. The newness of the present is framed continuously against what has been stored in memory of the past. Each new experience is capable of eliciting more past experiences. But the past is often remembered in the framed aspect of a passed opportunity or disappointment. With both the consciousness of change and the irretrievability of the past, we become wistful of things that never were nor can ever be. We look at our children with the hope of the present and tomorrow, but also with the implicit sense of comparison to one's own lost youth and what was denied.

At midlife, yardsticks become less important. In youth, the present is always evaluated against the goals one has set for oneself (goals that reside in one's ego ideal). Experiences are always judged against self-imposed yardsticks of accomplishment. As we get older we may actually achieve some of our objectives, but in attaining them they may seem hollow as compared with the richness of experience that was overlooked while pursuing "grander" things.

Emotions are less threatening in adulthood. In youth, certain feelings evoked anxiety and had to be repressed. These affects were anxiety-provoking to the young and dependent child, but not so much so now to the more seasoned and independent adult. In aging, circumstance will have required facing up to these threatening aspects of the self. In facing up to these powerful feelings, the sense of their power may be attenuated. The openness this engenders will generalize to many other feelings, whether sexual, aggressive, tender, or loathsome. The mature adult feels less need to control, hold on to, inhibit, censure, or strangle their emotional selves. When a threatening impulse reaches the threshold of awareness, the habitual defenses may not always trigger in automatic fashion; the texture and taste of each feeling is allowed some space to breathe.

The narrative level of consciousness development is postconventional, but not yet postlinguistic. It uses the social conventions of language to liberate itself from social conditioning, but it has to do so reflectively, using language as a tool of thought. Language possesses both constraining and transcending features. It frees our thinking from biological and cognitive limits, but it also captivates us in the prison house of our own self-representations. The power of narrative stages of consciousness rests in the way that the fixity and constituted-ness of our egos is shaken up and later transmuted in the liberation of self-authorship. But, eventually the joys attendant on self-authorship themselves are exhausted. Although self-authorship frees us from conventionality and social conditioning, although self-authorship allows us to creatively and aesthetically "mix" ourselves up with the world, it still is founded in a self–other and self–world separateness that perpetuates suffering.

Narrative theory (Freeman, 1993) holds that we are forever fixed within the boundaries of intertextuality; we can never break out of the worlds of our interpretation and imagination. We can rewrite ourselves as we negotiate the fusion of different horizons. We owe the beauty and nobility of our lives to the fact that they are created in much the same way a work of art is created. But this is a double-edged proposition. We are still prisoners, however gilded the cage. And ultimately we come to see that all of our narratives come to an end and cause us suffering because they make us try to be something *other* than we are. To become what we *are* requires a transcendence of language itself, a transcendence denied by most who write of narrative, hermeneutics, and social constructionism.

* *

Randall (1995) provides a nice schematic to explain narrative. He distinguishes four levels of story:

1. Existence, or the Outside Story
2. Experience, or the Inside Story
3. Expression, or the Inside-Out Story
4. Impression, the Outside-In Story

Existence is what *is,* the ground of our being, what is before us and what remains after us, and what we are even prior to story. It is the

Outside Story. When aspects of existence are taken up by our narrating minds we convert the events of existence into experience, we make them part of the Inside Story. In turn, we give expression to parts of our Inside Stories—but only parts—in words, images, or whatever, what it means to be our Inside Story in forms communicable to others. This is the Inside-Out Story. In turn, our Inside Story is affected by impressions, impressions we receive from others of the way things are, and the way existence is. These impressions become part of the Outside-In Story.

As we develop, we mold much of our Inside Stories according to patterns set for us by others, by impression, from Outside-In Stories. But as we become adults we may find these impressions too constricting. We may find that our Inside Stories do not contain enough of what we intuit as our existence.

> A basic goal of psychotherapy, we could say, is to coax more of the contents of the first level onto the second, and more of the second onto the third. Put another way, it is to help us have more of our lives at our disposal, meaning more of our existence incorporated into our experience and more of our experience available for expression. In addition, we could say, a goal of therapy and education alike is to enlighten us sufficiently to critique the stories others read into our lives outside-in, rendering them therefore less influential on, and less constricting of, the form and content of the stories we tell others inside-out. (Randall, 1995, p. 62)

We construct our Inside-Out Stories to include more of our Inside Stories, which in turn are demanding that we include in the Inside Story more of the Outside Story. But I think this is doomed to failure. Story or fiction is inherently selective, inherently linear, and inherently biased. A story cannot contain everything or it would not be a story. A story that contained and included everything would no longer be coherent or integrated. Stories require that some aspects of experience be foregrounded and that others be backgrounded. But if we try to include everything from the background in the foreground, we will then have no foreground to speak of. And it is with this realization that we arrive at the end of narrative.

Randall's account is written entirely from within the personal stages, as I am defining them here. And his account contains within it the seeds of its own disequilibrium and its own transcendence, the beginnings of the postpersonal stages. Randall says that we cannot imagine a life not seen through the lenses of story or fiction or language.

> None of us 'interpets the raw world directly,' writes Annie Dillard.... We interpret our world and ourselves *through* the inventions of our imagination, *through* our fictions.' 'Humanity has but one product,' she claims,

> 'and that is fiction.' In fiction, art as invention converges with art as interpretation: 'all mental activity is selective and interpretative; all language is interpretative; all perception is interpretative; all expression and activity is interpretative. And all interpretations miss their mark or invent it, make it up.' (Randall, 1995, p. 70)

> Stories may or may not be inherent in events themselves—indeed it is hard to know what this would even mean—but *seeing* stories in events is so central an activity of the consciousness through which we *experience* events that, for us humans anyway, it comes down to the same thing. What sort of person can experience events in the raw, without recourse to beginnings, middles, and ends? Who can stare wide-eyed, and for how long, at things-as-they-are-in-themselves, in the moment, naked, outside of an interpretative context within which they are constructed, assigned a past, present, and future? Who can endure what writer Michael Crichton longingly labels 'direct experience' . . . ? Perhaps a newborn baby can; perhaps a 'pure' scientist can; perhaps a mystic can, or a master of Zen; perhaps a Sartre can. But can we? I believe not. However good for the soul it may be to bear reality 'in the now,' we are all, technically, living in 'bad faith.' (Randall, 1995, p. 93)

Randall stumbles up here against a contradiction in his own thinking that he is not yet ready to see. Zen Masters *are* no different than we. They possess the same human "nature" as any of us. Indeed, it is this perception, the perception that the master is no different than the student, that is often said to characterize those who have attained enlightenment. The necessity of fiction, of imposing stories on the flow of experience, is not a given of the human condition, but a necessity only of a certain level of consciousness.

While there are forces within impelling us forward to more transcendental stages of consciousness, there are also forces within that hold us back. And at the late personal stages one of these conservative forces is the desire for control and the need for prediction. What becomes of our world and of our self when we can no longer know who we are or what we will be? What happens to our security, our territory, our sense of closure, when we feel that all our narratives are as fragile as gossamer and as impermanent as the dew in the morning?

As we grapple with contradictions in our thoughts, as we bump up against resistances set up by the "real world" to the fulfillment of our projections, as we glimpse gaps in the stability of our conceptions, and as we intuit a fluidity underlying the apparent stability of our self-images, we are forced to let go of our attempts to always *know* what is happening. We acknowledge how frail are our schemes for knowing as we try to fit more of existence into our experience. The narrative imperative contains a contradiction it cannot solve: existence cannot be fitted within experience, reality will not be bent to the Procrustean bed of interpretation, however sophisticated, dialectical, relativistic, metasystematic, or constructivist the scheme of interpretation. No matter how open we are to restorying our lives, no matter how willing we are to listen hermeneutically to the stories of others, no matter how receptive we are to being changed by life's events, we cannot frame the universe, however big the frame. Life cannot be pictured. And this is what I believe Buddhists mean when they say that phenomena are empty, void, *shunyata*.

With this insight, a revolution takes place in the way we apprehend the world. We begin to allow the world to penetrate our lives more, we begin to give up the attempt to always "know" the world within our schemes or simulations. These schemes are founded in the imperative of knowing, the imperative of prediction and control, and at bottom, in our souls, we learn that neither the world nor ourselves can be predicted or controlled.

* *

Despite some claims that the bond between word and world is broken, with its emphasis on storytelling and its view that lives are stories told and that understanding can only be a hermeneutic encounter with others' lives as texts, I would like to argue that the narrative approach requires a conception of psychological reality. Stories told are told about something: narratives have a referent, a self that is wrapped in story. Otherwise, any story at all could be told and any would be just as valid as any other. We have a sense, wherever that sense comes from, that some stories, some accounts, are more authentic than some others. The narrative and social constructionist approaches have to be modified to allow for a modicum of psychological realism. I would like to suggest that constructive developmental psychology can help to read what is "real" and how what is real develops. And this real is not reducible to the socially constructed. I would like to provide some indications of a developmental reality that seems to be shared by a number of writers on development.

On the other hand, it should still be emphasized that our conceptions of a self are going to be permeated by the available stories and ideas in circulation in our culture. Our language and culture are going to affect how we conceive of ourselves. Therefore, we have to develop multiple methods of observation and theory construction so as to reveal the commonality across persons and cultures. Psychological models possess greater validity if they reveal underlying patterns and commonalties in spite of such different theoretical vocabularies and different methods of observation. Psychological models also possess greater scope when they facilitate communication between different theories.

Once we have a general conception of development, we can then say what it is our stories are attempting to describe. Without a conception of development we cannot say what the trajectory of our selves is apart from whatever we ascribe by means of our stories. Once we can state what the paths of development consist of we can then decide if our stories are authentic to the lives they are meant to describe.

Some writers on narrative address what constitutes *development* in narrative. Freeman (1993) does not refer explicitly to stages of narrative development but he does refer to a process of developmental transition between one narrative conception and the next, more developed one. In analyzing the ways writers have constructed and presented themselves in autobiography, he notes the following characteristics that occur in transition from one story to a new more comprehensive story. First occurs the *recognition* that something is wrong, then a *distanciation* from the problem. Reflecting on it, the narrator articulates the story and effects some change in the way he or she narrates the story. Finally, there is *appropriation*. But while affirmation is made, it is never final, as there are always new stories to be written and rewritten.

Freeman often discusses what it means to speak of a progression or improvement in narrative constructions. Because constructions have a fictive nature and because all interpretation of narratives themselves presuppose narrative frameworks on the part of interpreters—whether on the part of psychologists or therapists or educators— the implications of relativism are inescapable. And one of these implications is the questioning of whether any one interpretation is better than any other. Without an answer to this question, what becomes of the authority of social scientists?

Freeman answers this by pointing to how the writers of stories themselves evolve new narrative constructions. As they break out of prior narrative frames and juxtapose older conceptions to new ones, they can identify how the newer constructions are changed. Freeman writes,

> We must still ask: Is this new truth necessarily 'better' or just different? It certainly could just be different sometimes: we get a new angle on a book we are reading, see it in a different way from how we had. But our new reading can surely be better as well. How do we know this? Precisely by its juxtaposition to the old one, which becomes exposed as inadequate in the very process of its being replaced. 'The "former" prejudice is not simply cast aside', therefore: 'whatever replaced it cannot present its credentials until the position under assault is itself unmasked and denounced as prejudice'. Thus, 'Every "new" position which replaces another continues

Narrative

> to need the "former" because it cannot itself be explained so long as it knows neither in what nor by what it is opposed.' (Freeman, 1993, p. 142)

> The notion of 'better', therefore, derives not from a omparison of two readings held fundamentally apart from one another, but from their relationship, from the transformation of one into the other: 'Now,' you might say, 'I have a more adequate—comprehensive, complex, aware, integrated, whatever—understanding of this thing before me.' Needless to say, this too will change, and our humility, perhaps even our humiliation, will return once more: How could I have missed it? How could I have failed to see? How could I be so ignorant, stupid, naive, and just plain wrong? But we ought not to move too far in this direction: again, our own hermeneutical position has changed. Should we ever kick ourselves for our former foibles? Certainly, but only if there is good reason to believe that our previous interpretations were inadequate given the situation we were in at the time. (Freeman, 1993, p. 143)

Freeman seems to be identifying how development can be understood. I hope to provide some indication of how we might begin to understand narrative development from the point of view of theories of cognitive and ego development.

CHAPTER 9

Epistemic Knowing

RELATIVISTIC KNOWING

I believe that the current interest in narrative psychology and narrative therapy is connected to some general intellectual trends that have been current throughout the second half of the twentieth century. One of the most important of these intellectual trends is *postmodernism* (Gergen, 1991). Postmodernism has a number of intellectual sources and can be characterized in number of different ways. One characteristic of it is the divide it establishes between *word* and *world,* or between *text* and *reality* (Freeman, 1993). Postmodernism holds that what we commonly take to be descriptions of a world "out there" are, in fact, only forms of discourse or text. It holds that such descriptions are socially constructed and possess, at most, consensual truth. These descriptions function within language practices, which are rooted in discourse communities, that is, social groups. One cannot evaluate or understand the meaning of a statement without reference to the language practices and discourse communities of which it is a part.

This way of thinking of things is offensive to most conventional thinkers, upsetting everybody from Christian fundamentalists to scientific positivists. Postmodern thinking is said to precipitate moral vertigo. It also unleashes a backlash of condemnation from both the moral right and the idealistic left. Those who espouse postmodernism are accused of corrupting the young and unseating the gods. Who is right? How can we address the controversy? How can we come to understand what and how to believe in such a polarized debate? Developmental research may provide us with an answer.

In the domain of *epistemic* knowing, four bodies of research converge in characterizing *only* higher-level intellectual development as capable of grasping the socially discursive nature of truth claims. William Perry (1970) refers to it as "commitment in relativism," Patricia

King and Karen Kitchener (1994) describe their stage seven as the realization of the constructed and social nature of reality descriptions, Mary Belenky (Belenky, Clinchy, Goldberger, & Tarule, 1986) refers to higher level intellectual development as "constructed knowing," and Jan Sinnott (1984) shows that the capacity for relativistic postformal operations involves understanding how interpersonal reality is co-created. These achievements are all guided by the insight that knowledge claims are relative to the discourse practices from which they arise: that when we as humans talk of reality, we can never escape the fact that we are always constrained by the structures and processes that shape how we talk. Furthermore, there is no *extralanguage* realm to which we can refer without using the very language into which we are socialized.

In describing the college age population of the 1950s and 1960s, William Perry found that freshman students often manifested what he termed an *epistemological dualism*, which is the felt sense of Authority as residing "out there" (Perry, 1970). With development in college, Perry found that students' perceptions of the role of Authorities in determining truth and knowledge underwent profound qualitative changes. As a result of exposure to competing and diverse pluralistic claims, some Authorities are judged to be wrong. Later more room is allowed for areas of disagreement, but these uncertainties are seen as temporary: Authorities will get the right answers with time. Later, these areas of uncertainty and disagreement are accorded a larger space in the students' intellectual universe, to the point where the student may rely only on opinion in many matters. Otherwise, they still rely on Authority in areas of certainty. But with the understanding of relativism, students perceive all areas of knowledge as uncertain, all truth claims as relative to frames of interpretation, and all knowledge as inherently subjective. This is relevant to narrative approaches: before a rewriting of the self can occur some kind of break with our conventional selves and conventional authorities has to be made.

The break with Authority is necessary before Commitments can be made. These Commitments can be understood in narrative terms as a deliberate writing of the self. Perry distinguishes between Commitment with an uppercase "C" and commitment with a lowercase "c," and argues that the former can be made only after the failure of certainties that results from higher epistemic development. Once Commitments are made, epistemic agency can be experienced as residing within. In Positions Six through Nine, Perry postulates that initially single Commitments are made, then multiple Commitments, and then finally the dialectical coordination of partial and contradictory Commitments.

Basseches (1984) has pointed out that some *Commitments* may in fact be *commitments,* and that Perry may have conflated the two. Lowercase style commitments are commitments made without the benefit of the full exploration of relativism. Uppercase style commitments are made with the full acknowledgment of relativism and uncertainty. Hence, Perry may have assessed his students at levels of Commitment prematurely. If people are making lowercase style commitments for life, this may explain why it is that later in life many people undergo such turbulent midlife crises and experiences of the sort described in Levinson (Levinson et al., 1978) and Gould (1978).

For the sake of brevity, I shall summarize Perry's nine positions as only four: dualism, multiplism, relativism, and commitment. *Dualism* is an epistemological position where students see Truth as residing with Authorities. To learn means to adopt the views of Authorities. Positions are categorized as Right versus Wrong, Good versus Bad, and We versus Them. *Multiplism* is the position that follows. In it, unlike before, students see many areas of knowledge as problematic and uncertain; when uncertainty prevails, students rely on their intuition or their subjective preferences. When many opinions exist on an issue, students uphold the view that any one position is as good as any other. Later, in *Relativism,* students see that opinions can be compared and contrasted rationally; doing so means to take into account that all knowledge is relative to a frame of reference and that all knowing involves the interpretive activity of a subject. Finally, with *Commitment,* students begin to construct lifelong orientations, values, or choices that are guided by rational truth claims, but which are nonetheless informed and permeated by points of view or frames of reference that have nonrational components.

I think it is important to note that in the higher-level Perry positions knowing is construed as inseparable from its embedding frame of reference or point of view, and that with maturity people can act on rather than from within thought systems or frames of reference. I think that these qualities of thinking are often necessary to spiritual paths because individuals have to question received beliefs and examine the limits of thinking so as to transcend thinking and rationality, a transcendence required in most accounts of spiritual awareness.

Several approaches to Perry measurement leave out Positions Six to Nine, the positions involving Commitment, arguing that Perry has confused epistemic or intellectual development with ethical or identity development (Baxter- Magolda & Porterfield, 1988; King & Kitchener, 1994). Perhaps it is difficult to operationalize or measure Commitment, but I do not think this justifies truncating Perry's scheme. Perhaps narrative approaches can take up where these epistemic approaches have left off, and begin to include identity issues in their conceptions of young adult development.

Perry's theory has been studied by many researchers. Various measures have been constructed and tested with different populations (Baxter-Magolda & Porterfield, 1988; Moore, 1982). Perhaps the most rigorous of the Perry researchers are King and Kitchener (1994), and their various colleagues. In their investigations into their Reflective Judgment Model, they have eliminated the last three Perry positions (in the abbreviated version presented here, the Commitment stage) and have organized the remaining six positions into seven levels of epistemic cognition. Paraphrasing King and Kitchener, these can be summarized into the following statements:

1. What I observe to be true is true. This is termed the "copy view of knowledge," that knowledge is absolute.
2. There is a true reality that can be known, but not by everybody. Hence, the need for authorities who do know.
3. Truth is temporarily inaccessible, even for authorities, but will be known at some point in time. In the meantime, rely on "feelings."
4. Reality cannot be known with certainty and knowledge claims are purely idiosyncratic.
5. Objective reality doesn't exist; there is only the subjective interpretation of data. Beliefs are justified only *within* a domain where legitimate interpretations can be made, but no comparisons can be made *across* domains.
6. While objective knowledge is not possible, some claims can be judged as better founded than others. There are principles of inquiry that are generalizable across domains.
7. Interpretations of the world can be synthesized into claims about the nature of the world. Therefore, knowledge must be constructed. We need to build coherent explanations.

Note in the following example the use of narrative in Stage 7 reasoning:

> One can argue here that one is a better argument than the other. One is more consistent with the evidence. What I am really after is a story that is in some sense intelligible and as intelligible as possible.... So it's very much a—I don't think it's as much of a puzzle solving as it is trying to get the narrative straight. (Davison, King, & Kitchener, 1990, p. 271)

The first four stages are more detailed explications of the first two presented here and the last three are a more detailed outline of the third stage. Their data are gathered from analyses of the protocols of students' reflections on truth claims made in four different domains of learning. King and Kitchener have

- Demonstrated high interrater reliability for the coding of their interviews
- Performed test–retest correlations to indicate stability or reliability of assessment
- Performed interproblem correlations to indicate that different domains have moderate cross-domain consistency
- Statistically tested the sequentiality of the proposed stages in the model
- Measured both longitudinal and cross-sectional validity showing reliable developmental progression
- Shown significant relationships to other domains, particularly moral and identity development, thereby supporting the construct validity of both the model and instrument and demonstrating that Reflective Judgment is required for the moral and identity domains
- Shown that the lion's share of stage increase is due to education and not age per se

I think that what is most relevant to the present topic is the emphasis the model places on how students evolve from adherents of the "copy theory" of knowledge to a social constructionist view of knowledge—that is, from a view that perceives learning as consisting of merely passively reflecting what exists in the real world and in the minds of authorities to a view that sees all knowing as inherently subjective and arrived at by forms of rational inquiry, inquiry carried out in social contexts by means of discourse practices. This insight into the social nature of thought may be necessary before what I am defining here as the representational or personal level of consciousness can be transcended.

The insight into the social relativity of thought and world-views is necessary before a true appreciation of the ubiquity and inescapability of narrative is possible. King and Kitchener's stage seven is a epistemological prerequisite to Commitment, which I am defining as the intellectual insight that choices are truly valid only after the choices made by others are exhaustively questioned. Stories that we live out because we are socialized into believing them are not the same as stories that we invent and construct for ourselves.

Critiquing the male biases they perceive as evident in Perry's work, and echoing some of the criticisms made by Gilligan of Kohlberg's moral developmental theory, Belenky et al. (1986) retrace the positions of Perry's scheme of epistemological and intellectual development, and propose to change the metaphor of knowing suggested by Perry as *vision* to one of a metaphor of knowing as *voice*.

Women's voices are first described in the scheme as *Silenced,* particularly in cases of abuse and neglect. But for most women, voice begins to emerge as *Received,* taking in the voices of others and unable to act on or evaluate what is taken in. Later there is a reaction to the objective and external voices of Authority and a turning within to listen to and develop the voice of *Subjectivity*—gut feeling and intuition. Women's experiences of this position differ radically from men's because they do not relate with or identify with the systems of power, authority, and knowledge as men do. Faced with the need to communicate and defend points of view, women evolve into *Procedural knowing,* learning the systems, methods, languages, and concepts of externally defined disciplines. Procedural knowing takes two forms: *separate knowing,* which is similar to Perry's relativism, practicing objective analysis and argument; and *connected knowing,* engaging in empathic relatedness and experiencing. Finally, the inner and outer voices are coordinated in the position of *Constructed knowing,* in which the relativity of knowledge is embraced at the same time as the self becomes more integrated in the process of knowledge construction.

They argue that a capacity for mature narrative is not really possible until the perspective of constructed knowing. We can conclude then, as was the case for Perry, and for King and Kitchener, that constructed knowing is a prerequisite for narrative knowing.

> During the process of self examination, women feel a heightened consciousness and sense of choice about 'how I want to think' and 'how I want to be.' They develop a narrative sense of the self—past and future. They do not want to dismiss former ways of knowing so much as they want to stay alert to the fact that different perspectives and different points in time produce different answers. They begin to express an interest in personal history and in the history of ideas . . . how truths even within the self are mutable— a matter of personal history, circumstance and timing—and how internal truths may conflict and change with time. (Belenky et al., 1986, pp. 136–137)

There are two important assertions made in *Women's Ways of Knowing* that need to be addressed. One is that these stages or positions are really developmental levels. The other is that there really are sex differences between men and women in the ways in which epistemic development unfolds.

Because Belenky and her colleagues employed a simple interview method, sampling their subjects at only one point in time, they cannot confidently attribute sequentiality to their positions because they do not take measurements from their subjects over time. Furthermore, they provide no statistical tests regarding the relationships between their positions and age. Neither do they attempt to relate their positions, as measured, to other stage models that have psychometric validity.

Roxie Orr and Mary Luszcz (1994) have carried out research addressing a few of these questions. They showed that relativistic operations, as assessed by Jan Sinnott's method of content analysis, were positively correlated to constructed knowing and negatively correlated to procedural knowing, but not related to received or subjective knowing.

To explicate this claim we turn now to a consideration of Jan Sinnott's work. Jan Sinnott (1984) reported a method of assessing relativistic operations, operations that she claimed were *postformal* operational ways of thinking, that is, operations that succeed formal operations. She operationalized relativistic operations as consisting of:

- Metatheory shift: an intentional alteration of one's set of *a priori* assumptions and hence of the types of solutions proposed.
- Problem definition: when subjects are explicit about the way they have formulated the problem to themselves for their own purposes. The formulation might or might not involve a metatheory shift.
- Process/product shift: when the outcome or solution is stated in relation to the processes of reasoning that led to it.
- Parameter setting: when the subject goes beyond the stated situation and sets parameters or variables that will be used to formulate relationships whether or not the parameters are altered to arrive at different solutions.
- Pragmatics: when the subject selects one of several variant formulations of a problem for practical reasons.
- Multiple solutions: when the subject explicitly notes that differing processes or *a priori* lead to different valid solutions.
- Multiple causality: when subjects acknowledge that events are multiply determined and that outcomes are the result of numerous interactions.
- Paradox: when the problem is stated as containing apparently conflicting interpretations.

The findings reported by Orr and Luszcz provide a demonstration of convergent validity for both Sinnott's and Belenky's schemes. That is, they both appear to be measuring the same things. Further research needs to confirm whether the stages are truly sequential and truly postformal.

The other problematic assertion made in *Women's Ways of Knowing* is that there are clear-cut sex differences in the way that men and women negotiate their epistemic development. Orr and Luszcz show quite clearly that the sex differences asserted by Belenky and company do not appear as robust as might be expected. They did not find differences between men and women on the measure of constructed knowing, nor did they find sex differences in the measures of relativistic operations. Furthermore, there were no differences in received knowing. However, females showed more evidence of subjective knowing and men showed more evidence of procedural knowing. This is similar to the debate initiated by Gilligan regarding so-called sex differences in moral judgment. When all the data are in, it appears that such a claim was premature: according to Walker (1989) and many others, the proposition that there are sex differences in moral development is not borne out.

To return to our main point, what Perry, Kitchener and King, Belenky, and Sinnott concur on is where epistemic knowing develops. It is the constructivist interpretation that all knowing is relativistically constructed by knowing subjects in interaction and discourse, and therefore that no truth exists outside of the domain of human rationality.

On the one hand, this is a sophisticated intellectual achievement that can open vistas of experience and knowing not possible before. On the other hand, this achievement undermines confidence in metaphysical and moral certainties—a dizzying prospect. Michael Chandler wrote of the problem of doubt, calling it the "Othello Effect" (1987). It is the giddy and starkly cold sense of standing by oneself on the summit of intellectual and moral achievement and realizing that there is no warmth to be had except for the fire burning within.

And while it may appear that there is no stable frame of reference, no Archimedean point of certainty in the natural world, it is also apparent that the only credence that can be ascribed to being is the credence that we, as humans, give to being. The things that are, that make up our world, have meaning such as is invented by us alone. And, by way of consolation, knowing that we make these worlds together somehow brings us closer together, softening and warming the cold isolation of epistemological loneliness.

One of the elements of the worlds that we construct and that we invent for society is how we know ourselves, that is, our *egos*: those parts of our being that we present and project to both ourselves and others by way of talking them into being. Ego is a mode of knowing that is socially constructed. And to that extent, the reality of ego is really a matter of storytelling: stories we tell for others and stories we tell for ourselves. Any substantial or foundational knowledge we think can be derived from such storytelling is, at bottom, an illusion—an illusion that nevertheless binds us to the worlds we create. It is an illusion because we take this storytelling activity as evidence of a real entity that is solid and substantial; in fact, the supposed entity does not exist apart from social processes. The "entity-" or "being-status" of ego is a function of interaction in the social domain. It is only by reifying an aspect of language and social expectations that we attribute ontological realness to the ego.

DIALECTICAL KNOWING

Several writers on adult development have used a model of dialectic to describe the more complex reasoning that matures later in life (Basseches, 1984; Kramer, 1989; Pascual-Leone, 1983; Riegel, 1973). Dialectic is defined by Basseches (1984) as developmental *transformation* occurring through *constitutive* and *interactive* relationships. Dialectical thinking in turn is described as thinking that uses models of "dialectic" to understand various kinds of phenomena. It locates the phenomena within systems or patterns that undergo dialectical transformation. Basseches has argued that dialectical thinking is *metasystematic,* possessing some of the properties of Piaget's formal operations, on which products it operates, and that dialectical thinking is *postformal,* a state of higher equilibrium emerging after formal operations. Although not composed of reversible operations, dialectical thinking has its own form of equilibrium. It is applicable to a broader sphere of application than formal operations, which are based on "closed-system" models, which are of limited value for understanding open, interacting systems.

I would like to suggest that dialectical thinking may be more relevant to reasoning about narrative than to reasoning about the physical properties of objects and that it may be incorrect to assume that dialectical thinking is a reequilibration of formal operations. The latter are described (Inhelder & Piaget, 1958) as the system of 16 binary operations (essentially the propositional calculus) and the INRC group. These structures are said to constitute the logical structure required to solve problems in physics such as the balance beam task or the chemical task of isolating variables to produce given effects. Dialectical thinking is said to operate on the products of these operations as formal operations are said to operate on the products of concrete operations, hence dialectical thinking is described by Michael Commons (Commons et al., 1984) as third-order operations. However, it is not clear that dialectical thinking succeeds formal operations. "Dialectical schemata," as described by Basseches, are not really described with reference to any of the properties of formal operations. As well, Basseches inferred the existence of dialectical schemata from the coding of interview transcripts the subject matter of which was defining the nature of education; and did not base them on asking subjects to reflect on actions involving balance beams or isolating chemicals to produce a certain color. Further discussion regarding the problematic status of dialectical thinking as a post-formal phenomenon can be found in Irwin (1991).

In fact, dialectical thinking may have little to do with formal operational thinking. Perhaps dialectical thinking develops parallel with formal thinking. Perhaps we should not connect dialectical thinking with reasoning about the properties of physical systems and apply it instead to the properties of reasoning about the constructed life worlds of historically situated humans. Taking as its proper object life stories and identities, dialectical thinking is appropriate to analyzing the interaction between different narrative constructions as they evolve over time, constituting each other as they also transform each other. Persons who reason by means of the dialectical "moves" described by Basseches would have a different understanding of how they construct their own identity and life story than subjects who evidence little dialectical thinking. The dialectical thinkers' approach regarding their stories would be consistent with what Kegan (1994) characterizes as fifth-order postmodern consciousness (see below).

Michael Basseches (1984) wrote of a postformal, metasystematic stage of reasoning termed *dialectical*. He originally argued that dialectical thinking succeeded formal operations, taking as its object systems organized by formal operational structures. Whether or not Basseches' appropriation of Piagetian stage theory is valid to describe uniquely adult modes of reasoning, there is evidence that dialectical thinking is found more often with adults than with adolescents or children when studied with his method of coding. Dialectical thinking was said by Basseches to be manifested in 24 moves of thought or schemata that ideally constituted an organized whole. An example of one such move is the thesis–antithesis–synthesis movement in thought.

Dialectical thinking seems to be more sophisticated than strictly relativistic or epistemic operations and some schemata are found more rarely than relativistic reasoning. For the purpose of identifying possible antecedents to spiritual development, what is relevant to note is the manner in which dialectical thinking emphasizes change in thinking and reasoning. For example, one of the four categories of dialectical schemata is motion-oriented schemata. Examples of these schemata are the avoidance or exposure of reification, objectification, and hypostatization or the schemata for seeing events as moments of a process. The former points to the secondary reality of things as opposed to processes and the latter points to how things are what they are only as moments in an unfolding process. Another category of dialectical schemata is relationship-oriented schemata. One example of these is the scheme of internal relations: objects are what they are by virtue of the network of relationships in which they are embedded.

These schemata, and many others, are relevant and necessary to spiritual understanding, particularly in Buddhism. Fundamental to the Buddhist perception is that all things are in a state of becoming; all things are impermanent. Suffering is due to the ego's inability to accept this fundamental fact. The end of suffering is to stop resisting change by effectively letting go of clinging and grasping to forms of solidity. It is the ignorance of ego, and the ego's tendency to hold on to its thought projections, which leads to grasping and clinging. The highest levels of meditative insight involve perceiving the emptiness of the self and of all things. Emptiness is the perception that the essence of all things is "no-thing," that is, that each thing has no self-subsisting reality or inherently existing self-nature apart from the flow of the phenomenal world.

While many of the models proposed to describe adult stages were developed to go beyond Piaget's description and "Beyond Formal Operations," I would like to suggest that they went beyond Piaget only in the sense of depth and not breadth. Stages of reasoning were elaborated that extended a stage model of cognitive, intellectual, or epistemological development further into adulthood without significantly modifying the domain the stage model was intended to describe. Pascual-Leone and Irwin (1994a, b) have proposed a more extensive stage model describing personality structures to account for dialectical thinking. On my own, I have proposed (Irwin, 1996) that we situate dialectical thinking within the domain of narrative reflection about self and other, and not graft it on to Piaget's stages, which were intended to model reasoning about closed physical systems.

CHAPTER 10

Knowing the Self

ROBERT KEGAN

When we consider either common sense notions or more "sophisticated" psychological notions about what maturity is, most people, including most psychologists, would assert that independence, self-direction, autonomy, or agency are all highly desirable characteristics to possess. Furthermore, they might argue that these characteristics clearly distinguish fully functioning and developed persons from those we might think of as less mature or less developed.

Yet evidence seems to suggest that this picture of maturity is incomplete and one-sided. At higher stages of development, individuals are described as going beyond a maturity that emphasizes only independence and autonomy; their maturity is as much about being embedded, connected, and related to others as it is about being independent and directed by volition. Previous conceptions of maturity as consisting only of autonomy seem at best one-dimensional and isolating, at worst, even narcissistic.

One stage model that questions traditional notions of what defines maturity, and that posits a higher stage going beyond strictly autonomous conceptions of maturity, is the theory of Robert Kegan (1982, 1994). Kegan labels the self-authoring stage, the stage of autonomy and agency, the *Institutional.* This is the stage when the individual goes beyond the conventional and embedded *Interpersonal* orientation. At the Institutional stage people are said to author their own being, to own their ideas and relationships rather than be owned by them. With the attainment of the Institutional stage, individuals are freed from their embeddedness in the social, their groundedness in the interpersonal. They can stand apart from their relationships, which up until now have defined them as who they are. They can begin to construct meanings and values for themselves. The concern at the Institutional Stage is with self-authorship and self-determination.

But for some, the Institutional balance comes to be experienced as limiting, as constricting and isolating. Independence and autonomy are perceived as empty and flat. Self-authoring and self-regulation feel somehow hollow. People emerging from the Institutional stage may feel like they would rather not be so in-control-all-the-time, always holding the reins of identity tightly. They desire to go with the flow of experience, to drift with the winds of change, to let go emotionally, physically, and mentally.

Feelings that before had been identified with feelings of freedom and strength—autonomy and self-initiation—are now experienced as staleness, dryness, and emptiness. The language Kegan uses to describe the Institutional reveals its limits: the Institutional self is concerned with self-maintenance and self-control. Life is viewed as an enterprise, feelings are conceived as things to be administered and regulated. The abstract identity of the Institutional requires continuous self-talk and self-surveillance.

As the evolving self transcends the Institutional, Kegan writes that it becomes more porous: more able to let things out and more able to take things in. This change can lead to feelings of ecstatic abandonment and transcendent intimacy. But it can also sometimes lead to a loss of self-esteem and a loss of meaning—at least as understood from the old perspective. The *Interindividual* stage involves

> the relaxation of one's vigilance, a sense of flow and immediacy, a freeing up of one's internal life, an openness to and playfulness about oneself.... the same loosening up may be experienced as boundary loss, impulse flooding, and, as always, the experience of *not knowing*. This last can speak itself in terms of felt meaninglessness. (Kegan, 1982, p. 231)

Experiences affect and penetrate the self. No longer surveying the body and emotions from some "higher" cognitive center of administration and surveillance, one is more tolerant of and more open to sensual feelings, more perceptive of emotions and more aware of the depth and breadth of concrete experiences. But this can threaten values based in the old Institutional self: values based on predictability, on self-consistency, on self-maintenance, on sticking to the project by which one had defined the identity.

Building on the theories of Kohlberg, Piaget, and Loevinger, Kegan claims that developmental transformations in the underlying structure by which subject–object relations are differentiated account for changes across the life span which he and his colleagues identify using the Subject–Object interview. The logic of development is described as a successive disembedding or decentering from within what one takes to be the organization of how one structures self and world. With development, each organizing subject becomes an object or content for an emergent new form or structure.

Kegan's Subject–Object interviews assess unself-conscious epistemologies, or what we might call principles of meaning coherence. The content of the interviews is generated from real-life experiences and involve emotional, cognitive, intrapersonal, and interpersonal concerns. These interviews are transcribed and content analyzed by a rigorously developed coding scheme. Kegan reports interrater reliability estimates ranging from .75 to .90 and a test–retest reliability of .83, as well as high consistency across alternate forms, different domains, and test items. Regarding validity, Kegan cites high correlations with like interviews.

In 1994, Kegan cited the research of Lisa Lahey, who carried out Subject–Object interviews on her subjects' love life and work life with 22 adults. Subjects were interviewed annually for 4 years and then again 5 years after that. Lahey made six reliable distinctions between any two orders of consciousness:

- 3, a clear stage 3,
- 3(4) where a person has begun to separate from that order,
- 3/4 where both exist but 3 predominates,
- 4/3 where the 4th predominates,
- 4(3) where 4 predominates but must work at not letting 3 intrude,
- until finally a clear 4.

Subjects were no more than one discrimination apart in both interviews in 18 of 22 cases.

Stage changes were almost always in the direction of greater complexity, and from one year to the next there never was movement of more than one-fifth of a position. No evidence of stage skipping was found. Also of note: with a larger composite sample of 282 subjects, approximately one half to two thirds have *not* achieved the fourth order, the Institutional.

In Kegan's theory, the infant begins in the *Impulsive* or first-order stage, taking the actions and sensations of its reflexes and of its sensorimotor schemes as object to emerging impulses and perceptions. These impulses become object to the subject, which is now the needs, interests, and wishes of the *Imperial stage* or second order of consciousness in childhood. These needs are in turn decentered and become object at the *Interpersonal stage*. Dominated by its embeddedness in the conventional, objective, symbolic, and moral, it is only at the third-order consciousness that a child is clearly socialized, identified with its social roles and rules. The Interpersonal in turn becomes object to the *Institutional* or fourth order. The Institutional is autonomous and systemic. The highest level of development is reached when the Institutional is decentered and becomes content to the form of the *Interindividual*, an organization that is intersystemic and dialectically interactive, rather than autonomous.

Kegan's most recent exposition of his theory (1994) takes an explicitly narrative turn. With the developments throughout the third, fourth, and fifth orders, Kegan employs the metaphor of *authoring*. At the Interpersonal third order, the self is described as subject to authority rather than self-authoring. At the third order, infallible guides and traditions are sought and adhered to. The self is made up by its beliefs, roles, and values, the assumptions of which are taken as true. Third-order consciousness is lived by its plot line or script and is relatively unaware of the stories in which it is embedded, with the result that it is authored by them. The source of this authoring is the prescribed roles and prescriptions dictated by society and internalized by means of socialization as ego ideals which are externally defined.

With the fourth order, the self becomes author of its own being, the writer of the dramas it invents, and these dramas are based on self-chosen and autonomous systemic principles. The self is capable of becoming separate from its story, with the consequence that it experiences what Kegan calls the loss of community and the loss of "gods." This requires that the self become the maker, author, and critiquer of its narrative constructions. Belief systems and scripts are taken as objects by an emergent identity that no longer is owned by prescribed or received roles and values. At the fourth order, we can speak of a form of personal authority.

At the relatively rare Interindividual stage, the individual enters what Kegan calls the postmodern era of personal development. The self loosens its identifications with its self-chosen systems, ideologies, its forms of personal authority, and its mechanisms of self-control. Autonomy, independence, and essence are questioned. The self is experienced and defined as much by what it is not as by what it is. Rather than identify with any particular self as system, it identifies with the interaction between systems that make up the world of which it is a part. Emotional experiencing is allowed a full range because no emotion, good or bad, can now so easily threaten this more open perspective. Others must no longer always be changed because they too make up a part of the whole in which one interacts. The self engages as much in deauthoring as in reauthoring.

CHANGES IN THE VERTICAL ORGANIZATION OF EGO

The process of development in the early years can be characterized as primarily becoming acculturated into stories, dramas, and roles that are externally defined. Whether you consider the theories of Kohlberg, Loevinger, Kegan, Armon, or Labouvie-Vief, there is agreement that early development is one of "taking in" the values of the culture. To function in a civilized world, we have to take on the symbol systems of our parents and internalize the means of self-control we learn from our culture. Before we can be *postconventional* we have first to become *conventional*. Higher development is a postconventional relativization of and separating away from cultural norms. This is so that we have an authentic self, a self that constructs and has meaning, rather than a self that is constituted by meaning.

Drawing on her work in measuring ego development, defense mechanisms, and investigating how subjects of various ages interpret texts, Labouvie-Vief (Labouvie-Vief, 1990, 1994; Labouvie-Vief, DeVoe, & Bulka, 1989; Labouvie Vief, Hakim Larson, DeVoe, & Schoeberlein, 1989; Labouvie-Vief, Hakim-Larson, & Hobart, 1987) proposes the following model of the life course. Progressing from childhood into adolescence we develop a cognitively centrred control of our emotional and bodily selves to cope with the demands of living in a socialized universe. To do this, we become decentered from our immediate experiences. We objectivise our thoughts and decontextualize our language so as to adapt to and fit into systems of cultural meaning making. But once we attain maturity we have the opportunity to reconnect to our immediate experiences, to make our thinking more subjective, and to recontextualize our language in figurative and intuitive, emotional and physical ways, so that our cognitive–affective balance becomes lateral instead of hierarchical.

> To become a competent member of the collective, the youth needs to be able to dissociate impersonal, abstract and collective meanings from more concrete and personal meanings that carry a great deal of organismic significance. The focus is on the development of a strong ego and on the containment of instinctual processes. Hence, the individual evolves a "vertical" cognitive organization in which mental processes are understood to control or superordinate more organismic aspects of life. For the mature adult, however, it becomes evident that these mental ideals and objective structures are themselves symbolic of the subjective conditions of life.

> Hence, the individual learns to see through and beyond the "objective" to encode underlying conditions of human subjectivity. As a consequence, an epistemological shift is necessitated in which the organismic and inner dimensions are successively upgraded, permitting the individual to evolve a lateral or dialogic structure between rational and nonrational ways of processing. (Labouvie-Vief, 1992, p. 215)

Labouvie-Vief describes wisdom as the fruition of maturity and development. Wisdom consists of a realignment of the ego, a restructuring of the vertical organization by which mind, soul, or self controlled the organismic. As an unsocialized child we are said to be at the *Presystemic level*. At about late adolescence and early adulthood we enter the *Intrasystemic*. We are described as more independent, thinking by means of single systems based on fixed conventions and norms. These abstractions are employed in the monitoring of our internal lives. With further development, some of us reach the *Intersystemic* where we are said to evolve a dialectic for the coordination and relating of different systems. Conflict is acknowledged, but only partially integrated. Such conflict is often experienced in our emotional lives. Finally, with the achievement of the *Integrated level,* both change and difference are valued: the ego is more permeable to experience and has less need to control internal processes. But it is also at the same time more committed to its values and choices however nonabsolute they may be because they reflect internal and more intuitive realities. The distinction between the Intersystemic and the Integrated levels seems parallel to Pascual-Leone and Irwin's (1994a, b) distinction between the predialectical and dialectical periods (see below).

According to Labouvie-Vief, as the ego initially develops, the rule of Logos subordinates that of Mythos. *Logos* is knowledge that is arguable and demonstrable, analytically defined with both accuracy and validity. Meaning is located apart from change and involves stable systems of description and categorization. *Mythos* is knowledge based in narrative, plot, the human drama and the dialogue it engenders among its participants. Thinker and what is thought about are experienced nondualistically. Mythos is grounded in particular experience; Logos is based on what is abstracted from experience. As the ego matures in adulthood, Mythos is accorded as much validity—if not more—than Logos.

Labouvie-Vief equates her distinction between Logos and Mythos with the distinction Bruner draws between *paradigmatic* and *narrative* forms of knowing. Accepting her account, we may have to reconsider whether Bruner's two modes are parallel forms of knowing, as he seems to have done, and consider instead whether the narrative form of knowing may be more advanced or developed than the paradigmatic.

One difference between Logos and Mythos, or the paradigmatic and narrative ways of knowing, is in how Mythos accords a greater role to the self in the construction of knowledge than does Logos. Throughout the constructivist adult developmental field there seems to be general agreement that as individuals mature they question objectivity and embrace subjectivity. Rather than claim that truth exists "out there," that it can be obtained by careful observation, mature people become increasingly aware of the subjective element in their knowing. With this awareness of subjectivity comes the acknowledgment of the role of interpretation in knowledge claims. At higher levels of development, after subjectivity is granted a larger role in the process of knowledge construction, it is coordinated with objectivity in a dialectically unfolding dialogue in which the dualism of subject and object begins to break down and become transformed.

Applying this idea to an understanding of narrative, it may not be clear to less developed individuals that the lives of both themselves and others can be seen as stories that are fictional, and are therefore largely invented. Earlier in life there is a tendency to see the roles and rules of life choices as *given* things that have to be taken on like store-bought clothing from the rack of matching sets. In maturity, the adult may come to perceive that clothing can be tailored individually, integrating their selves with the variety of forms culturally available.

With development into connected knowing in the sense of Belenky et al. or into the Perry positions of Commitment, adults appreciate how paths taken and life choices made are not preordained or fixed. What one comes to be and how one defines oneself can be creatively transformed by intuition, affect, the bodily, and the personal, as in the Mythos of Labouvie-Vief. Identities need not be formed only out of conventional prescriptions and interdictions. Psychological and organismic processes can be combined with social norms and canonical life scripts in a dialectical synthesis that enables truly innovative life choices.

Some researchers who have focused on the structuring of ego or self have noted that earlier development in childhood and adolescence involves increasing control of emotion and experiencing, whereby the body and affect are regulated from "higher" centers of cognition that contain the internalizations of cultural roles and rules. Later in adulthood this process is undone. With movement out of the Institutional balance of Kegan or out of the Intrapsychic stage of Labouvie-Vief, cognitive and affective processes become related in a more lateral or horizontal manner. The self is therefore more open to intuitive and affective processes. There is an opening up to what is inside. By opening up to what is inside, the self is better able to open up to what is outside as well. Speaking of early ego controls, Labouvie-Vief wrote:

> From the midteens to early twenties, emotional control is based on the notion of an ideal abstract state. Emotion language now is preoccupied with the mental control of emotions or the failure of such control. Emotions and actions are justified by social norms binding for all, whereas their characterization as private, organismic processes is almost entirely absent. Overall, the language of emotions is one of containment and repression rather than vividly felt emotional experience. (Labouvie-Vief, 1990, p. 73)

But with maturity, this orientation is experienced as one-sided and unnecessary. Labouvie-Vief writes, "Aware that organismic processes have their own lawfulness that is only obscured and even distorted with excessive efforts at censoring, the individual now explores and acknowledges inner tendencies" (1990, p. 74)

Labouvie-Vief construes both adolescent identity formation and the achievement of formal operations as both extensions of the process of subordinating the individual to the conventions of the collective. Other theorists, such as Kohlberg, Piaget, or Marcia (1980), have described adolescent achievements in more positive terms. But theorizing from the point of view that there *are* higher stages of human development, Labouvie-Vief conceptually situates both identity achievement and formal operational structures as belonging to conventional and conformist levels of development. In this way, they are similar to earlier interpersonal roles and concrete operational thinking structures, but only more abstracted and disembedded from the particularities of unique interpersonal realities, and therefore more adapted to interpersonal reality in general.

Labouvie-Vief identifies this development with social evolutionary adaptations to the more structured, hierarchically stratified and codified urban societies that evolved out of earlier agrarian cultures. This evolution, in turn, paralleled the change from oral culture to literate culture. Society required a differently socialized individual who could adapt to, and assume, more abstract and departicularized roles. These roles embodied more general rules that were not contingent on the immediate presence of concrete persons and actions and that could be organized in terms of the hierarchically arranged structures prevalent in society.

While we may construe adolescent and early adult evolution as eventuating in greater agency or autonomy, Labouvie-Vief perceives it also as resulting in further alienation from our being. The more individuals identify with and embrace the abstract identity required of them in society, the more they will become estranged from their inner being. Midlife individuation is about getting behind this mask of civil propriety, opening up to what lies within, acknowledging the shadow side of the personality, and experiencing emotions and bodily desires less as processes that are threatening and requiring control, and instead experiencing them more as internal sources of wisdom and experience.

In childhood, adolescence, and, indeed, much of adulthood, the ego develops as a means of internalizing collective representations which in turn subordinate imaginative, intuitive, and organismic experiences. These representations are shaped and informed by shared collective meanings as they are structured by language, dominant narratives, and discourse practices. When internalized as cognitive structures, they ensure that individual desires and wishes are consonant with social realities. Identity is an achievement that requires that the individual accept collective representations of self and others as definitive of self. This process acts to socially regulate instinctual life, a life that becomes subordinated to abstract and collective roles and rules, a process that is necessary if society is going to perpetuate its institutions from generation to generation.

From the point of view of spiritual development and higher stages of consciousness, identity can be construed as having a reference point by which the world is totalized—and the practice of meditation is about giving up that reference point—that is, giving up credentials and thereby having an immediate and naked openness to the phenomenal world. Seen this way, relativistic and dialectical thinking are abstract cognitive methods of coordinating these different world totalizations. This process, when understood as narrative, eventuates in the perception that all of these worlds are fictions, fictions that are scaffolded by language. Spiritual transcendence is a matter of leaping beyond all points of reference, all forms of language-mediated filters, and becoming naked to the phenomenal world.

Midlife individuation, and the setting outward on a spiritual path, can be understood as psychologically evolving beyond the dominance of the reified reality of the collective, with its social meanings, roles, and rules. While much of our interpersonal behavior and social practices require the internalization of shared patterns, the role of these internalized structures becomes refigured in our psychological landscapes as more space is allotted for directly felt experiences and intuited realities that may not even be represented in the dominant forms of collective discourse. In fact, many felt experiences and bodily realities have been habitually suppressed or even repressed as we have accommodated to social realities, particularly in childhood when we had no choice but to internalize what we perceived around us.

As Labouvie-Vief writes (quoted earlier),

> a major task is to give up identification with the conscious ego and to open oneself to the more organismic self processes in which the ego is embedded. . . . the self is this more inclusive embedding and regulating process, and the major task of midlife is to give up the egoic, idealized definition of self and open oneself up to this broader organismic structure. (Labouvie-Vief, 1990, p. 74)

For example, rather than projecting evil as something that only exists without, we become more open to acknowledging the evil that exists within. Labouvie-Vief has documented the decline with age of denial and projection as habitual defense mechanisms, a decline that occurs in higher levels of ego development. We are more open to accepting those parts of ourselves not scripted by our conventional roles and identities. Opening up to what's inside, we can transform or sublimate these tendencies, rather than deny or repress them.

THE MIDLIFE CRISIS IN DEVELOPMENT

In narrative psychology, a major task for therapy is to give voice to aspects of clients' lives that currently dominant discourses stifle. White and Epston (1990) think that therapeutic interventions work by attending to experiences not fitting the dominant story.

> persons experience problems, for which they frequently seek therapy, when the narratives in which they are "storying" their experience, and/or in which they are having their experience "storied" by others, do not sufficiently represent their lived experience, and that, in these circumstances, there will be significant aspects of their lived experience that contradict these dominant narratives. (White & Epston, 1990, pp. 14–15)

This sense of the insufficiency of one's life story, the sense that aspects of one's internal life are not adequately storied, is particularly common during the midlife crisis, as described in the research of both Daniel Levinson (Levinson et al., 1978) and Roger Gould (1978).

One of the characteristics of midlife is the emerging, yet uneasy, sense of the partialness and one-sidedness of the life structure—the life structure being how one connects one's motivations and desires and internal life with the broader world in which one lives. Narrative theorists would construe the self-structure as a type of life story. The identity constructed in early adulthood, while adequate to the demands of coping with and getting by in the domains of work and family, is now felt as incomplete. Aspects of lived experience were not attended to in elaborating an identity in youth and young adulthood and, in fact, were actively pushed out of awareness as the younger adult tried to adhere to an ego ideal now felt as defined more by the categories of others than by self-chosen and internally authentic themes.

Levinson describes development as the course of the self-structure as it evolves through life. The self-structure is based on choices made, and choices involve both positive and negative elements, aspects to include and aspects to exclude. The self-structure can only be built out of the materials available in the prevailing culture. How these materials are synthesized into a viable structure enabling individuals to negotiate their roles in marriage and work, church, school, and community, determines the quality of the self-structure. Above all, the self-structure is an adaptation to the tribe, and although we can describe the adult self-structure as more synthesized and more self-regulated than the early accommodations of childhood, it is still fundamentally an internalization of roles and rules that had to be learned.

The midlife crisis can be broken down into three aspects:

1. As one arrives at midlife, one's life structure is more likely to be perceived as incomplete and insufficient. A feeling of staleness and boredom pervades; one feels that one's life script is routine or conventional. The loftier elements of the project or dream, which made the more prosaic aspects of life more endurable, are seen now as unattainable and impractical. The self-deceptions marshaled during early adulthood so as to successfully perform one's roles become more apparent now that it may not be so necessary to keep one's nose to the grindstone. Less willing to accept the compromises made, the sacrifices agreed to, and the obligations assumed, the maturing adult surveys a now subjectively constrained and limited future, and feels that changes have to be made.
2. Liberated from internalized prescriptions and interdictions, no longer so obsessed with external achievements, there is an "opening up to what's inside" (Gould, 1978). Desires that in childhood were repressed because there just simply was not the mental equipment to contain them, are now attended to, reassessed, and even allowed expression.
3. Of course, from a conventional perspective, the social consequences of opening up to what's inside may not be acceptable. Jung spoke of one of the tasks in later life as acknowledging and working with one's shadow, those disowned and projected aspects of the self that were earlier rejected as incompatible with the ego ideal. Gould writes that we have to live with the evil within.

> As children, before we had the mental capacity to control ourselves in any other way, we controlled our desires by refusing to know what they were.... Now we are thirty to forty years older and more capable. We can afford to know what we feel because, and only because, we now have the mental strength to control our desires. We can contain a passion without acting on it. (Gould, 1978, p. 295)

> To achieve an adult sense of freedom, we must pass through periods of passivity, rage, depression and despair as we experience the repugnance of death, the hoax of life and the evil within and around us. To enjoy full access to our innermost self, we can no longer deny the ugly, demonic side of life, which our immature mind tried to protect against by enslaving itself to false illusions that absolute safety was possible. (Gould, 1978, p. 218)

Levinson's initial model was based on research conducted with 40 adult males initially selected in 1969: biologists, novelists, executives, and blue-collar workers. He interviewed each of them for several hours and conducted follow-ups. From the transcripts of the interviews, Levinson and his co-workers abstracted a model of the life course of the self-structure, a model articulating how there were seasons of life that manifested regular patterns that Levinson linked to specific ages. His model emphasized how periods of stability alternated with periods of transition. Oddly enough, the periods of transition occur at the ages of 30, 40, 50, and 60, while the periods of stability occur in the midpoints of each decade.

Within the self-structure, Levinson identified a representation, an image, what Levinson sometimes calls a "dream," of what the self is, an image that is inherently partial and one-sided and incomplete, but that guides the project or journey of the self. The awareness of the insufficiency of the dream never reaches a point of critical mass until the midlife crisis, when the neglected aspects of self and experience draw attention away from the constricting adult definition of self maintained up until now. As much as the dream may embody and realize many ideals and aspirations, it also includes many elements of self-deception.

The self-structure is the result of the choices undertaken during the manufacture of the identity of adolescence. It is now tested on the high waters of adult life. This means that the adult identity still contains elements of the childish qualities of ego: its rigid prescriptions, its dos and don'ts, and its defenses against demons and monsters, as well as its collection of sensible rules and prohibitions, noble projects and ideals.

For our purposes, we are focusing on the most critical transition period of the model—the midlife age crisis at age 40. Levinson identified it as the most serious and most potentially disturbing. It threatens the self-structure, the stable identity achieved up to this point, and often precipitates divorce, abrupt career change, alcoholism and substance abuse, and sometimes spiritual confusion and angst.

We might identify a number of "causes" of the midlife crisis: psychological, sociological, or anthropological. But the one that is most obvious and most unavoidable is the biological. Undeniably, we are aging. Mortality and death are no longer a matter of conjecture, no longer merely hypothetical. Death and age are no longer things that happen only to other people. By now we have lost one or both of our parents or some of our relations and maybe some close friends. Those who remain are looking old, graying, aging or becoming ill. And we are facing our first illnesses, the first signs of our own deterioration.

And this implodes on our dream, our self-structure, which to be actualized had always implicitly contained the assumption that we would live indefinitely. The dream does not include its own terminus, its own finality. "Happily ever after" does not allow for cancer or Alzheimer's.

The is illustrated by the story of Siddhartha Gautama, the historical Buddha. As a boy and as a youth, Siddhartha was kept inside the castle by his father, who did not want his son exposed to the miseries of mortals. He was sequestered and kept away from unpleasantness. But as he grew older, Siddhartha became restless and wanted to see what lay beyond the castle walls. He ordered his servant to prepare his chariot and was taken out to the streets of the city, where in succession, he saw an old man, a sick man, and a dead man. And it was this experience that caused Siddhartha to give up the things of this world and take up the life of a holy man.

This story can be interpreted as representing the condition of youth regarding old age and misery. By virtue of the protection afforded by our youth and by the solicitous attentions of society, we are not really exposed to death and mortality while young. As we go out into the world we have to face mortality nakedly, without the comfort of mother, without the stories of the nursery.

Levinson drew heavily on the theories of both Erik Erikson and Carl Jung when he interpreted his interviews. From the latter, he borrowed the concept of *individuation.* Jung had shown how we could understand the personality as characterized by the relative predominance of thinking, sensation, feeling, or intuition. Up until midlife, most people can be characterized as emphasizing only one of the four biases. But at midlife, the other biases make their demands on the self-structure. Jung also wrote of how, at midlife—*the noon of life,* as he called it—the shadow side of our personality asserts itself.

Levinson describes a decreased concern for making it in the "tribe" at midlife. The tribe is society. By terming it a tribe, Levinson is implicitly emphasizing the more archaic elements of social life and adaptation. Social life bequeaths to us many beneficial things, but the vestiges of our archaic past haunt us in the stifling identities society forces us to assume, identities that many argue are forever decided. Many civilized virtues that we esteem so highly are, in fact, the product of the evolutionary necessity of each individual fulfilling a narrowly circumscribed position in a hunting-and-gathering tribe.

As I showed earlier, our identities are simulations that we present to others in a social universe so that we may predict and control ourselves as well as enable others to predict and control us. The trick of the game—and it is, ultimately, a game—is to believe that these simulations are "real." There are times in life when the probability increases that we may see through these simulations, when the crack in the armor of personality reveals chinks through which the light can show through. One of these times is adolescence; another time is the midlife crisis.

Ultimately, Levinson's model adheres to the continuity of the self-structure, and after the midlife crisis, the age 40 period of transition, Levinson felt that the self-structure rebuilds and goes on, and that at age 50 another period of transition will take place, and then another at age 60. But he felt that the self-structure nevertheless persists. He conceived of the self-structure as the psychological bridge between self and society, and theorized that the role of society in the equation of the self continues well into maturity. But I want to suggest that the role of society in constituting the self-structure can be transcended in the case of some paths of development, and that the ego, identity, self-structure—call it what you will—may be transcended altogether.

At this point, I shall introduce a caveat. My intention is only to outline a path of *optimal* development. This model allows for and acknowledges that not all individuals will follow this path; indeed, most never move beyond the midway point of the scheme. Whether we describe these variations as just a part of normal human variance, or whether we describe these variations as failures of growth, or deviations from a natural course, is ultimately an empirical question.

Many psychological models of development do not contain stages of higher development. Assuming such stages *do* exist, there are two ways we can explain the paucity of the frequency of higher stages. In the entirety of the human population, these stages are relatively rare: most people simply do not reach them. Consequently, when we consider actual studies carried out that include older samples, it is no wonder that psychology does not have well-established models for higher human development. But there is also the issue of operationalization. For a construct to have a place in a psychological model, it must be measured. If there is no extant measure for a construct, there will be no way to look for its occurrence, no way that it will appear in our observations. Our theories have to tell us that a certain rock exists before we can look underneath it. Without a method of measurement, we cannot record, we cannot observe, and we cannot quantify.

The midlife crisis is a time when the conditions are ripe for change. In some cases, this change can precipitate a spiritual transformation. But for many, indeed most, the self-structure will be reconsolidated in maturity. The midlife crisis provides a period of transition, and if the conditions are right, the spiritual spark may be ignited and the ego will embark on the path of its own undoing, its unraveling into egolessness. But some people do not respond well to the midlife crisis. And some people continue on in their lives in a decidedly secular way.

In childhood we take in visions of perfection and ideas of how things can be (often based on our parents' ideas of how things should be). In psychoanalysis, these are called *introjects.* In adolescence we take in yet more abstract and conceptualized versions of these same things. Part of our personality is the goals and images of perfection that we hold (literally). Levinson thought that we start to lose many of these images or visions in midlife. Once we closely look at, critically examine, and let go of many of our ideals, so many of which are based on and grounded in an essentially childish way of apprehending the world, we can begin to discover who we really are. Such a discovery can be both exhilarating and terrifying.

In childhood we developed many primitive mechanisms to achieve self-control and mastery over our unpredictable emotions and our volatile musculature. This was because we did not have the mental ability, the cognitive equipment, to control ourselves by any other means than repression, denial, and exclusion. But with maturity, and with more sophisticated and more powerful modes of knowing ourselves, we can allow ourselves to experience what we did not allow ourselves to experience in childhood. We can acknowledge feelings and affects that in childhood might have threatened our precarious accommodation to reality. We can give way to or provide a psychological space for previously taboo feelings. We can now more benignly constrain aspects of our selves rather than shut them off entirely, because we can know without having to act, without having to discharge powerful negative feelings. The childhood controls, which have been ingrained into our cognitive–affective habits and which have been imprinted into the musculature of our armored bodies, can be uprooted and exposed to the light of day. Gould defines maturity as "the release from arbitrary constraints" (1978, p. 321). In Buddhist paths, particularly the Tantric, practice includes the transmuting of passions, and this is possible once we remove the harshly punitive and primitive childhood controls constructed around the superego.

As we let go of and relinquish childhood voices, we have the possibility of an inner directedness not heretofore experienced. This inner directedness can express itself in many ways.

For example, with midlife there is more openness to sexual and sensual experiences. Wilber (1993, 1996a) has characterized his *Vision-Logic Stage* as centaurlike, based on a reintegration of the physical and mental. Labouvie-Vief (1994) shows in midlife how the ego structure becomes less hierarchical, less organized around top-down executive control structures that contain and repress organismic structures, how organismic processes can coexist with the mental rather than be controlled and subordinated by it. Kegan (1982, 1994) speaks of the *Interindividual Stage* as more relaxed, more accepting of emotional and physical experiences. Loevinger (1976) wrote of her *Autonomous Stage* that it was more open to and appreciative of sensual experiences (pp. 25–26).

I would like to propose that we can get "sexier" with age. I would like to do this in blatant contradiction to our culture's infatuation with youth and its exclusive identification of sexuality with youth. And we get sexier not by slavishly adhering to the prescriptive models of sexuality provided us by the media, but by opening up to and responding to the inner currents of a sensuality we inherit from our primal psyches, a sensuality labeled "polymorphously perverse" by Freud.

JUAN PASCUAL-LEONE

A process analytic approach may help to elucidate some of the psychological mechanisms responsible for the changes observed at midlife. Most generally speaking, a process analytic approach is one that analyzes phenomena down to the basic mechanisms of the brain. Pascual-Leone first applied his process analytic approach to explicating Piaget's stages of cognitive development, arguing that the apparent qualitative changes in thinking structures that Piaget found were due to quantitative increases in processing capacity in the brain.

One of the characteristics of higher-order development that researchers have identified as unique to mature development is a toleration of and openness to contradiction (Basseches, 1984; Pascual Leone,

1983; Riegel, 1973). This new attitude toward contradiction allows a person to operate on the products of propositional thinking in the sense of dialectical postformal logical thinking (Basseches, 1984) or to dialectically process the competing partial self-systems of the ego. I will adopt the latter approach here.

In Pascual-Leone's work (Pascual-Leone, 1983, 1990a,b; Pascual-Leone & Irwin, 1994a,b), the basic unit both of the brain and of mental life is the scheme. A scheme is a pattern of coactivation among neuronal assemblies. A scheme consists of releasing and effecting components. These embody the conditions for the scheme's activation and the effects such schemes take when applied.

Executives are higher level schemes that function as plans. Executives also have releasing and effecting components. Often the releasing components are activated by affects or perceptions or other executives. Executives can set task goals and allocate mental energy or attention, either by "boosting" other schemes by interrupting the activation of task-irrelevant schemes.

Mental energy is one type of silent resource, the brain's endogenous and physiological source of mental activation. Silent resources work alongside the schemes to codetermine the brain's activity. M, or mental attention, is one such resource that grows over the lifetime and determines the span of working memory, and indirectly the unfolding of the Piagetian stages, according to Pascual-Leone.

Among other things, silent resources and schemes determine what can be "centrated." Centration is the central bottleneck, the span of working memory, setting limits on what can be processed in consciousness.

Affects also reside in the brain and can serve as sources of mental activation. Affects are an endogenous source of energy connected to instincts and also are represented themselves as schemes in specific regions of the brain.

Ego is a complex set of executive structures that coordinate affect schemes with executive and cognitive schemes, what we commonly refer to as personality. Ego is a repertoire of cognitive–affective schemes, and can be analyzed into functional categories.

The two main categories of Ego are *Ego Core* and *Ego Milieu,* the true self and the circumstantial self, the latter consisting of others, the world, the superego, and the ego ideal.

The *Ego Core* or true self consists of what Pascual-Leone calls the I-self and the Me-self. The *I-self* is the operative side of the self, the self as subject. The *Me-self* is the figurative side, the self as object, the self as known by society and history.

The I-self consists of Agency and Soul. *Agency* is linked to power affects, to mastery and independence. Agency consists of I-can and I-will. *I-can* is constituted of task executives that get things accomplished and *I-will* consists of meta-executives that embody life projects and motives.

Soul is linked to warmer affects, consisting of Communion, Passion, and Ethos. *Communion* consists of executives that mediate empathic affects in interaction with others. *Passions* involve self-oriented emotions. *Ethos* is the more developed and mature of the Soul repertoire, coordinated out of Communion and Passions, as well as reworked elements of the ego ideal.

Collectives are complex mental structures that coordinate self and others, the Ego Core and the Ego Milieu. Collectives are like scripts that coordinate the various roles self and others play in specific contexts. Collectives begin to develop in childhood and are generally not consistent across different contexts or different life scenes. This inconsistency is suppressed in youth by mental interruption, an endogenous hardware resource, which in turn is directed by activated executive structures. But mental interruption declines at midlife so that inner contradictions can no longer be avoided or denied.

A distinction within dialectical operations can be made between negative and positive hermeneutics. In the case of *negative hermeneutics,* the self reluctantly grants the existence of its various collectives. But when *positive hermeneutics* develop, the self processes the contradictions posed by such collectives positively. Prior to both dialectical stages, the younger adult holds out for the possibility that a unified self-system can be managed, but with the increasing acknowledgment of the competing representations of self, the fictive nature of idealizations is granted.

In Pascual-Leone and Irwin (1994a,b), we explained midlife changes by reference to decrements in central inhibitory mechanisms that function to screen out the awareness of the compartmentalization of partial self-systems. With the weakening of this selective mechanism, a mechanism that contributes to maintaining the illusion of a stable unified self, the self must confront the inconsistencies and duplicities of its various contextualized selves. As individuals age, they can no longer deny the multitude of *limit situations* that force themselves on consciousness: death, mortality, suffering, illness, and so forth. The cohesiveness of life projects and ego ideals is harder to maintain given the onslaughts of fortune and time.

With these changes taking place, one more readily acknowledges the fictive nature of one's self-authored identity and story. One can risk becoming more "permeable," less rigid and more open to emotional and figurative processes, less controlled and controlling. With an enhanced perspective on one's identity, one can afford to relax, appreciate humor, and be less serious. One can also appreciate things "spiritual," have less of a self-aggrandizing desire to conquer the world, and have more concern for issues of generativity (Erikson, 1963).

This does not mean that stories or narratives are no longer needed, but perhaps that they can be invented more playfully and flexibly. The adult works with a wider and richer canvas of life than in childhood, more from the palette of experience. Colors are selected from a wider spectrum, textures are vivified, and forms expanded. Breaking free of a pastel existence, a more vivid and vibrant approach is risked. The adult opens to the shadow self and those aspects of self not granted a part in the drama of one's more daytime and conventional life.

Being forced to process competing and often contradictory partial self-systems requires changes in our normal modes of conceiving of identity. We may no longer be masters in our own home. It is no longer possible to maintain the self-deceptions and defenses by which we sustain our cherished identities. These identities were initially constructed in adolescence and early adulthood when it was easier to ignore the messy and unpleasant aspects of our lives. But as we mature, we cannot continue to ignore our own sufferings and weaknesses, nor those of others.

In addition to positing organismic processing factors as causing age-related changes in adulthood, I think we can point to general characteristics of midlife aging as responsible for problematizing the narratives of our identities and making us face our internal contradictions. As we enter midlife, we are forced to face our finitude. As Levinson (Levinson et al., 1978) showed, the issue of mortality at midlife affects us with a poignancy unlike any earlier period in our lives. While it is commonly thought that adolescents believe they can live forever, by the time we reach our midlife we can no longer project our yearnings into an infinitely extendable future. We feel ourselves aging: graying, wrinkles, bulging paunches, less reliable memories, and slower reaction times. We may have our first operation or serious illness. We note the passage of time at high school reunions and family get-togethers—how our friends and relations have become more "weathered" or "seasoned" (all euphemisms). While in our youth our parents may have provided us with assurances of solidity and composure, we now watch as they become old and die. And while our children provide us with a connection to youth and exuberance, we cannot fail to notice how quickly they grow up.

Our ideals and projects have had sufficient time to be jarred by the slings and arrows of outrageous fortune. We realize we may never obtain that home we used to dream of. Our children do not turn out perfect. We never have enough time to read the books we know of or travel to the countries we have read about. As more New Year's Days pass, we realize our resolutions have become empty, banal, or repetitive. We fail to reach the highest level in the company. Nor do we achieve the most proficient knowledge in our field or the highest skill level possible in our profession. And there is less time to improve on what we have achieved.

The first noble truth of Buddhism is that life is suffering. You can only enter onto the path of Buddhism when you know this thoroughly (Patrul, 1998). When we are young, we are sheltered from suffering by our parents and the institutions of our society. When we become adolescents and then young adults, we shelter ourselves from suffering, and the constant reminder provided by our young and healthy bodies reinforces the security. But in maturity, we know suffering more truthfully and accurately than we ever could before. Acknowledging and accepting suffering, not defending and escaping from it at every chance, is a prerequisite to beginning a spiritual path. With the acknowledgment of suffering, you can begin to see who you are, and not only the version of yourself that you want others to see.

In youth, as we grow and mature, it seems that we get more self-reliant and more independent. For most people, the sense of self-esteem and autonomy tends to increase. In effect, our egos get stronger and more assured. But with midlife and further development, holes appear in our confidence, gaps occur in the stream of narrative chatter by which we sustain our identities. Pascual-Leone explains this gap as occurring as a result of an openness to contradiction, and this openness in turn is explained by a biologically based decline in the ability to interrupt incompatibilities. When we can no longer interrupt or screen out the incompatibilities in our self- and other-representations, we are ready to let go of the solidity and substantiality of the self. We are ready for the transcendence of the ego.

CHAPTER 11

Social and Moral Knowing

LAWRENCE KOHLBERG

In 1969, Kramer and Kohlberg reported some anomalous results regarding research on stages of moral development. Young people who had been scored as at stage four, a very high and relatively rare finding, were found to be regressing back to stage two. According to the tenets of stage theory, this should *not* be happening. Young people, who had been reasoning in terms of maintaining the social order and taking the point of view of rules and roles, were regressing back to reasoning from self-interest and instrumental exchange. Many of these young people were on the campus of Berkeley in the 1960s.

Kohlberg decided that there was something wrong with the scoring system and revised it. Instead of moving from stage four to stage two, under the newly revised scheme, people moved from *stage four* to *stage four and a half*. And it is the nature of what comes after stage four that we are most concerned with in this book. Stage four is the second of the two conventional stages. For Kohlberg, "conventional" is about reasoning from the social perspective, the social system. And by the time that an individual has attained the conventional stages, the social system is internalized and the self as the actor is identified with the roles and rules of the system.

Most people in Kohlberg's scheme never achieve stage four, so the finding did not emerge early on in research with the theory. But, by and large, Kohlberg's model has held up to testing (Kohlberg, 1976). Raters can be trained to achieve reliable levels of scoring, subjects do move through the stages one after another, the stages can be found in other cultures, and moral developmental stage level does predict such things as level of faith.

The following outline of Kohlberg's stages is adapted largely from Cole and Cole (1996).

Preconventional

Stage 1: Punishment and Obedience. Kohlberg described this as a literal obedience to rules simply to avoid punishment. While Stage 1 avoids the power of authorities, it is primarily egocentric and does not consider the interests of others. Only physical consequences are used to judge actions.

Stage 2: Individual Instrumental Purpose and Exchange. Stage 2 is based on needs and the exchanges that result from a calculation of their demands. Rules are followed because they help satisfy someone's interest. Fair is defined as an equal exchange. Stage 2 clearly differentiates its own interests from those of others.

Conventional

Stage 3: Mutual Interpersonal Expectations, Relationships, and Conformity. Stage 3 is identified with playing "the nice role," having concern for others, and adhering to loyalty and trust. Stage 3 follows rules and expectations. What others expect defines what is good. Mutual relations are paramount. Stage 3 typifies the golden rule of putting yourself in the other person's shoes.

Stage 4: Social System and Conscience Maintenance. Stage 4 is about doing one's duty, upholding order and the welfare of the group. Laws are upheld unless they conflict with other social duties. Stage 4 believes in keeping the institution going. His or her sense of self-respect is based on keeping to obligations made. Stage 4 takes the viewpoint of the system that defines the rules and roles. Individuals are considered in terms of their place in the system.

Postconventional

Stage 4/5: The first of the postconventional stages, stage 4/5 makes choices that are personal and subjective, based on emotions and not on conventional roles or rules. Conscience is arbitrary and relative. The Stage 4/5 perspective is outside of the system. Often commitments cannot be made. Obligations are often chosen that are socially defined but there are no general principles for such choice. I believe this stage is important because it makes more salient how postconventional reasoning differs from conventional.

Stage 5: Prior Rights and Social Contract. Stage 5 upholds basic rights, values, and contracts even when they conflict with the group. For Stage 5, people hold different opinions and rules are relative, but rules should be upheld in the interest of the social contract. Relations are entered into as contracts or commitments. Stage 5 upholds the maxim that the greatest good is for the greatest number and will perform a rational calculation of overall utility in making a social decision. Stage 5 has a prior-to-society perspective and differentiates moral and ethical points of view.

Stage 6: Universal Ethical Principles. Particular laws rest on general principles. When laws violate these principles, Stage 6 acts in accord with the principle of justice. Justice can be defined as the equality of human rights and the respect for the dignity of human beings as individuals. Abstract principles are used to generate decisions. There is a moral point of view from which existing social arrangements are derived. Stage 6 respects others as ends and not as means.

* *

There have been controversies. John Gibbs (Gibbs, Basenger, & Fuller, 1992) has claimed that researchers cannot reliably differentiate the postconventional stages. This means that Stage 6 may not exist separately apart from Stage 5. Carol Gilligan (1982) has claimed that Kohlberg's theory reflects his male bias in the extent to which it emphasizes reasoning from abstract principles rather than from situated caring. She claimed that as a consequence of this, females were assessed at lower levels than males. Gilligan's claim has not held up. Lawrence Walker (1989) showed clearly that males and females do not differ significantly on moral stage.

And Kohlberg himself added a seventh stage, based on purely theoretical considerations (Kohlberg & Ryncarz, 1990). The seventh stage asks the question why be moral and not the question how to be moral. Stage 7 individuals see from a cosmic perspective from which things are accepted as is. The tension between what *should* be and what *is* is resolved. Suffering is accepted and transmuted.

As I have noted, what is most significant for our purposes here is to observe how moral development passes through preconventional, conventional, and then postconventional stages. We begin as children in a fundamentally egocentric and presocial state. With sufficient cognitive development, we become able to internalize the roles and rules of a social system to the point where we identify with that system and, in fact, have no perspective apart from that system. As children and as adolescents, we see ourselves as objects residing within that system. But then later, with postconventional moral development, we begin to disembed and stand apart from the system, to have a perspective on the system from above, as it were.

As we begin to analyze what occurs in the postconventional stages, for Kohlberg, things get unclear. Controversy ensues as to what universal stages all people must pass through. And I think that is because we will not find what is universal at these higher stages by focusing only on moral development. It is as possible to observe hedonistic anarchy as it is to observe Gandhian virtue, both of which are postconventional moral positions. And in the higher reaches of human development and spirituality, we are as likely to observe "crazy wisdom" as we are to observe the unfolding of the life of the Bodhisattva.

CHERYL ARMON

Cheryl Armon makes a nice distinction between *individuality* and *autonomy* that is relevant to describing precisely what is occurring at around roughly midlife in a few individuals (Armon, 1989). In her six-stage model of the Good Life, she describes a transition from a stage four *Individuality* to a stage five *Autonomy*.

Stage 4 is described as an individuated self-system that holds self-chosen values and aims. Only at Stage 4 is there the freedom to go against consensual norms and to tolerate extreme variability. Stage 4 can embrace a form of relativism where anything can be of value. Society as a unit is conceptualized, which had not been the case before. Stage 4 has difficulty balancing the respective claims of a society that requires order and the need for the individual to be constrained by that order and still be fulfilled. Overall, the self is separate from society so as to maintain "individuality."

Stage 5 emphasizes generalizable abstract criteria rather than individual feelings and preferences: not the self choosing the values, but the worth of the values themselves. Value relativism is rejected. Society is conceived as created out of the collective lives of individuals just like the self. Good is based on general standards for the justification of ideal values. Society is viewed as a medium of communication, a web of social relations, where the relations between self and society define the units that are constituted. Self is seen as inextricably connected to others. Individuals realize that the self's creation is dependent on society.

Working with researchers such as Albert Erdynast and influenced by the approach of Kohlberg, with whom she studied at the Harvard Graduate School of Education, Cheryl Armon devised the Good Life Interview (Armon, 1984, 1989). It consists of:

1. The subdomains of good work, good relationships, good education, the good of truth, knowledge, beauty, religion, and sexuality,
2. Real life experiences when goods conflict, and
3. Real life experiences when making moral judgments.

Interviews are carried out with standard questions and follow-up prompts. These interviews are taped, transcribed, and then content analyzed by raters who are trained to achieve respectable levels of agreement. Armon reports that the Good Life stages fit well within the empirical requirements of a structural stage model: clear-cut stage advancement with age, no stages skipped, no stage regression, no postconventional stages reached before a certain adult age. The Good Life stages are highly correlated with moral development stages and they continue to develop into adulthood, although the rate of development decreases.

Armon's Good Life stages can be divided into three levels, consistent with many of the models presented in this book. These are the Preconventional, the Conventional, and the Postconventional.

Preconventional

Stage 1: Egoistic. Concerned with the gratification of desires, the realization of fantasy, and having a good experience, the Egoistic equates doing good with having good experiences. Stage 1 is physicalistic and sensory. The good and the bad are dichotomized.

Stage 2: Instrumental. Stage 2 serves the individual's interests, distinguishing motives and intentions and contemplating consequences. Stage 2 desires to be praised and to satisfy material wants. For Stage 2, the Good Life consists of those things which serve the individual's interests, making no distinction between what is desired and what is desirable. Stage 2 has a strong need for others, but also a desire for independence and freedom.

Conventional

Stage 3: Altruistic. Based in an affective sense of happiness and positive interpersonal experience, Stage 3 promotes the mutuality of self and others. Good is the absence of bad feelings. Stage 3 operates in accordance with group-approved virtues in the immediate social world.

Stage 4: Individuality. The good is an expression of the individual's self-chosen interests and values. The theme of Stage 4 is meaning, in a personal sense, at the same time adhering to moral and social norms. Activities express self-chosen internalized interests and values where ends are freely chosen. Society must be maintained in harmony with the individual's pursuit of the Good Life.

Postconventional

Transitional Stage 4/5: Subjective Relativism. Stage 4/5 stands outside moral and social norms and is subjective and relative, based on what the individual *feels* is right.

Stage 5: Autonomy. The good is the result of applying a consistent ethical philosophy with the individual as an autonomous agent engaged in productive meaningful activities. Stage 5's perspective is broadened to include the societal perspective, balancing responsibility to self and to society. Values are constructed autonomously, worthy for all persons and judged by objective standards. Interdependence of self and others is a requirement of self-realization. Things are pursued for their own sake and because they are ideal for all persons.

Stage 6: Universal Holism. Although not discussed in all of her accounts of the development of the Good Life because there is as yet no empirical justification for its existence, Stage 6 holds to a grand conception of "humanity" or "nature" where the Good is universalized and where there are principles of justice and respect for all persons.

CHAPTER 12

Cosmic Knowing

SUSANNE COOK-GREUTER

Susanne Cook-Greuter is a researcher from Harvard University who has studied with Robert Kegan and has been an active member of the Society for Research in Adult Development for several years. She has researched the ego development model of Jane Loevinger and has scored thousands of protocols using the Washington University Sentence Completion Test. She has focused on the later stages of ego development, and has made distinctions in the data that Loevinger's method of analysis did not reveal. Cook-Greuter has argued for the existence of higher stages in the model than Loevinger argued for (Cook-Greuter, 1990, 1994, 1995). In the following presentation of her work, I am relying on her most recent (Cook-Greuter, 1995) terminology.

In the period of life with which we are concerned (the postconventional or postpersonal stages, what Cook-Greuter calls the *Construct-Aware*), people are described as changing in a number of significant ways. One aspect of such a change is a new attitude toward language. In earlier stages of development, language is valued because it affords communication, enabling people to cognitively package reality into discrete entities on their conceptual maps. In later mature stages, language is experienced as filtering the underlying reality and therefore leaving out the richness of experience. People at the Construct-Aware stage yearn to apprehend an unfiltered reality, a reality of flux and change not tied down with conventional labels and definitions.

People experience a new attitude toward the functioning of ego at higher stages as well. Whereas in earlier stages of development, people take a certain self-reflective pleasure and delight in working with their complexity and contradiction—that is, in thinking about themselves—with higher development in the Construct-Aware stage, people question their "objective self-identity" altogether, no longer wishing to be in control in the ways they have been. From the point of view of an emerging maturity, self-control has required being too watchful, too vigilant, of the image of self as presented in the social theater of the mind. Self-consciousness is experienced as a form of limitation. People at the Construct-Aware stage intuit another mode of being based on noncontrol, on an "unboundedness," a mode of experiencing liberated from deep-rooted habits, a mode of existing that does not require effort, that is grounded in "radical openness," a mode of being that is not grounded in ego. On the downside, however, this change in attitude toward ego can increase levels of anxiety, lower self-esteem, heighten loneliness, and even lead to moments of the feeling of being "nothing."

Cook-Greuter labels this level the *Construct-Aware*. She notes that this transition is equivalent in significance to the development from the *prerepresentational* to *representational* stages in childhood, which required extensive social mediation in the form of language learning. Likewise, the Construct-Aware transition, as the linking stage from what is termed *representational* to *postrepresentational* development, may require very specific cultural supports, supports of an altogether different nature from those required in childhood, supports that do *not* require further socialization. Cultural supports are needed that go beyond the simple internalization of norms and rules. These supports can include meditation techniques, lineages, and teachers.

Cook-Greuter shows that the Construct-Aware self is aware of the filtered nature of its world, contingent on language and on maintaining the illusion of a stable ego that is in control. When such a self is weary of its old habits and longs to break through to a more *immediate* reality, I would like to suggest that we describe the self as ready to take up spiritual practice. Switching our metaphors from auditory to tactile, we can describe the mature self as longing for a *naked* mode of experiencing. Meditation can be characterized as a disciplined practice in keeping contact with sensations at the raw and *unmediated* level, without the need for protective covers, without the need for conceptual filters.

Again, adopting another metaphor—this time a metaphor based on tactile experiences of effort and resistance—we can say that the change at this stage is a shift from a consciousness oriented to securing greater autonomy by means of greater control to a consciousness oriented to giving up control altogether. And this is how the practice of meditation is relevant: it involves learning a disciplined mindfulness that short-circuits the ego's constant need to control by grasping and clinging. Yet, while relinquishing control, meditation practice requires that we remain wide awake, that we be mindful. We cannot simply give in to whatever greed or lust or fantasies arise once conventional forms of self-control are discarded. Indeed, it would appear that meditation provides the solution to the unavoidable mental loops that Cook-Greuter identifies as existing at the Construct-Aware stage: how to use effort to get beyond control.

Cook-Greuter has studied ego development empirically, revealing changes we are equating here with transpersonal development. She uses as her source of data Jane Loevinger's Washington University Sentence Completion Test (WUSCT), a projective assessment instrument that asks subjects to complete in writing a set of 36 sentence stems with their own thoughts. She has analyzed her subjects' sentence completions reliably by a coding method that reveals developmental stages in levels of response.

Cook-Greuter proposed her Stage 5/6 while attempting to analyze data according to Loevinger's theory. Cook-Greuter began to differentiate Stage 5/6 (the *Construct-Aware*) from both Stage 5 (the *Autonomous*) and Stage 6 (the *Unitive*). She reports that she has developed a means of coding for distinctions between 5/6 and 6 and that she has been able to train novice raters to criteria (correlations were .79 to .95, Cronbach's alpha was .95, and percent agreement among raters was 93.3).

The characteristics of the Construct-Aware stage reveal a consciousness still embedded in ego, still immersed in personal levels of development, and still operating with the currency of representational thinking, but now yearning for an existence beyond such limitations, yearning for a *transpersonal* mode of being.

According to Cook-Greuter's revised version of Loevinger's model, a child comes into the world without an ego, without a differentiation of itself from the world around it. As the child begins to separate from the mother, he or she identifies first with impulses, and can only be restrained by rewards and punishments. This is the *Impulsive stage*. As the child learns how rewards and punishments operate in the external world, he or she develops the first forms of self-control—ushering in the *Self-Protective Stage*. But with the attainment of the *Conformist Stage*, the child identifies fully with the group. The child takes in the forms of socialization and identifies fully with them; in fact, the child has no self apart from the voice of others. The child (or adolescent) seeks approval, and thus is nice, complies, and cooperates.

But there is still as yet no internal, or what we might call *psychological,* life. There is no appreciation of a subjective life apart from group norms and reputations. As an internal life dawns, the child enters into the *Self-Aware stage*: the self becomes something distinct from norms and expectations, it becomes a distinct object of reflection, and therefore creates a space for exceptions to cultural expectations. With the attainment of the *Conscientious stage*, the older child or adolescent can be said to have its own self or identity apart from the group: rules are fully internalized, but are one's own in a more conscious and articulated manner—standards are self-chosen, traits are conceptualized as part of an interior world. Able to reason and reflect across time and society, the ego constructs a rich psychological causality. The mature youth is now ready to enter the adult world.

But that is not the end of development. After the Conscientious Stage is the *Individualistic stage*. The often simplistic ideals of youth are questioned; self-certainty gives way to the perception of internal contradiction. The self begins to distance itself from role identities; subjective experience is emphasized at the expense of the now-questioned status of "objective reality." There is an appreciation of development and an acknowledgment of the discrepancy between inner and outer reality. There is a greater tolerance of self and others and a greater appreciation of contradiction.

But as the *Autonomous stage* replaces the Individualistic, the self transcends and integrates psychological complexities even more. The role of conscience is attenuated, emotional dependencies are acknowledged rather than repressed, and sexuality is accepted more openly. People are construed as part of larger social totalities. As the self integrates more of its compartmentalized identities, it aims for a form of meaning based in self-actualization and self-determination. At the next stage, the *Construct-Aware*, the very substantiality of the self is questioned.

But even this stage is transcended in rare cases by the *Unitive stage*. Embedded in the process of creation, the Unitive self is based on a global and universal vision. The concrete and temporal are apprehended as part of the eternal. Things are accepted as they are. Ego boundaries are transcended. There is an immersion in the ongoing process of being. Whereas at earlier levels of development, the nothingness of the self is experienced as anxiety-provoking, at the Unitive stage the enlarged, open, and more relaxed self can accept that at the heart and bottom of its being it is truly a "no-thing."

KEN WILBER

Ken Wilber describes a particularly detailed theory of life-span development, particularly detailed in the richness with which he describes the higher stages, going beyond stages as they are usually described in Western psychology (Wilber, 1986a–c; 1993, 1996a,b). Broadly speaking, his lower stages draw on the theories and research of Piaget, Freud, Maslow, Loevinger, Kohlberg, and others, while the higher stages draw for their content on what Huxley called the "perennial philosophy" of mysticism. While Wilber is not a social scientist and has not carried out any empirical research on the validity of his stages, his work has been applied and modified by Eugene Thomas (1994) to the development of a coding system for the analysis of interview materials.

Wilber describes a series of nine structures that determine the predominant orientation of consciousness at each stage of development. He has presented numerous versions of his model and some versions have even more structures, but for this account I shall present his model as it appears in Wilber, (1986a–c, 1996a). For Wilber, each structure is itself a result of a negotiation of a particular *fulcrum* of development; at each of these fulcrums the individual either progresses to the next structure, or as a result of fixation, develops a particular pathology or developmental arrest. The basic process of development begins with a fusion at a particular structure. As development proceeds, the individual differentiates a new structure from the previous one. As the new structure is differentiated, it must then be integrated with the prior structure.

There are nine different structures. These can be divided into three levels. The first level is the *prepersonal.* In the prepersonal level the child develops the first rudimentary ego or mind. At Stage 1, the *Sensoriphysical stage,* the child is not differentiated from the physical world; the child is the sensorium of experience and his or her purely material interactions with it. As the child differentiates the physical body from the materiality of the world and of its mother, he or she develops an internal world of desires, wishes and images that are often not differentiated from the objects of those same images. This is Stage 2, the *Phantasmal-Emotional Stage.* It is narcissistic: the world is an extension of the emotional self.

With development into the *personal* levels the child can be said to have a mind. I think that what Wilber means by "personal" can be equated with what I am calling "ego." From images, the child develops to the capacity to have symbols. With symbols, the child can construct concepts. With the birth of the mental at Stage 3, the *Representational Mind Stage,* the child can separate the mental from the bodily, and therefore can control it (*and* repress it).

The next of the personal levels is what Wilber calls Stage 4, the *Role/Rule stage.* The child can combine and coordinate concepts into rules that govern behavior. The child is able to internalize these rules of behavior by identifying with them. These rules and norms can become scripts by which the child guides his or her behavior. Conventional moral judgment and behaviour follow from this capacity. The child is also capable of assuming roles and seeing how their actions appear from the perspective of others.

Whereas at the Role/Rule stage, the child is identified with the conventional norms of the social world, with development into Stage 5, the *Formal/Reflexive stage,* the child can see such conventional norms from the outside, as it were, taking a perspective on them, so that he or she can think about thinking. This is the distinguishing characteristic of the Formal/Reflexive stage: thinking can take its own products as objects. With this capacity, the individual—probably now an adolescent—develops self-chosen ideals, morals, beliefs, and ideologies. The adolescent can reflect on, choose, and change identities, often adopting an attitude of critical distance from sanctioned role identities and rules that earlier had regulated behavior.

The final stage of the personal is Stage 6, the *Vision-Logic stage.* Wilber often calls this stage *centauric* because it is based on an integration of mind and body not previously attained. Wilber holds that the mind and body are capable at this stage of being integrated because consciousness is now no longer exclusively identified with mind as it had been in previous stages; it now has a perspective on both mind and body, and can integrate them in a higher level of consciousness.

While the centauric possesses well-being, greater authenticity, and is reoriented in more organismic and existential ways, not all of the emotions and feelings that are available at this stage are positive or comforting. Many of the experiences at this stage are described in bleak and somber tones, because in many respects, this stage is the one most characterized as full of angst or dread. For a description, I shall quote extensively from Wilber's *A Brief History of Everything* (1996a, pp. 195–196).

> The whole point of the existential level [centauric] is that you are not yet in the transpersonal, but you are no longer totally anchored in the personal—the whole personal domain has started to lose its flavor, has started to become profoundly meaningless. And so of course there is not much reason to smile. What good is the personal anyway—it's just going to die. Why even inhabit it?
>
> The world has started to go flat in its appeal. No experience tastes good anymore. Nothing satisfies anymore. Nothing is worth pursuing anymore. Not because one has failed to get these rewards, but precisely because one has achieved them royally, tasted it all, and found it all lacking.
>
> And so naturally this soul does not smile very much. This is a soul for whom all consolations have gone sour. The world has gone flat at exactly the moment of its greatest triumph. The magnificent banquet has come

and gone; the skull grins silently over the whole affair. The feast is ephemeral, even in its grandest glories. The things on which I once could hang so much meaning and so much desire and so much fervent hope, have all melted into air, evaporated at some strange point during the long and lonely night. To whom can I sing songs of joy and exaltation? Who will hear my calls for help sent silently into that dark and hellish night? Where will I find the fortitude to withstand the swords and spears that daily pierce my side? And why even should I try? It all comes to dust, yes? and where am I then? Fight or surrender, it matters not the least, for still my life goals bleed quietly to death, in a hemorrhage of despair.

This is a soul for whom all desires have become thin and pale and anemic. This is a soul who, in facing existence squarely, is thoroughly sick of it. This is a soul for whom the personal has gone totally flat. This is, in other words, a soul on the brink of the transpersonal.

The implications are enormous for practicing clinical psychologists and therapists. If the developmental dimension is not recognized, and particularly the higher stages of consciousness development, when a client at the Vision-Logic stage presents the characteristics Wilber describes, mental health professionals may simply conclude that the client is suffering from clinical depression. They may then prescribe medication or treatment that will only succeed in delaying the client's development, alleviating or tranquilizing a pain that may be crying out to be experienced authentically in all its existential richness. Unacquainted with the possibilities of higher development and oblivious of the vicissitudes of consciousness at higher stages, the services of the mental health professional may be exactly what the client does *not* need.

Wilber differentiated various types of depression depending on the developmental level they arose from. Kegan (1982) has described a model for differentiating types of depression depending on developmental stage. Accepting this, it is necessary to distinguish where the depression is coming from developmentally and to adjust the treatment accordingly. Not only does depression vary along the developmental path, but is also often itself a sign of growth: growth entails loss, and depression *is* basically a reaction to loss.

In a society that values youth over age, pleasure over pain, security over uncertainty, and in a society that defines well-being simply in terms of economic indicators, it is unlikely that pain or loss will be perceived as an opportunity for growth. Development is not a bed of roses; growth is not *only* a natural flowering. It requires pain. Growth requires that we give up childish ways. It requires that we let go of our old selves with their accomplishments and securities. Perhaps our society as a whole is moving forward, as Wilber thinks. And part of this movement forward may be the understanding that there are higher reaches to human development that may challenge our narrow Enlightenment and scientific world-views. But if such social development does not proceed, then it is possible that aspirations for higher development may be interpreted as signs of pathology or even deviance.

I have made the focus of this presentation the Vision-Logic stage. With development into the transpersonal stages, individuals transcend both ego and representational mind. They begin to step off the wheel of *samsara*. These stages are more or less unique to the East, at least not described in most Western psychologies. Wilber draws on descriptions of advanced spiritual development found in Buddhist and Hindu Vedanta scriptures. The first transpersonal stage Wilber calls Stage 7, the *Psychic*. It is characterized by nature mysticism; often called the Path of the Yogis. The second transpersonal stage is Stage 8, the *Subtle*: it is characterized by deity mysticism and called the Path of the Saints. The third transpersonal stage is Stage 9, the *Causal*: it is characterized by monistic mysticism and called the Path of the Sages. After this stage, the individual transcends all stages and attains nondual mysticism, which absorbs all that had gone before. To the reader, these names may be nothing more than words without content: words pointing to a moon they have never seen in the daytime existence of their lives. Perhaps a metaphor might help.

In an interview with *The Shambhala Sun,* a Buddhist newsletter, Wilber (1996c) describes enlightenment by the metaphor of the wave. We are all waves, each of us part of the ocean, only we don't know it because we identify only with being little waves and cannot see the ocean of which we are a part, except as a whole lot of other little waves who often get in the way of our waveness. With enlightenment, we can see our true "Suchness," our true being, which in this metaphor is knowing the wetness of the waves. We do not have to become the biggest wave to see our wetness; we only have to know our own wetness to know that it is the same wetness as that of all the other waves. We do not have to know the particulars of all the other little waves to know ourselves; we need only know that by sharing in all the wetness we are a part of the ocean of existence.

Meditation develops what Wilber calls the *Witness*: our observing consciousness, which is not identified or attached to the objects that parade in awareness. The Witness really makes its appearance first at the Vision-Logic stage, the stage at which we begin to have a perspective on both our body and our mind. With right practice, we can go deliberately into this pure resting awareness, past all attachment, letting go of all we have been, and burning our karma by a kind of nonaction. After the last of the nine stages, the Causal stage, we let go of even this Witness and become one with the nondual ground of our being, which is pure Emptiness. This Emptiness is also the fullness of being, and in this state, there is a profound oneness of consciousness and the world.

CHARLES ALEXANDER

The next stage theory I shall deal with is a theory based also in Eastern philosophy, but which has been integrated with Western psychology, specifically developmental psychology. But it is a spiritual theory based, not in Buddhism, but in the Vedic tradition, specifically Vedanta philosophy as taught by Maharishi Mahesh Yogi. In the following account, I shall draw on the work of Charles Alexander, who was a professor at the Maharishi International University, and who presented his work in a number of forums, including the Society for Research in Adult Development, as well as in several publications that integrated Western and Eastern approaches (Alexander et al., 1990).

Alexander accepted the basic Piagetian stages of human development, and added his own stages in a manner similar to Wilber. Alexander begins with the Sankhya account of *levels of mind.* Mind begins at the level of *action* and the *senses,* which Alexander equates with Piaget's Sensorimotor stage. While the child may act on and take in aspects of the external world through its senses, there are no symbols, no permanent objects, nor is the self differentiated from its environment.

The next level of mind is *desire,* or the Early Representational, which is identified with Piaget's Preoperational stage. The child can form simple representations and maintain simple desires in his or her emerging consciousness, a consciousness that monitors both action and sensation. The child can use speech and can represent both self and others. The child is also capable of goal-directed behavior, but is fundamentally egocentric. Alexander identifies this level with Loevinger's Impulsive stage.

The next level of mind is *mind* per se, which Alexander equates with Piaget's Concrete Operations. It is the comparative thinking mind, which generates classes and relations. This level of mind steps back from the simple representational screen and coordinates perceptions and representations over time and space. Mind at this level can conserve, and it can decenter, but it can only think about the actual or concrete. Alexander seems to equate this level with Loevinger's Conformist stage.

Intellect is the next level of mind, which Alexander equates with Piaget's Formal Operational Stage. Intellect operates on concrete representations. It makes possible logical thinking, decision-making, and direction and order. Intellect subordinates the actual to the possible, and enables self-conscious reflection, precipitating both self-awareness and identity formation. Alexander equates Loevinger's Conscientious stage with the level of Intellect.

Intuition is the next level of mind. Alexander identifies it with the Post-Formal Operational stages, and it is the first level of mind with which we are chiefly concerned here. Intuition is relational, sensitive to the richness of context and the ubiquity of change. Intuition is holistic, less dominated by language and logical reasoning. Intuition integrates affect and intellect. Abstract thought is integrated with responsibilities, commitments, and needs. Intuition includes dialectical operations, whereby thinking embraces information not consistent with current constructs, enabling the relating of opposing systems. Alexander identifies Intuition with the Autonomous stage of Loevinger.

The next level of mind is termed *Ego* and is the point where unbounded pure consciousness connects with the current process of knowing. In Alexander's account, Ego is the transition from the Personal to the Transpersonal (note that Alexander means something quite different by the term *Ego* than the account of ego espoused throughout this book). Ego is equated with wisdom and the synthesis of opposing systems of thought. Alexander identifies Ego with Loevinger's Integrated stage.

Alexander also describes seven states of consciousness. The first are those with which we are familiar in our daily lives: *sleeping, dreaming,* and *waking consciousness.* These are available in all of the foregoing levels of mind. But with the development of the last two levels of mind, intuition and ego, there is an increased probability that the fourth, fifth, sixth, and seventh states will occur. The fourth is *transcendental consciousness,* which is the temporary experience of an inner unified unbounded Self transcending the boundaries between knower, known, and the process of knowing. The fifth is *cosmic consciousness,* in which the inner unified mind is maintained along with but separate from the active levels of mind. The sixth is *refined* or *glorified cosmic consciousness,* which consists of a profound intimacy between self and environment, whereby the sense of unity pervades more and more aspects of experience. Objects are seen not just as objects, but as part of a flowing field of energy with which the self feels related but still distinct from. The seventh is *unity consciousness,* involving the complete unification of all inner and outer worlds, such that all of reality is experienced as the self.

Generally, the main independent variable in Alexander's research is the practice of Transcendental Meditation (TM). To assess its efficacy, his researchers often use the Loevinger Sentence Completion Test as their dependent variable, and most often obtain significant effects: they have generally found that the practice of TM enhances the development of ego. But they also assess the efficacy of TM with other cognitive and neurophysiological measures, such as measures of intelligence, moral judgment, and EEG coherence. Alexander's own dissertation research provides a good illustration. He worked with prison inmates who practiced TM. Relative to controls, the TM practitioners demonstrated higher levels of ego development, generally moving from the Conformist to Self-Aware stages.

At the level of *intellect,* Alexander posits that *identity,* in the sense of Erikson, is constructed or achieved. Consistent with the analysis presented here, and congruent with any conception of human development holding that there are higher *postrepresentational* or *postpersonal* stages of consciousness, identity is described in such a way as to imply that it is both constrained and fictional. Alexander describes identity as an internalization of social roles, not a transcendence of those roles, and sees the project of identity as inherently flawed. Identity is a way of answering the question of what we *are* by constructing an answer in terms of what we *do;* consequently, identity fails to authentically answer the real question. Marcia's (1980) data on identity achievement were obtained by asking young people about occupation and ideology: about how they make money and how they adopt social belief systems and creeds. Defined in these terms, identity *is* conformist and socially referenced.

Both Alexander and Wilber ascribe to views of mind that see the emerging structures as deriving from inherent levels of mind. Wilber speaks of the Platonic doctrine of *anamnesis,* a view that holds that as we evolve, we recover or re-remember what we were. Alexander speaks of the growth of consciousness as deriving from a natural potential or tendency, but that potential is blocked from fulfillment due to external stress. He also describes the development of consciousness as *epigenetic,* and by that he means that the structures or patterns are present from birth and need only to be activated to emerge. From the perspective of both Alexander and Wilber, the path of human development is about an actualization of potentials *innately* present. Therefore, there *is* a direction to development, a path of unfolding, and there is a teleological purpose to existence.

From a more cultural and contextualistic perspective, the view that the structures of the mind are actualizations of potentials innately present is both romanticist and rationalist: we are good by nature and we already know everything we need to know from the day we are born (or earlier). While many have criticized the nativist view when it has been applied to the development of children, there are different implications when it is applied to the higher stages of consciousness development. Because these higher stages are about achieving knowledge that has traditionally been associated with metaphysical truth and insight, it appears that the romanticist and rationalist perspectives have a broader application, but also that new questions are raised about nativist positions.

If the nativists are correct, then there is nothing new under the sun. The higher stages of human development and potential are present from birth and have been with us since the dawn of human history. Cultural evolution makes no contribution to human development, but rather is significant only as a facilitator or inhibitor to the actualization of a blueprint laid down in our genes. Do we really want to believe that everything we learn is, in actuality, a *relearning*? What about the effects of language and the new technologies of social interaction? It is evident that there was a time, for example, when there was no written language. And the social conditions and the cultural technologies we currently take for granted are recent arrivals on the scene. Do these things only serve as soil for the "bringing out" of what is already present in the seed?

JAMES FOWLER

In sketching a model of the development of faith, James Fowler shows how his Stage 4 breaks from the conventional aspects of Stage 3 and constructs an identity in faith that is self-reliant and founded in conscious certainty (Fowler, 1995). But often, in midlife, this balance is threatened by unconscious and previously acknowledged forces. As he describes it:

> Restless with the self-images and outlook maintained by Stage 4, the person ready for transition finds him- or her-self attending to what may feel like anarchic and disturbing inner voices. Elements from a childish past, images and energies from a deeper self, a gnawing sense of the sterility and flatness of the meanings one serves—any or all of these may signal readiness for something new. Stories, symbols, myths, and paradoxes from one's own or other traditions may insist on breaking in upon the neatness of the previous faith. Disillusionment with one's compromises and recognition that life is more complex than Stage 4's logic of clear distinctions

and abstract concepts can comprehend, press one toward a more dialectical and multileveled approach to life truth. (Fowler, 1995, pp. 182–183)

Note the similarity between this description and that of Wilber's description of the Vision-Logic or Centaur stage quoted above. While the identity of Stage 4 is a hard-won achievement, often not constructed by the majority who remain in Stage 3, Stage 4 may appear to meet all our criteria of reason and adjustment, yet it is not enough. Because it is a choice, it is based as much on what is excluded as on what is affirmed, and it is what is excluded that demands attention at Stage 5. We are unconscious as well as conscious; we lose as much as we gain; we are the other as much as we are our selves. And it is this openness to paradox that characterizes Stage 5. And this openness dissolves the boundaries of identity achieved in early adulthood.

In his research, Fowler asked his subjects to describe their life experiences in the area of what he called "faith." Most broadly put, faith is our way of making meaning. As Fowler puts it, faith is our way of moving into "the force field of life," the fundamental category in the search for transcendence, an "alignment of the will" and "a resting of the heart." Most basically, faith is a verb, an "active mode of knowing, of composing a felt sense or image of the condition of our lives taken as a whole. It unifies our lives' force fields" (Fowler, 1995, p. 25).

While we may often equate faith with religion, this is not always the case. Fowler's model is meant to apply to the scientific agnostic as well as the believer, to the existential atheist as well as the churchgoing citizen, the dialectical materialist as well as the Jesuit priest, and to the Buddhist as well as the Protestant.

Fowler derived his model from an examination of interviews conducted with 359 subjects. He reports that his method of content analysis, which breaks faith down into seven aspects, possesses an interrater reliability of 85 to 90% agreement. His data are cross-sectional: that is, he only interviewed his subjects at one point in time. But he is able to extrapolate a development model by virtue of the age range sampled.

As the age of the subjects increases, the spread of scores across the six stages increases. Initially, subjects only fall within the early stages. With age, more subjects are identified at higher stages. But development is not a simple stepwise function of age; it appears that many people fail to develop beyond Stage 2 or 3, but the lower stages do decrease in frequency overall. Higher stages are only identified in older subjects. Stage 4 seldom appears before 21 years of age and Stage 5 never appears before 31 years of age. And the highest stages are quite rare: Stage 6 does not occur before 60 years of age, and then only with one subject.

Briefly, the stages are:

- *Undifferentiated Faith.* The child learns a basic sense of trust and love from the primary caregiver, but must contend with the fear of abandonment. The mutuality and trust established at this stage forms the basis for all later autonomy, hope, and courage, but a failure of mutuality can lead to excessive narcissism or isolation.
- *Stage 1: Intuitive-Projective Faith.* By three to seven years of age, the child has a mental life that is fantasy filled and imitative, influenced by examples and stories, a mental life that is intuitive and not restrained by logical thought. The child is dominated by perception, images, and feelings. His or her first self-awareness is primarily egocentric, and the first apprehensions of sex, death, and taboo occur. There is a danger that the child may become possessed by images of terror, or that his or her imagination may become exploited by excessive taboos and moral expectations.
- *Stage 2: Mythic-Literal.* By school age, the child can narrate his or her experience, that is, not just receive stories, but generate them as well. These stories express communal truths and beliefs that are appropriated literally as moral attitudes and rules. Imagination is now curbed and ordered. The child can take the perspective of others, but cannot step back from the flow of stories to reflect on them. The danger at this stage is an overcontrolling perfectionism or sense of badness.
- *Stage 3: Synthetic-Conventional.* Generally beginning in adolescence, authority is located external to the self, in the "they," but extending beyond the family. These different spheres demand that the adolescent orient to them, to synthesize values and information, to construct an identity and outlook. This is when the first personal myths are developed. Yet despite the feeling that choices and commitments have been made, the reality is that the self has been made by its choices and commitments, as defined by "they." Stage 3 is conformist in that it is attuned to the expectations and judgments of others. The adolescent exists in a world mediated by others' values and beliefs, and cannot step outside of it. The adolescent has an ideology but cannot objectify it, and is therefore unaware of having it. This is like the proverbial fish that is unaware of the sea in which it swims. The danger at Stage 3 is one of too much internalization impairing judgment or of betrayals that may occur, precipitating nihilism or a retreat to an extramundane God.
- *Stage 4: Individuative-Reflective.* At Stage 4 the reliance on external sources of authority is attenuated. The "tyranny of the they" is undermined. Authority is centered within the self. Stage 3 persons tend to reflect on the flow of their lives from within the flow, relying on

narratives. They lack the cognitive ability to step out of the flow. At Stage 4, they can transcend the life stream and compose a myth of their own past, present, and future. At Stage 4, responsibility is assumed for commitments, for the choice of a lifestyle, for having beliefs and attitudes. Identity is no longer defined by roles and meanings set by others. Meaning is composed as the awareness develops of even *having* a world-view. Having defined an explicit system of meanings, one's self and outlook are differentiated from those of others. Often changing the environment, such as going off to school or the army, effects a 3–4 transition, but this can be prevented by absorbing the self in fraternities and cliques or jumping into an early marriage. Many make the 3–4 transition in their 30s or 40s, and not in their 20s, and this often causes a more serious midlife crisis.

- *Stage 5: Conjunctive.* Stage 5 moves beyond the dichotomizing logic of either/or and sees both sides of an issue simultaneously. Stage 5 attends to the organic relatedness of things. Its mind set can be suspended, allowing a dialogical knowing whereby the known speaks its own language, whereby the knower and the known converse in an I–Thou relationship. Stage 5 integrates repressed compartments of its self, reclaims its past, and opens to the voices of a deeper self. Stage 5 can live with defeat and accept the reality of commitments it cannot deny. At the same time, Stage 5 becomes more porous and permeable, maintaining a vulnerability to the other, yet freed from the confines of tribe, class, religion, or nation. The danger at Stage 5 is in passive inaction or cynical withdrawal.

- *Stage 6: Universalizing.* Stage 6 seems to transcend all attachments to ego. As Fowler (1995) describes it,

> Heedless of the threats to self, to primary groups, and to the institutional arrangements of the present order that are involved, Stage 6 becomes a disciplined, activist incarnation—a making real and tangible—of the imperatives of absolute love and justice of which Stage 5 has partial apprehensions. The self at Stage 6 engages in spending and being spent for the transformation of present reality in the direction of a transcendent actuality. (p. 200)

Stage 6 lives in the reality of a God which "intends the fulfillment of creation and the unity of being." This unity is "richly plural and highly variegated, a celebration of the diversity and complexity of creation." The individual submits to the "Kingdom of God" defined by "a quality of righteousness in which each person or being is augmented by the realization of the futurity of all the others" (p. 205).

Stage 6 individuals shatter our notions of normalcy. They live on the side of transcendent actuality, universal compassion, and ultimate respect for being, rather than on the side of self-interest, parochial vision, and the measured standards of goodness and morality masking the concern of tribe or species.

Fowler's description of Stage 6 is permeated with Judeo-Christian language, involving "righteousness" and "the Kingdom of God." In fact, in reading his account, comparing this description to that of the other stages, it is apparent that his characterization owes more to literary sources than interview data. There was only one subject in his sample who was unequivocally scored at Stage 6.

Consistent with his Judeo-Christian outlook, Fowler's account of religious experience is framed as a relationship with a *transcendent* presence to which one relates by becoming an "incarnation" of its actuality. This contrasts to a perception of being that apprehends the sacred in *immanent* terms: one in which self and universe are fused to such an extent that one's secular nature is not experienced apart from being.

Fowler states that his stages have a normative dimension, a dimension that provides a criterion of determining what is "good faith," defined as that which is free of "idolatrous distortions." How we conceive of higher stages also informs how the lower stages are conceptualized. Yet he also states quite clearly, in full awareness that 93.4% of his subjects are born into the Judeo-Christian heritage, that "I fully expect that our present stage descriptions will undergo a significant process of elimination of Western and Christian biases and that the genuinely structural features will emerge with greater clarity" (1995, p. 298).

At this point in time, it seems to me that what is common to the foregoing structural stages of higher human development (Cook-Greuter, Wilber, Alexander and Fowler) is that they go beyond ego, that they are transpersonal. Given that Fowler's account of Stage 6 is based on only one subject (unless we include Fowler himself in this stage!) and also that it is based largely on an extrapolation from literary sources, it is best to exercise caution when interpreting the generality of his highest stage.

Conclusion

So there it is. I have assembled evidence to suggest that there is some kind of order or pattern to how humans develop, of how we grow from childhood to adolescence to adulthood.

Weaving together the ideas of Freud, Piaget, Darwin, and Buddha, I have created a picture that combines psychoanalysis with cognitive development, evolutionary biology with Eastern mysticism.

And the central concept, which provides the pivot around which all of the other constructs revolve, is Ego.

Ego is defined in a way that is somewhat different than either psychoanalysis or even Buddhism. Whereas Buddhism speaks of ego without necessarily positing that it have a particular developmental course, and psychoanalysis presents ego as a relatively permanent fixture in the room of the rational mind, I have presented ego as a social and developmental artifact that serves evolutionary and social purposes. This ego is also a source of suffering and separation that we need to transcend, a view I share with Buddhism and a view that differentiates my thinking from most of psychoanalysis.

Ego is essentially self-representation, taking an image of self as real and grasping on to it, holding on to it, clinging to it—as change threatens from all corners.

Ego is that capacity that enables us to take ourselves as objects, to see ourselves in the inverted gaze of self-observation that we construct so as to control ourselves, that we may gain greater favor in the court of social approval.

Ego is what makes us safe, what makes us predictable, what makes us solid, sane and stable in a world that is in essence

> "like a dream, a phantom, a drop of dew, a flash of lightning."

Ego is also what keeps us separate and distinct, what keeps us opposed to and different from others, others whom we also learn to construe as similar objects like ourselves, objects interacting with our objectlike being as we float in empty space, where contact is defined as the bumping together of objects.

The entire reality-creating enterprise is a ruse "designed" to ensure both the transmission of genetic material and the perpetuation of social control.

Reality-creating, or what I have referred to as *simulation capacity,* is a product of evolution, as are all our behaviors, and this reality-creating behavior survives because it creates a realm of trial and error selection in our minds that does not terminate the existence or the appendages of the trial maker.

For most individual lives, and indeed for most of social history, the story of conventional ego and consciousness development has been the *only* story. We are *only* these ego-bounded beings that I have described. And we are only the products of evolutionary and social development.

But a study of human ideas, of philosophies and of art, reveals a more spiritual story that goes beyond the mundane one, a story that transforms and transcends the day-to-day reality of our conventional existence.

Similarly, a study of human development reveals a progression of the "soul" that goes beyond the mundane. The literature of the perennial philosophy and of mysticism has documented this for years, and now the study of consciousness and of development has yielded techniques of content analysis and of statistics that trace the same progression of the soul.

Most people develop through stages of cognitive, social, moral, and ego development that lead from the preconventional to the conventional, from the prepersonal to the personal, from the prerepresentational to the representational.

And some people go further: they develop from the conventional to the postconventional, from the personal to the transpersonal, and from the representational to the postrepresentational.

And it is this latter shift that is of primary concern here. At this stage in the turning around of consciousness, there is frequently breakdown and crisis, chaos and disruption. There is loss and a falling apart as we divest ourselves of our old skins of conventional and personal existence. In some cases there is a return of the repressed, a loss of inhibition, a sexual awakening. But ultimately, there is a realignment of the thinking and feeling minds and an undoing of social conditioning.

While the story of development from the preconventional to the conventional is easily recognized and understood, the shift from the personal to the transpersonal is not so easily apprehended.

Conclusion

Our mainstream culture does not really provide a support system for these kinds of changes. It is rather in our more marginal subcultures that support systems can be found: in the arts, in literature, in mystical teachings, and in the esoteric.

I am certainly not treating the kinds of things that are on display on grocery store checkout counters. This is a reality that most of our media, our marketplace, and our political system has little use for, targeted as each of these is to the common denominator. And because our worlds are socially constructed, this makes it often hard for those undergoing such changes to even believe these changes are real or amount to anything of significance.

The existence of such realities is not always grasped within the walls of academe or the mental health profession, or even within religious institutions. It is hoped that this book, and others like it, can contribute to an awareness or understanding—in the sciences, the arts, and the humanities—of the existence of higher stages of consciousness, of the transpersonal, and of the post-conventional.

I have recently taken refuge and Bodisattva vows under Penor Rinpoche, head of the Nyingmapa branch of Tibetan Buddhism and am undergoing *ngondro* practice.

I have had a lifelong interest and fascination with Buddhism and the philosophies of the Rast. In my youth I embraced the path of dharma for a time, but did not pursue it wholeheartedly because I still had identity issues to work out. But now in my midlife, in "my winter of discontent," I believe that I have unraveled the narrative basis of that identity and am ready to shed most of what we commonly take for granted as "personality."

In the words of my teacher, "The old proverb says, when the student is ready, the guru appears. The meaning of that is, when the mind of the student is ready, the guru is recognized."

I hope that some of the research and the ideas I have presented here contribute something to the understanding of what it may mean to be "ready."

References

Anderson, J. R. (1980). *Cognitive psychology and its implications.* San Francisco: Freeman.
Alexander, C. N., Davies, J. L., Dixon, C. A., Dillbeck, M. C., Druker, S. M., Oetzel, R. M., Muehlman, J. M., & Orme-Johnson, D. W. (1990). Growth of higher stages of consciousness: Maharishi's Vedic psychology of human development. In C. N. Alexander & E. J. Langer (Eds.), *Higher stages of human development: Perspectives on adult growth* (pp. 286–341). London: Oxford University Press.
Alexander, C. N., Heaton, D. P., & Chandler, H. M. (1994). Advanced human development in the Vedic psychology of Maharishi Mahesh Yogi: Theory and research. In M. E. Miller & S. Cook-Greuter (Eds.), *Transcendence and mature thought in adulthood: The further reaches of human nature* (pp. 39–70). Lanham, MD: Rowman & Littlefield.
Armon, C. (1984). Ideals of the good life and moral judgment: Ethical reasoning across the life span. In M. L. Commons, F. A. Richards, & C. Armon (Eds.), *Beyond formal operations: Late adolescent and adult cognitive development* (pp. 357–380). New York: Praeger.
Armon, C. (1989). Individuality and autonomy in adult ethical reasoning. In M. L. Commons, J. D. Sinnott, F. A. Richards, & C. Armon (Eds.), *Adult development: Vol I. Comparisons and applications of developmental models.* (pp. 179–196). New York: Praeger.
Bakan, D. (1966). *The duality of human existence: Isolation and communion in Western man.* Boston: Beacon Press.
Balk, D. E. (1995). *Adolescent development: Early through late adolescence.* Pacific Grove, CA: Brooks/Cole.
Basseches, M. (1984). *Dialectical thinking and adult development.* Norwood, NJ: Ablex.
Baxter-Magolda, M. B., & Porterfield, W. D. (1988). *Assessing intellectual development: The link between theory and practice.* Washington: American College Personnel Association.
Belenky, M. F., Clinchy, B. M., Goldberger, N. R., & Tarule, J. M. (1986). *Women's ways of knowing: The development of self, voice, and mind.* New York: Basic Books.
Berger, P. L., & Luckman, T. (1967). *The social construction of reality: A treatise in the sociology of knowledge.* New York: Anchor/Doubleday.
Brookfield, S. (1986). *Understanding and facilitating adult development.* San Francisco: Jossey–Bass.
Bruner, J. (1986). *Actual minds: Possible worlds.* Cambridge, MA: Harvard University Press.

Bruner, J. (1990). *Acts of meaning.* Cambridge, MA: Harvard University Press.
Campbell, J. (Ed.). (1971). *The portable Jung* (R. F. C. Hull, Trans.). New York: Viking.
Chandler, M. (1987). The Othello effect: Essay on the emergence and eclipse of skeptical doubt. *Human Development, 30,* 137–159.
Chodron, P. (1997). *When things fall apart: Heart advice for difficult times.* Boston: Shambhala.
Cole, M. & Cole, S. (1996). *The development of children* (3rd Ed.). San Francisco: W.W. Freeman.
Commons, M. L., Armon, C., Kohlberg, L., Richards, F. A., Grotzer. T. A., & Sinnott, J. D. (Eds.). (1990). *Adult development: Vol. II. Models and methods in the study of adolescent and adult thought.* New York: Praeger.
Commons, M. L., Richards, F. A., & Armon, C. (Eds.). (1984). *Beyond formal operations: Late adolescent and adult cognitive development.* New York: Praeger.
Commons, M. L., Sinnott, J. D., Richards, F. A., & Armon, C. (Eds.). (1989). *Adult development: Vol. I. Comparisons and applications of developmental models.* New York: Praeger.
Cook-Greuter, S. R. (1990). Maps for living: Ego-development stages from symbiosis to conscious universal embeddedness. In M. L. Commons, C. Armon, L. Kohlberg, F. A. Richards, T. A. Grotzer, & J. D. Sinnott (Eds.), *Adult development: Vol. II. Models and methods in the study of adolescent and adult thought* (pp. 79–103). New York: Praeger.
Cook-Greuter, S. R. (1994). Rare forms of self-understanding in mature adults. In M. E. Miller & S. R. Cook-Greuter (Eds.), *Transcendence and mature thought in adulthood* (pp. 119–146). Lanham, MD: Rowman & Littlefield.
Cook-Greuter, S. (1995). *Comprehensive language awareness: A definition of the phenomena and a review of its treatment in the postformal adult development literature.* Unpublished manuscript, Harvard University Graduate School of Education.
Cote, J. E., & Levine, C. (1987). A formulation of Erikson's theory of ego identity formation. *Developmental Review, 7,* 273–325.
Cote, J. E.. & Levine, C. (1988a). A critical examination of the Ego Identity Status Paradigm. *Developmental Review, 8,* 147–184.
Cote, J. E., & Levine, C. (1988b). On critiquing the Identity Status paradigm: A rejoinder to Waterman. *Developmental Review, 8,* 209–218.
Davison, M. L., King, P. M., & Kitchener, K. S. (1990). Developing reflective thinking and writing. In R. Beach & S. Hynds (Eds.), *Developing discourse practices in adolescence and adulthood* (pp.265–286). Norwood, NJ: Ablex.
Dawkins, R. (1990). *The selfish gene.* London: Oxford University Press.
Descartes, R. (1998). *Discourse on method and the meditations.* New York: Viking.
Erikson, E. (1963). *Childhood and society* (2nd Ed.). New York: Norton.
Fancher, R. E. (1979). *Pioneers of psychology.* New York: Norton.
Festinger, L. (1957). *A theory of cognitive dissonance.* Stanford, CA: Stanford University Press.
Fisher, H. (1995). *Anatomy of love: A natural history of mating, marriage, and why we stray.* New York: Fawcett.
Fowler, J. W. (1995). *Stages of faith: The psychology of human development and the quest for meaning.* San Francisco: HarperCollins.
Freeman, M. (1993). *Rewriting the self: History, memory, narrative.* London: Routledge.
Freud, S. (1975). *Civilization and its discontents* (J. Riviere, Trans.). London: Hogarth Press.
Freud, S. (1976). *Introductory lectures on psychoanalysis* (J. Strachey, Trans.). London: Penguin.

Fromm, E. (1960). Psychoanalysis and Zen Buddhism. In E. Fromm (Ed.), *Zen Buddhism and psychoanalysis* (pp. 77–141). New York: Harper and Row.
Gergen, K. J. (1991). *The saturated self: Dilemmas of identity in contemporary life.* New York: Basic Books.
Gibbs, J. C., Basenger, K. S., & Fuller, R. L. (1992). *Moral maturity: Measuring the development of sociomoral reflection.* Hillsdale, NJ: Erlbaum.
Gilligan, C. (1982). *In a different voice: Psychological theory and women's development.* Cambridge, MA: Harvard University Press.
Goldstein, J. (1976). *The experience of insight: A natural unfolding.* Santa Cruz, CA: Unity Press.
Gould, R. (1978). *Transformations: Growth and change in adult life.* New York: Simon & Schuster.
Gruber, H., & Voneche, J. (Eds.). (1977). *The essential Piaget.* New York: Basic Books.
Hayward, J. (1987). *Shifting worlds changing minds: Where the sciences and Buddhism meet.* Boston: Shambhala.
Howard, G. S. (1991). Culture tales: A narrative approach to thinking, cross-cultural psychology, and psychotherapy. *American Psychologist, 46*(3), 187-197.
Inhelder, B., & Piaget, J. (1958). *The growth of logical thinking from childhood to adolescence* (A. Parsons & S. Milgram, Trans.). New York: Basic Books. (Original published 1955)
Irwin, R. R. (1991). Reconceptualizing the nature of dialectical postformal operational thinking: The effects of affectively-mediated social experiences. In J. D. Sinnott & J. C. Cavanaugh (Eds.), *Bridging paradigms: Positive development in adulthood and aging* (pp. 43–57). New York: Praeger.
Irwin, R. R. (1996). Narrative competence and constructive developmental theory: A proposal for rewriting the *Bildingsroman* in the postmodern world. *Journal of Adult Development, 3*(2), 109–125.
Itard, J.M.-G. (1962). *The wild boy of Aveyron* (G. & M. Humphrey, Trans.) New York: Appleton–Century–Crofts.
Josselson, R. (1987). *Finding herself: Pathways to identity development in women.* San Francisco: Jossey–Bass.
Keen, E. (1986). Paranoia and cataclysmic narratives. In T. R. Sarbin (Ed.), *Narrative psychology: The storied nature of human conduct* (pp. 174–190). New York: Praeger.
Kegan, R. (1982). *The evolving self: Problem and process in human development.* Cambridge, MA: Harvard University Press.
Kegan, R. (1994). *In over our heads: The mental demands of modern life.* Cambridge, MA: Harvard University Press.
Kitchener, K. S., & King, P. M. (1994). *Developing reflective judgment: Understanding and promoting intellectual growth and critical thinking in adolescents and adults.* San Francisco: Jossey–Bass.
Knowles, M. S. (1980). *The modern practice of adult education: From pedagogy to androgogy.* London: Cambridge University Press.
Kohlberg, L. (1976). Moral stages and moralization: The cognitive-developmental approach. In T. Lickona (Ed.), *Moral development and behavior.* New York: Holt, Rinehart & Winston.
Kohlberg, L., & Kramer, R. (1969). Continuities and discontinuities in childhood and adult moral development. *Human Development, 12,* 93–120.
Kohlberg, L., & Ryncarz, R. A. (1990). Beyond justice reasoning: Moral development and consideration of a seventh stage. In C. N. Alexander & E. J. Langer (Eds.), *Higher stages of human development: Perspectives on adult growth* (pp. 191–207). London: Oxford University Press.

Kramer, D. A. (1989). Development of an awareness of contradiction across the life span and the question of postformal operations. In M. L. Commons, J. D. Sinnott, F. A. Richards & C. Armon, (Eds.), *Adult development: Vol. I. Comparisons and applications of developmental models* (pp. 133–159). New York: Praeger.

Labouvie-Vief, G. (1990). Wisdom as integrated thought: Historical and developmental perspectives. In R. L. Sternberg (Ed.), *Wisdom: Its nature, origins and development*. London: Cambridge University Press.

Labouvie-Vief, G. (1992). A neo-Piagetian perspective on adult cognitive development. In R.J. Sternberg & C. Berg (Eds.), *Intellectual development* (pp. 52–83). London: Cambridge University Press.

Labouvie-Vief, G. (1994). *Psyche and eros: Mind and gender in the life course*. London: Cambridge University Press.

Labouvie-Vief, G., DeVoe, M., & Bulka, D. (1989). Speaking about feelings: Conceptions of emotion across the life span. *Psychology and Aging*, 4(4), 425–437.

Labouvie-Vief, G., Hakim Larson, J., DeVoe, M., & Schoeberlein, S. (1989). Emotions and self regulation: A lifespan view. *Human Development, 32,* 279–299.

Labouvie-Vief, G., Hakim-Larson, J., & Hobart, C. (1987). Age, ego level, and the lifespan development of coping and defense prosesses. *Psychology and Aging,* 2(3), 286–293.

Laing, R. D. (1979). *The divided self.* New York: Penguin

Levinson, D. J., Darrow, C. N., Klein, E. B., Levinson, M. H., & McKee, B. (1978). *The seasons of a man's life.* New York: Knopf.

Lewis, M. (1993). Self-conscious emotions: Embarrassment, pride, shame and guilt. In M. Lewis & J.M. Haviland (Eds.), *Handbook of emotions* (pp. 563–573). New York: Guilford Press.

Loevinger, J. (1976). *Ego development.* San Francisco: Jossey–Bass.

Lowen, A. (1975). *Bioenergetics.* New York: Penguin.

Luria, A.R. (1973). *The working brain.* New York: Penguin.

Marcia, J. (1980). Identity in adolescence. In J. Adelson (Ed.), *Handbook of adolescent psychology* (pp. 159–187). New York: Wiley.

Merriam, S. B., & Cunningham, P. M. (Eds.). (1989). *Handbook of adult and continuing education.* San Francisco: Jossey–Bass.

Miller, G. (1991). *The science of words.* New York: Scientific American.

Moore, W. (1982). *Measure of intellectual development: A brief review.* Baltimore: Center for Application of Developmental Instruction.

Orr, R., & Luszcz, M. (1994). Rethinking Women's Ways of Knowing: Gender commonalities and intersections with postformal thought. *Journal of Adult Development,* 1(4), 225–233.

Packer, M. J. (1991). Interpreting stories, interpreting lives: Narrative and action on moral development research. In M. B. Tappan & M. J. Packer (Eds.), *Narrative and storytelling: Implications for studying moral development* (pp. 63–82). San Francisco: Jossey–Bass.

Pascual-Leone, J. (1983). Growing toward human maturity: Toward a metasubjective theory of adulthood stages. In P.B. Baltes & O.G. Brim (Eds.), *Life-span development and behavior* (Vol. 5, pp. 117-156). New York: Academic Press.

Pascual-Leone, J. (1990a). An essay on wisdom: Toward organismic processes that make it possible. In R. J. Sternberg (Ed.), *Wisdom: Its nature, origins, and development* (pp. 244–278). London: Cambridge University Press.

Pascual-Leone, J. (1990b) Reflections on life-span intelligence, consciousness, and ego development. In C. N. Alexander & E. J. Langer (Eds.), *Higher stages of human*

development: Perspectives on adult growth (pp. 258–285). London: Oxford University Press.
Pascual-Leone, J., & Irwin, R. R. (1994a). Noncognitive factors in high-road/low-road learning: I. Modes of abstraction in adulthood. *Journal of Adult Development, 1*(2), 73–89.
Pascual-Leone, J., & Irwin, R. R. (1994b). Noncognitive factors in high-road/low-road learning: II. The will, the self, and modes of instruction in adulthood. *Journal of Adult Development, 1*(3), 153–168.
Patrul, R. (1998). *The words of my perfect teacher.* Boston: Shambhala.
Perry, W. (1970). *Forms of intellectual and ethical development during the college years.* New York: Holt, Rinehart & Winston.
Polkinghorne, D. E. (1988). *Narrative knowing in the human sciences.* Albany: State University of New York Press.
Popper, K. (1963). *Conjectures and refutations: The growth of scientific knowledge.* New York: Harper & Row.
Randall, W. L. (1995). *The stories we are: An essay on self-creation.* Toronto: University of Toronto Press.
Riegel, K. (1973). Dialectical operations: The final period of cognitive development. *Human Development, 16,* 346–370.
Sarbin, T. R. (1986). *Narrative psychology: The storied nature of human conduct.* New York: Praeger.
Seligman, M. E. P. (1990). *Learned optimism: How to change your mind and your life.* New York: Simon & Schuster.
Sinnott, J. D. (1984). Postformal reasoning: The relativistic stage, In M. L. Commons, F. A. Richards, & C. Armon (Eds.), *Beyond formal operations: Late adolescent and adult cognitive development* (pp. 298–325). New York: Praeger.
Thomas, L. E. (1994). Cognitive development and transcendence: An emerging transpersonal paradigm of consciousness. In M. E. Miller & S. R. Cook-Greuter (Eds.), *Transcendence and mature thought in adulthood: The further reaches of adult development* (pp. 71–87). Lanham, MD: Rowman & Littlefield.
Trungpa, C. (1995). *The path is the goal: A basic handbook of Buddhist meditation.* Boston: Shambhala.
Vygotsky, L. S. (1978). *Mind in society: The development of higher psychological processes.* Cambridge, MA: Harvard University Press.
Walker, L. J. (1989). A longitudinal study of moral reasoning. *Child Development, 60,* 157–166.
Washburn, M. (1994). *Transpersonal psychology in psychoanalytic perspective.* New York: State University of New York Press.
White, M., & Epston, D. (1990). *Narrative means to therapeutic ends.* New York: Norton.
Wilber, K. (1986a). The spectrum of development. In K. Wilber, J. Engler, & D. P. Brown (Eds.), *Transformations of consciousness: Conventional and contemplative perspectives on development* (pp. 65–105). Boston: Shambhala.
Wilber, K. (1986b). The spectrum of psychopathology. In K. Wilber, J. Engler, & D. P. Brown (Eds.), *Transformations of consciousness: Conventional and contemplative perspectives on development* (pp. 107–126). Boston: Shambhala.
Wilber, K. (1986c). Treatment modalities. In K. Wilber, J. Engler, & D. P. Brown (Eds.), *Transformations of consciousness: Conventional and contemplative perspectives on development* (pp. 127–159). Boston: Shambhala.
Wilber, K. (1993). *Grace and grit: Spirituality and healing in the life and death of Treya Killam Wilber.* Boston: Shambhala.

Wilber, K. (1996a). *A brief history of everything.* Boston: Shambhala.
Wilber, K. (1996b). *The Atman Project: A transpersonal view of human development.* Boston: Shambhala.
Wilber, K. (1996c, September). Big thinker: The kosmos according to Ken Wilber. *The Shambhala Sun.*
Zimbardo, P. (1999). *Psychology and life.* New York: Longman.
Zukov, G., & Finkelstein, D. (1994). *The dancing Wu Li Masters: An overview of the new physics.* New York: Bantam.

Index

Abandonment anxiety, 60
Adaptation, 126
   regressive and progressive, 52
Agency, 25–28, 149, 156
Aging, 127–128
Alexander, C. 183–186
   action and senses, 183
   cosmic consciousness, 184
   desire, 183
   Ego, 184
   ego development, 185
   epigenesis, 185
   on identity, 185
   intellect, 184
   intuition, 184
   and Loevinger, 184
   mind, 183
   refined or gloried cosmic consciousness, 184
   seven states of consciousness, 184
   transcendental consciousness, 184
   Transcendental Meditation (TM), 185
   transpersonal, 184
   unity consciousness, 184
Alienation, 156
Altruistic stage, 174
Anatta (selflessness), 13
Anicca (impermanence), 13
Anxiety, 18, 62, 106
Archetypes, 3
Armon, C., vi, 153, 172–174
Armoring, 56, 59
Artificial intelligence (AI), 70
Asch, S., 68
Attachment, 40, 42
Attention, 6, 73
   as process, 28

Attribution theory, 101
Authoring, 152
Authorities, 58, 128
Authority, 113, 138
Autistic stage, 59
Automatization, 56, 58, 62, 71, 74, 85
Autonomous stage, 164, 177, 178
Autonomy, 54, 149, 156
Autonomy stage, 172, 174
Awareness, 70

Bakhtin, M., 112
Basseches, M., vi, 139, 145–148
Behaviorism, 115
Belenky, M., 136, 142–143
Bodhisattva vows, 193
Bottom-up processing, 70, 115
Bruner, J., 111, 115, 121, 122, 154
Buddha, 8, 161
Buddha Nature, 13
Buddhism
   First Noble Truth, 168
   Nyingmapa, Tibetan, 193
   Soto, 9
   Tantric, 164
   Theravada, 9
   Tibetan, 9
Burroughs, W., 8

Causation, 22
Centration, 70, 71
   and language, 83
Chandler, M., 144
Change versus development, 29–31
Chomsky, N., 115

Christ, 8
Chunking, 71, 101
Civilization, 50
Cognition
  architecture of, 70
  as conformist, 67
  evolution of, 65
  as fixation of belief, 66
  of self, 67, 75–76
  and social world, 67–69
  and surveillance, 67
  as transformation, 77
Cognitive dissonance, 101
Cognitive revolution, 115
Cognitive structures, 115
Commitment, 138, 139, 155
  defined, 141
  and identity, 140
Communion, 25–28
Concrete operations, 42
Conditioning, 51
Conformist stage, 177, 185
Confounds, 23
Conscience, 46, 55, 57, 96–97
Conscientious stage, 103, 178
Consciousness
  development of, 3
  definition of, 6
  early, 7
Construct-Aware stage, 175–176
Constructed Knowing, 142
Constructionism, psychological, 42, 144
Control, 23, 54, 155, 176
Conventional stages, 153, 169
Cook-Greuter, S., vi, 175–178
Copy theory of knowledge, 141
Correlation, 22
Cote and Levine, 94–95
Cultural supports, 176

Dalai Lama, 8
Dawkins, R., 82
Death, 161
Defense mechanisms, 57, 158
Denial, 158
Depression, 62, 106, 119, 181
  levels, 181
  types of, 16
Descartes, R., 38

Development, 29–31
  conceptions of, 4, 29
  direction of, 185
  higher, 3
  levels, 14
  limits, 18
  process of, 25
  social, 5
  spiritual, 3, 5, 24
  universality of, 30–31
Dialectical knowing, 145
Discourse community, 137
Dreams, 159, 160, 161
Dualism, 138, 139
Dukkha (sorrow), 12, 50

Eastern philosophy, 16–19
Ego, 31–33, 44, 74, 145
  definition of, v, 191–192
  development of, 61, 127
  and id, 51
  as illusion, 19
  positive aspects of, 18
  representation of self, 7
  stages of, 175
Ego ideal, 7, 94, 97, 127, 159
Ego strength, 153
Egoistic stage, 173
Egolessness, 12
Emotions
  and aging, 129
  control of, 156
  primary and secondary, 95
Emplotting, 117
Emptiness, 147, 183
Enlightenment, 46
Epigenesis, 30
Epistemic knowing, 137
Epston, D. 122, 124, 158
Erdynast, A., 173
Erikson, E., 161
Evil, 158, 159
Experiments, 23
Externalization, 124

False self-system, 96
Family drama, 62
Fast-mapping, 44

Index

Festinger, L., 101
Fiction, necessity of, 132
Fisher, H., 104
Formal operations, 4,6, 145
Foregiveness, 50
Foucault, M., 8, 124
Fowler, J., 186–190
  Conjunctive stage, 187, 189
  definition faith, of, 187
  Individuative-Reflective stage, 186, 188
  Intuitive-Projective stage, 188
  Judeo-Christian bias of, 190
  Mythic-Literal stage, 188
  and normativity, 190
  research, 187
  Synthetic-Conventional stage, 186, 188
  and transcendence versus immanence, 190
  transpersonal stage, 190
  Universalizing stage, 189
Freeman, M., 112, 117, 134
Freud, S.
  on conscience, 46
  on happiness, 51
  id and ego, 51
  influence, 58
  on maturity, 6
  nirvana principle, 52
  Oedipus complex, 53
  polymorphous perversity, 164
  on repression, 49
  superego, 55
Funk, J. vi
Fundamental Attributional Error (FAE), 101
Future, 38

Games, 162
Gandhi, M., 8
General Adaptation Syndrome (GAS), 52
Generativity, 3, 167
Genetic epistemology, 4
Gestalt, 116
Gibb, J., 171
Gilligan, C., 142, 171
Good Life Interview, 173
Gould, R., 125, 158–164
Guilt, 95
Gurus, 193

Guttmann, J., vi

Happiness, 51
Hatching phase, 60
Head size, 41
Heisenberg Uncertainty, 120
Hermeneutic circle, 114
Heteronomous morality, 55
Hierarchical integration, 29
Higher stages, paucity of, 162
Howard, G., 122
Human beings, as a species, 40, 49, 87
Huxley, A., 179
Hysteria, 119

Identity, 31, 45, 59, 125, 126, 127, 160, 167, 185, 193
  and conscience, 94
  and dreams, 103
  as form of ego, 7
  and guilt, 98
  as individuation, 97
  as internalization, 106
  Labouvie-Vief on, 156
  as limitation, 93
  at mid-life, 158
  and role, 99, 118
  and sex, 98, 103
  statuses, 99, 100
  widening circle, 93
Ideologies, 119
Irwin, R., 147, 154
Imperial stage, 151
Impermanence, 147
Impulsive stage, 151, 177
Independence, 149
Individualistic stage, 178
Individuality, 172, 174
Individuation, 3, 156, 161
Information processing, 115
Institutional stage, 103, 149, 152, 155
Instrumental stage, 173
Integrated stage, 154
Integrity, 3
Interindividual stage, 150, 152, 164
Interpersonal stage, 149, 152
Intimacy, 98, 104
Intrasystemic stage, 154

Introjects, 163
Introspection, 102

James, W., 117
Josselson, R., 99
Jung, C., 127, 159, 161

Karma, 14, 51, 63, 75
Keen, E., 197
Kegan, R., 103, 113, 122, 146, 149–153, 164, 175, 181
Kerouac, J., 8, 28
King, 138, 140–142
Kitchener, P., 138, 140–142
Kohlberg, L., 169–172
   and Armon, 173
   and conventional morality, 60
   and Gilligan, C., 142
   and heteronomous morality, 55
   research, 169
   sixth stage, 6
   stages, 55, 170–171
   seventh stage, 171
   values, 153
Kramer, R., 169

Labouvie-Vief, G., vi, 102, 127, 153–158, 164
Lahey, L., 151
Language, 43, 44, 74, 76
   as amplifier, 79
   as communication, 80
   and computers, 88
   in Construct-Aware stage, 175
   evolution of, 82
   as externalization, 80
   and historical relativism, 88
   as organ, 81–82
   orthography, 81, 86
   and printing press, 88
   as scaffolding, 83
   as scripts, 85
   selection of, 81
   sequentiality, 85
   as simulation, 79, 81–83
   in stories, 85
   teaching, 84
   and technology, 87
   written versus spoken, 79, 83, 88–89

Leaving Los Vegas, 28
Levinson, D., 104, 127, 158–164
Lewis, M., 95
Life structure, 158
Loevinger, J., 103, 164, 175
Logos, 102, 154
Lowry, M., 28
Luszcz, M., 143

Maharishi Mahesh Yogi, 183
Marcia, J., 99, 185
Master narratives, 121
Master stories, 109
Maturity, 149
Mediation, 45
Meditation, 8, 107
   breath, 10
   in Construct-Aware stage, 176
   readiness for, 15
   reasons for, 15
   shamatha, 9
   thinking in, 11
   variability of, 15
   vipashyana, 9
   and Witness, 182
Memes, 82
Memory, 62
   long-term, 70
   span, 71
Mid-life crisis, 139, 157, 160, 161, 169, 193
Milgram, S., 68
Mind in evolution, 35–36
Mindfulness, 51, 75
Monasticism, 105
Monogamy, 104
Morphology, 85
Moral development
   seventh stage of, 3
Mortality, 120, 161, 167
Mothering, 45
Mudras, 10
Multiplism, 139
Mutations, 35–36
Mythos, 102, 154

Narcissism, 60
Narratives
   authenticity, 133
   as break or rupture, 121

Index

Narratives (cont.)
  canonicity, 121
  capacity, 116
  and Constructed Knowing, 142
  contradiction, 132
  definition of, 110
  and fiction, 120
  frameworks, 68
  as freedom, 112
  and future, 113
  and intention, 114
  and interpretation, 119
  intertextuality, 116, 130
  levels of consciousness, 130
  metaphors in, 110–111
  and paradigmatic approach, 111, 115, 154
  and past, 113
  and postmodernism, 117
  progression, 134
  psychology, 101
  therapy, 122–125
  on world and word, 116
Nationalism, 69
Ngondro, 14, 193
Nirvana principle, 52
Noble savage, 41
Nonegoic core, 60
Novels, 117
Nyingmapa, 193

Object permanence, 60
Object relations theory, 59–62
Objectification of self, 57
Objective world, 154
Oedipal stage, 60
Offspring, helplessness of, 40
Operationalization, 163
Optimal development, 162
Orr, R., 143
Othello effect, 144

Packer, M., 120, 121
Pain, 181
Panopticon, 124
Pascual-Leone, J. 147, 154
  affects, 165
  Agency, 166
  attention, 165

Pascual-Leone, J. (cont.)
  centration, 165
  Collectives, 166
  Communion, 166
  contradiction, 164–165, 168
  dialectics, 166
  Ego, 165
  Ego Core, 163
  Ego Milieu, 163
  Ethos, 166
  executives, 165
  hermeneutics, 166
  I-can, 166
  I-self, 165
  I-will, 166
  inhibition, 166, 168
  Me-self, 165
  mental attention, 165
  mental energy, 165
  midlife, 166
  Passions, 166
  Piaget's stages, 164
  process analysis, 164
  scheme, 165
  silent resources, 165
  Soul, 166
  working memory, 165
Penor Rinpoche, 193
Perennial philosophy, 179
Permanent object, 42
Perry, W., 137, 138–140
Personality, 53, 58
Personhood, 18
Phonology, 85
Piaget, J., 115
Pleasure principle, 49, 52
Polymorphous perversity, 164
Popper, K., 82
Positivism, 115
Postconformist stage, 8
Postconventional morality, 8, 153, 171, 192
Postformal operations, 143
Postlinguistic stage, 8
Postmodernism, 137, 146, 152
Postpersonal stage, 8, 185, 192
Postrepresentational stage, 176, 185, 192
Practicing phase, 60
Pragmatics, 85
Pragnanz, 116
Prediction and control, 109
Presystemic stage, 154

Primal alienation, 60, 96
Primal repression, 60, 96
Procedural Knowing, 142
Processing limits, 71
Project of self, 160
Projection, 158
Psychoanalysis, 191
Psychology
  attitude toward spirituality, 16
  Western, 16–19
Puberty, 98
Punishment, 45, 56

Racism, 69
Randall, W. 121, 130
Random assignment, 23
Rapprochement phase, 60
Reality-creating, 192
Reality principle, 49
Received Knowing, 142
Reflective Judgment, 140–142
Refuge vows, 193
Regression, 169
Relativism, 138, 139
Relativistic operations, 143
Reliability, 22
Religion
  according to B. Russell, 68
  versus spirituality, 19–22
Repression, 49,
  defined, 50
  origin of, 61
Retrieval, 70
Right Effort, 27
Rousseau, J., 41
Roles
  and rules, 125
  as stories, 118,

Samsara, 47, 50, 63, 182
Sankhya levels of mind, 183
Sartre, J.P., 116
Science, 22–24
Scripts, 69, 107, 125
Seasons of life, 160
Secondary subjectivity, 44
Selection, 35
  and spirituality, 4

Self
  as concentric rings, 44
  construction of, 42
  versus ego, 31, 158
Self-Aware stage, 177, 185
Self-consciousness, 63
Self-control, 163
Self-deception, 159
Self-directed learning, 84
Self-direction, 149
Self-esteem, 95, 97
Self-fulfilling prophesy, 69, 101–102
Self-knowledge, 39
Self-perception theory, 69–102
Self-Protective stage, 177
Self-regulation, 54
Self-structure, 159, 162
Self-talking 21, 32
Seligman, M., 106, 123
Selye, H., 52
Separation, 25
Separation anxiety, 40
Separation-individuation, 60
Sex
  in adolescence, 98
  in midlife, 164
Sex differences, 144
Shadow, 159, 161
Shambhala Sun, 182
Shunyata, 133
Siddhartha Gautama, 105
Silenced Knowing, 142
Simulation, 23, 35–39, 44, 76, 192
Sinnott, J., vi, 138
Social constructionism, 69, 84, 141
Social determinism, 19
Social world, evolution of, 38
Socialization, 53
Society, notion of, 20
Society for Research in Adult Development (SRAD), 175, 183
Spiritual development, 62, 76
Spirituality versus religion, 19–22
Stages, adult, 147
Stories, 101, 111, 112, 117, 119, 126, 130, 145, 158, 167
Subjective Relativism, 174
Subjective world, 155
Subjectivity stage, 142
Subject-object relations, 150

Index

Subject-Object Interview, 151
Suffering, 147, 168
Sumegi, A., vi
Superego, 46, 94, 97
Symbiotic stage, 59
Syntax, 85

Tappan, M., vi
Telos, 29
Theory of mind, 42
Therapy
  as excavation, 120
  as new religion, 21
  types of, 21
Thomas, E., 179
Three Marks of Existence, 12
Top–down processing, 70, 115
Transcendence, 62–64
  of ego, 46
  as universal, 46
Transcendental Meditation (TM), 185
Transpersonal stage, 192
Tribe, 127, 162
Trungpa, C., 10

Unique outcomes, 124
Unitive, 177, 178
Universal Holism, 174
Unwelt, 77

Validity, 22
Value orientation stages, 94–95
Variables, 22
  dependent, 23
  independent, 23

Vedanta, 183
Vygotsky, L., 124

Walker, L. 144, 171
Washburn, M., 96, 103
Washington University Sentence Completion Test (WUSCT), 175, 177, 185
White, M., 122, 124, 158
Widening circle, 42
Wilber, K., 178–183, 187
  anamnesis, 185
  Causal stage, 182
  centauric, 180
  existential level, 180
  Formal/Reflexive stage, 180
  fulcrums, 179
  and personal levels of development, 179
  Phantasmal-Emotional stage, 179
  Prepersonal stage, 179
  Psychic stage, 182
  Representational stage, 179
  Role/Rule stage, 179
  Sensoriphysical stage, 179
  spectrum of consciousness, 14
  Subtle stage, 182
  Transpersonal stages, 180, 182
  treatment modalities, 14
  Vision Logic, 164, 180
"Wild Boy of Aveyron", Victor, 41
Will, 27, 28
Wisdom, 154, 184
World-creating processes, 125

Zabuton, 9
Zafu, 9
Zimbardo, P., 68